THE PRESENT SOUTH

PROBLEMS OF
THE PRESENT SOUTH

A DISCUSSION OF
CERTAIN OF THE EDUCATIONAL, INDUSTRIAL
AND POLITICAL ISSUES IN THE
SOUTHERN STATES

BY

EDGAR GARDNER MURPHY

NEGRO UNIVERSITIES PRESS
NEW YORK

Originally published in 1904
by the Macmillan'Company

Reprinted 1969 by
Negro Universities Press
A DIVISION OF GREENWOOD PUBLISHING CORP.
NEW YORK

SBN 8371-1912-X

PRINTED IN UNITED STATES OF AMERICA

To My Sons

DU BOSE AND GARDNER
MURPHY

PREFACE

With two exceptions, the papers here included have been prepared for this volume and have not heretofore appeared in print. Even in these exceptional instances the chapters have attained only a small private circulation, and they are here presented in a somewhat altered form. While, therefore, the volume is thus so largely and so directly representative of matter that has not before found its way to print, I am aware that certain repetitions will be noted. These are chiefly due to the fact that the book has but one essential theme, and that each chapter is an attempt — from a somewhat different point of view — to discuss this one subject. The volume is an effort to contribute, from a standpoint within the life and thought of the South, to the discussion of the rise of democratic conditions in our Southern States. The problems of the South — industrial, educational, political — appear as phases of the essential movement toward a genuinely democratic order.

The limitations of space have made it necessary to postpone the discussion of some of the topics which it seemed desirable to include. Chapters upon "The Negro Tax and the Negro School," — a more explicit discussion of the proposal to accord to the negro schools only the amount collected from

negro taxes; "The South and the Amendments," —
a criticism of the proposal to enforce the terms of
the Fourteenth and Fifteenth Amendments by Con-
gressional action; "The Broader Emancipation," —
a more definite study of the progress of the negro
since the Civil War; "Commerce and the Common
Schools," — a discussion of the direct relation of
public education to the general economic efficiency
of the people; these, and a number of chapters
dealing with some of the less familiar phases of our
social and political development, may possibly find
place in a later volume.

The chapters just named, as well as those here
published, have been written — as already suggested
— from within the life and thought of the South.
They assume, however, no representative finality.
They are not intended as an authoritative interpretation of Southern opinion. Their essential conclusions will be rejected by some forces within the South
and accepted by others. Their service — if they are
to prove of service at all — will be found, however,
not in the immediate evidences of agreement or disagreement, but in such contributions as they may
offer toward that slowly forming, collective verdict,
in reference to Southern issues, in which the public
opinion of our whole country, North and South, will
gain at length its rational and articulate expression.
Popular judgments, operative as living social forces
upon a large and inclusive scale, act and react upon
the national character. To contribute, however in-
adequately or imperfectly, to their formation is a
legitimate and honorable interest.

This volume offers, moreover, no dogmatic "solution " of the problems with which it deals; least of all have I ventured to engage in the familiar occupation of "solving the negro question." The great problems of life are never solved in any mathematical or final sense. They are solved only in the sense that life becomes adjusted to them, or in the sense that their conflicting or complementary elements find a working adjustment to one another, an adjustment consistent, in larger and larger measure, with wisdom, right, happiness; but always coincident with the possibility of misconception and with recurrent periods of acute antagonism. The problems of racial cleavage, like the problems of labor and capital, or the problems of science and religion, yield to no precise formulæ; they are problems of life, persistent and irreducible. And yet they are subject to approximate adjustments, increasingly righteous, intelligent, and effective, and yielding an increasing measure of social peace, of industrial co-operation, of individual freedom and happiness. It is in this sense that the word "solution" is employed in the pages which follow. Toward the establishment of such a working adjustment of the factors of any national problem it is well to labor, in order that the problems of American life may become the occasions of a keener and more widely distributed sense of social obligation, a larger and saner political temper, a purer civic devotion, rather than the occasions of national demoralization.

While, therefore, these chapters are written from within the South, written by one who through birth, education, training, has shared its traditions and its experience, they have been written within the national perspective. More than once I have expressed the conviction that, in a certain local and palpable sense, the peculiar problems of the South are sectional in their form. And yet such a view is in no way inconsistent with the contention that the time has now come when every problem of every section of our country is to be conceived in the terms of the Nation's life.

E. G. M.

MONTGOMERY, ALABAMA,
March 5th, A.D. 1904.

CONTENTS

xi

THE OLD IN THE NEW

THE PRESENT SOUTH

CHAPTER I

THE OLD IN THE NEW

In the year 1865, at the close of the final catastrophe of the Southern arms, the following declaration was made in London, England, by the late T. H. Huxley. Mr. Huxley, man of science and man of letters, speaks as one in detachment from the local and partisan passions of the long controversy, but also as one who is, upon the whole, in sympathy with the contention of the North. His words have specific reference to the issue of emancipation.

"The question," he observes, "is settled; but even those who are most thoroughly convinced that the doom is just must see good grounds for repudiating half the arguments which have been employed by the winning side, and for doubting whether its ultimate results will embody the hopes of the victors, though they may more than realize the fears of the vanquished. It may be quite true that some negroes are better than some white men; but no rational man, cognizant of the facts, believes that the average negro is the equal, still less the superior, of the average white man. . . .

"But," continues Mr. Huxley, "whatever the position of stable equilibrium into which the laws of social

3

.

gravitation may bring the negro, all responsibility for the result will henceforth lie between Nature and him. The white man may wash his hands of it, and the Caucasian conscience be void of reproach for evermore. And this, if we look to the bottom of the matter, is the real justification for the abolition policy." [1]

It seems difficult to escape the conclusion that, in Mr. Huxley's thought, the policy of emancipation represented the rejection, rather than the expression, of responsibility. The negro was to be freed from slavery in order that the Caucasian might be freed from obligation.

One is amazed to realize that an Englishman of such varied learning and of such masterful acumen should have had so imperfect a perception of the essential temper of American life. The issue of emancipation carried no such significance to the North. It bore no such significance to the South.

The broader heart and the higher conscience of Southern life have often found utterance in the decisions of Southern courts, and in the declarations of press and pulpit. These expressions have represented, especially, the slaveholding class, the class which had been most directly involved by the policy of emancipation, and the class, therefore, which might have been expected to cherish an attitude of deliberate irresponsibility. Yet, in striking contrast with Professor Huxley's words, are the following paragraphs

[1] T. H. Huxley, " Emancipation — Black and White " (1865), in " Science and Education," pp. 66, 67, D. Appleton & Co., New York. Mr. Huxley included the address, unchanged, in the latest edition of his works.

from one of the most intensely Southern of Southern publicists, one high in the counsels of the Confederacy, an ex-slaveholder, a veteran both of the Mexican War and of the War between the States, — all in all, perhaps, in these recent years, the most typical representative of the old South. It was at Montgomery, Alabama, — the first capital of the Confederacy, — that the late J. L. M. Curry addressed these words to a Southern audience on the evening of May 9, 1900.

"We have heard much already," said he, "and will hear more before we adjourn, of slavery. It was an economic curse, a legacy of ignorance.

"It cursed the South with stupid, ignorant, uninventive labor. The curse in large degree remains. The policy of some would perpetuate it and give a system of serfdom, degrading to the negro, corrupting to the employer. The negro is a valuable laborer; let us improve him and make his labor more intelligent, more skilled, more productive. . . . Shall the Caucasian race, in timid fearfulness, in cowardly injustice, wrong an inferior race, put obstacles to its progress? Left to itself, away from the elevating influence of contact and tuition, there will be retrogression. Shall we hasten the retrogression, shall we have two races side by side, equal in political privileges, one educated, the other ignorant? Unless the white people, the superior, the cultivated race, lift up the lower, both will be inevitably dragged down.

"Look at these roses on this platform. They have been developed from an inferior plant by skilled culture into gorgeous American Beauties. So it is with other flowers and fruits; so with animals, and so it is with men. Eight hundred years ago our ancestors were pirates, careless of laws, either of God or man, and yet by culture and education, and discipline and free institutions and liberty of worship, they have been made the people that they are to-day. God's throne is justice and right and truth. Unseat Him from that throne and he becomes a demon; and so will sink our Southern civilization into infamy if we are guilty of cruelest injustice to an inferior race, whom God has put into our hands as trustees for their elevation and improvement, and for His glory." [1]

As I heard Dr. Curry's words, I do not know which was the more inspiring, the moral virility with which he spoke, or the earnest and impassioned approval with which his audience responded to his message. For the words were as typical as the man. They were not an exceptional declaration. Such words from Curry, and from others like him, had long been familiar to Southern ears. There was not a Southern legislature to which Curry himself — by special invitation — had not brought a like appeal again and yet again. There was always something leonine in the regal and commanding power with which his eye flashed his instinctive scorn of wrong, and with which his voice thundered the realities of that moral obligation which binds the strong man to the weak. There was something deeply veracious, something restorative of one's essential confidence in life, to note that the highest appeal to the people whom he addressed was always followed by the most spontaneous and most serious tribute of applause.

[1] See Report of the Conference of the Society for the Consideration of the Race Problems and Conditions of the South, published by the B. F. Johnson Publishing Company, Richmond, Virginia, pp. 112, 113.

The measure of the Southern conscience cannot be taken from the expressions that have sometimes greeted an unintelligent censure from without. It is only when a people, united by a common suffering and bearing a common burden, are overheard in their converse with one another, it is only when the South speaks freely to the South, that one may catch that real spirit of *noblesse oblige* which has so largely dominated the development of Southern life. It is one of the incredibilities of history that in the world's discussions of the South the occasional victories of impatience should loom so large, and that the South's far greater victories of magnanimity should loom so small. There is, indeed, nothing more characteristic of the Southern temper — whatever the suggestion of Mr. Huxley's inference — than that deep note of responsibility which sounds through Dr. Curry's words. The sense of responsibility may express itself wisely or mistakenly, perversely or constructively, but whatever the form of its expression, the consciousness of obligation is not absent.

It is, therefore, by no accident of language that this sense of responsibility, as expressed in the words just quoted, should define, under certain characteristic assumptions, the policy of the South in reference to the negro. There is a distinct assumption of the negro's inferiority; but there is also a distinct assumption of the negro's improvability. It is upon the basis of this double assumption that the South finds its obligation. If the negro were not peculiarly in need of progress, or if the negro were utterly incapable of progress, the problem of his progress could bring no especial burden to the South. Recognizing the double fact, first the fact of the negro's need and then the fact of the negro's promise, the South, as suggested in our quotation, has conceived her responsibility both as a policy of supreme self-interest and as an obligation of Christian stewardship.

This sense of responsibility is the present residuum of the moral forces of the old South.   It is a natural and legitimate development.   It was under slavery that men learned the oppressive significance of the negro's heritage from barbarism.   It was under slavery that men first learned the presence of those latent capacities by which the negro has so often transcended the limitations of that heritage.   It was through the bond of slavery that the wiser South was taught, in the light of an immediate self-interest, the advantage to the white man in the negro's integrity and skill, — the disadvantage, indeed the peril, to the white man in the negro's inefficiency and vice. Finally, it was through this bond of slavery that the truer South was taught, in the countless daily appeals of the negro's absolute dependence, — the appeal of ignorance to knowledge, of weakness to strength, of suffering to a sympathetic and interested power — the spirit of that tender and generous paternalism which so often made the master a sort of feudal providence to those in servitude.

If the rigors of slavery made it a system of bondage to the negro, its responsibilities made it also a system of bondage to the master.   There were many men to whom these responsibilities brought moral disaster, men who abused authorities which were so much greater than flesh and blood should wield.   There were other men, however, whose genius, half domestic

and half executive, set the ideal of the institution,
and as controversy gathered about the institution
they became the more sensitively jealous of this ideal
—holding it up to themselves and to one another,
and attempting, ever the more seriously as the quarrel
raged, to discharge its responsibilities, and to justify,
by a broader solicitude and a more considerate kindliness, the awful prerogatives of the master. Yet the
issue of this struggle was, to many, but a heavy
and saddened heart. The burden was too great, and
emancipation brought a quick sense of inexpressible
relief. Emancipation did not, however, remove the
negro. The negro remained and the white man
remained. Their proximity to each other was as palpable, as inevitable, as ever. The burden was lightened,
was altered in its form, but the fact of responsibility
continued, and the ideal of responsibility could not
perish. The appeal of the weak still came up to
the hearts of the strong. The crude necessities of the
ignorant and the helpless still asked an answer. The
habitual directions of moral interest are not easily
overcome, and the strong custom of a protective and
directive oversight still bound the white man to the
fortunes of his humbler fellows.

At this point in the new development of the relationship between the races, and across the many lines
of its promise, — its promise to the negro and to the
peace of the South, — there crashed the congres-
sional policies of reconstruction. I enter here upon
no criticism of these policies in detail. I pause only
to point out their direct effect upon that sense of
responsibility to which slavery had contributed. The
policies of reconstruction represented two cardinal

movements of purpose. One was the withdrawal of
political and civic power from those, especially those
in official position, who had borne arms against the
United States. This effort was an expedient of distrust. It was as natural as it was unintelligent, and
it was as successful as it was mischievous. Those
who had borne arms, especially those in positions
of responsibility, were largely the slaveholding class,
the representatives of the aristocracy, the men who
were the heirs of the broader and nobler traditions
of the South. They were most generously disposed
toward the freedmen. They were most scrupulously
faithful to the terms of their surrender. They, like
men, had fought it out; and they, like men, had
accepted the verdict in containment, if not in full
content. The measures of reconstruction took power
from them, leaving power in the hands of the young
and the irresponsible. When these men came to
their throne and faced the presence of the negro, it
was as though a Pharaoh had arisen who knew not
Joseph. It was from their ranks that the more vio-
.lent measures of the Ku-Klux Klan too often gained
support. Nor had they faced the bitter realities of
war. They knew not therefore, they could not know,
the cost and the worth of peace.

The old South was the real nucleus of the new
nationalism. The old South, or in a more general
sense the South of responsibility, the men of family,
the planter class, the official soldiery, or (if you
please) the aristocracy, — the South that had had
power, and to whom power had taught those truths
of life, those dignities and fidelities of temper, which
power always teaches men, — this older South was

the true basis of an enduring peace between the
sections and between the races. But a doubt was
put upon its word given at Appomattox. Its representatives were subjected to disfranchisement. Power
was struck from its hands. Its sense of responsibility was wounded and confused.

This was not all. The suffrage which the masters
were denied was by the same act committed into the
hands of their former slaves, vast dumb multitudes,
more helpless with power than without power. Men
from afar, under whose auspices this new preroga-
tive was bestowed, were present to instruct them,
not in fitness for it, but in its apt and grateful use.
The negro masses, upon the suffrage as a basis, were
reorganized out of their old economic and human
dependence upon their masters of the past, into a
formal political dependence upon the vague and
beneficent authority which had freed them. I write
primarily, not in order to accuse, but in order that
we may understand.

The effect of the new alliance of the freedmen, the
effect upon their own relation to the political reorganization of Southern society, must be evident.
The strong and effective forces which had secured
this new alignment were soon withdrawn. The
actual reorganization of the South was left, as was
inevitable, to the resident forces of Southern life.
The new allies of the freedmen could not share in
so short a time that identity of interest in the soil,
in the intimate fortunes of the South, which the
negro had once felt. The agents of reconstruction
who remained were just strong enough to modify
this feeling in the negro, to make the negro distrust

the South and to make the South distrust the negro.
They were not strong enough seriously to contribute,
or to aid the negro in contributing, to the rebuilding
of the political commonwealth. With the checking
and the confusion of their sense of responsibility
toward the blacks, it is therefore not unnatural that
the negro's older allies should have omitted him from
even a humble partnership in the task of rehabilitation. To the consciousness of the South, engaged
in a desperate struggle for unification and for reinte-
gration, the ballot of the black man thus unfortunately represented not only a negro suffrage, not only
an incompetent suffrage, but an alien suffrage.

The political reorganization which was proceeding
was all the more difficult because the South was just
entering, by pain and sacrifice, into the crucial movement of the century. The historian of institutions
must perceive that the real struggle of the South from
the date of Lee's surrender — through all the accidents
of political and industrial revolution — was simply
a struggle toward the creation of democratic conditions. The *real* thing, in the unfolding of the later
South, is the arrival of the common man. Southern
development is, in its essence, but an approach to
democracy, to democracy not merely as a theory of
administration, but as an expression of society itself.

The thinking and responsible life of the South, as
we have seen, had been an aristocracy. We may
note the fact without criticism, for it was inevitable.
We may note its passing without regret, because its
passing was the deeper emancipation — an emancipation which is bringing to the South a richer and
larger life than the older age, with all its charm and

fulness, could have dreamed. Yet men have often
failed to realize the drastic conditions of reorganization into which Southern experience was compelled,
both by the issue of the Civil War and by the federal
policies which followed. It was nothing less than
the reconstitution of an aristocratic society under
democratic conditions. The change was inevitable,
but the effort to *force* the change, to create it " over-
night," to take an aristocratic civilization and to ham-
mer it into another shape between sundown and sunup,
to create republican institutions by military power, to
inaugurate freedom by force and a democracy by
martial law, was — in the nature of the case — impossible. And for two reasons. Democracy is a thing
of growth and not of fiat; and democracy, of all the
forms of governmental or constitutional life, is the
very form which cannot be nailed on from outside.
It is by its very essence a form of government proceeding from within. It is an instinct of life before
it is an organization of society. Because democracy
is an institution of freedom, the very effort to force
democracy is its denial and subversion. There has,
therefore, never been a cruder oligarchy than that
represented by the reconstruction governments of the
Southern States.

Yet, under all the conditions of the new order, the
movement toward democracy — however thwarted or
embarrassed — made gradual progress. Civilization
must be reattempted, society must become a coherent
and stable force; life, liberty, and property cried out for
government. The only existent forms of government
were democratic. Democracy was the assumption of
civilization; and therefore the thought and purpose

of the South attempted their own reorganization under
the new conditions. The aristocracy, however, could
no longer stand alone. It could not express itself, it
could give neither currency nor efficiency to its conceptions, it could not create government nor administer laws, except by some deeper alliance with human
numbers. The aristocracy could furnish leadership,
but the people must furnish votes.

There were but two quarters from which the volume of coöperation could be increased. The older
civilization had contained two great classes of "non-
participants." First were the slaves. We have seen
the working of the forces and the rise of the conditions which made it unnatural and impossible for the
aristocracy — still, as yet, the leaders of the new
order — to turn for coöperation to the blacks. The
removal of their own civil disabilities had not made
the leaders of the aristocracy forget. Nor had the
negroes themselves forgotten either their natural
gratitude to their new masters or their unnatural
suspicion of the old. In the movement toward
democracy, in spite of whatever theoretic inconsist-
ency, the conditions thus made it impossible to
include the blacks.

In the older civilization, the other class of non-
participants were the non-slaveholding white men.
I use the term non-participants in what is, of course,
a broad and general sense, a sense in which I have
employed many of the expressions of this chapter.
Non-participants they were, but some of them were
men of wealth and influence. As a class, however,
the non-slaveholding white men had been outside
the essential councils of the South. Many of them

voted; some of them, through sheer personal distinction, had entered the ranks of the privileged, but as
a whole they stood aloof; they were supposed to follow where others led; they might furnish the ballots,
but the "superior" class was supposed to provide the
candidates for important office. There was no intimate or cordial alliance between their forces and the
forces of the aristocracy. Multitudes of them were
left wholly illiterate. White illiteracy at the South
long antedates the Civil War. In 1860, less than
1 per cent of the adult native white population of
Massachusetts were illiterate; in Pennsylvania, less
than 3 per cent; in Connecticut, less than 1 per cent;
in New York, less than 2 per cent: but of the adult
native white population of Virginia, in 1860, more
than 14 per cent could not read and write; in Tennessee, more than 16 per cent; in North Carolina,
more than 21 per cent.[1] To the white non-participants of the older civilization the aristocracy turned
instinctively, however, in its reorganization of the

[1] This striking contrast between the civilizations of the North and
the South is largely due to the historic difference in the attitude of the
respective sections toward the education of the masses. Says James
Bryce, "In old colonial days, when the English Commissioners for
Foreign Plantations asked for information on the subject of education from the governors of Virginia and Connecticut, the former replied, 'I thank God there are no free schools or printing-presses, and
I hope we shall not have any these hundred years;' and the latter,
'One-fourth of the annual revenue of the colony is laid out in maintaining free schools for the education of our children.'"—"The
American Commonwealth," Third Ed., Vol. I, Chap. XLIX, p. 618.
Thomas Jefferson, in his effort to secure the foundation of public
schools in Virginia, points, in vigorous fashion, to the contrast between
the policy of Virginia and the liberal policy of New York. See Letter
to John Cabell, Washington Edition of Jefferson, Vol. VII, pp. 186,
188; Ford Ed., Vol. X, pp. 165, 167.

South. The alienation of the negro and the menace of negro power not only eliminated the negro from the attempted reorganization of government, but operated also as a constraining force to draw together the separate classes of the stronger race, and to fuse them — men of ignorance with men of culture — into a racial unity far more powerful, far more effective, than the South had known before.

Politically, industrially, and I had almost said socially, this fusion is now practically complete. Still there are, in the white population, large numbers of the illiterate; but in the distribution of political and industrial responsibilities the South knows no longer the old distinctions of clan and class. The line of illiteracy is now local rather than social. It is a phenomenon conspicuous in rural localities, conspicuous nowhere in the cities. The democratizing of the South has assimilated within its progress all the classes and factions of its white people. The aristocracy exists no longer as a distinct political or industrial force. The expanding and enlarging life of democracy has included in the conscious movement of our civilization the most important of the non-participants of the older order. It is one of the far-reaching achievements of a democratic age.

I have said that the old South was the true basis of the new nationalism. It has also been the real basis of the new democracy. It is true that it has maintained at the South the old consciousness of importance — a consciousness which still impresses itself upon the life of the Nation, and which has been wholly unmoved by the fact that the South contains to-day but one-fourth of the white population of the land. It has maintained the old self-confidence, both in counsel and in action. It has maintained, in large degree, the old reverences and the old assumptions of social usage. But, chiefly, it has maintained, as one of the deepest forces of its social heredity, the old sense of responsibility toward the unprivileged. It is this force which has given distinction and beauty to the alliance between the aristocracy and the common people.

It is in its surrender to this force that the old aristocracy has passed away. It is in response to this force that the plain people have arrived, have arrived through the manifestation of those latent powers of initiative, those native capacities of energy and purpose, which have proved the amazement of the historian. Where the aristocracy has been sometimes faithless to its broader mission, the plain people have often wrested the rights which have been denied. In more than one locality the common people have ruthlessly assumed the reins of power; it is a phenomenon attended by its perils as well as by its inspirations. But upon the whole it is chiefly by coöperation that the white solidarity of the South has been secured, a solidarity which has been the broader ground of the new democracy, and which has sought a larger social unity upon the basis of unity of race. As a basis for democracy, the conscious unity of race is not wholly adequate, but it is better as a basis of democratic reorganization than the distinctions of wealth, of trade, of property, of family, or class. The passion for rehabilitation has swept the circle of social life, and has included every child within its policies. Through large sections of the South it has made the enthusiasm for popular education a form of civic piety. The cause of the common schools has become, not only a tenet of patriotism, but a social faith. It has entered the programme of politics. Popular education is to-day the theme of debate before multitudes gathered in humble "meeting-houses," or on the quiet hillsides under the open sky, or in the forest pulpits of the rural church. The debate proceeds, often attended by larger audiences and a deeper interest than any that attend the partisan discussions of the political campaign, a debate characterized by no clatter of the demagogue, but by that note of seriousness found in a man's voice only when he talks of the intimate realities of his domestic or religious experience. This is no vision of far-distant possibilities. It is a story of the present. Does it mean merely that democracy is being attempted? It means rather that democracy — so far — has been achieved. Democracy in its essence has arrived when the rich man and the poor man, the man of the professions and the man of trade, the privileged and the unprivileged, unite to build the common school for the children of the State. It means that the non-participants have come to take their part, in a certain high and liberal sense, not only as the factors of government, but as the heirs of a larger world.

And what of that other class of the "non-participants" in the older civilization? What of the negro? It was inevitable that thus far he should have been largely omitted. It was inevitable that the movement of democracy should have first included the non-participants of the homogeneous population. But is the

negro to be omitted in perpetuity? Is the organization of democracy in our Southern States never to
include him? Is he never — as a factor of government and as the heir of a free and generous life — to
be accepted as a participant in our civilization?

Such questions necessitate the definition of certain
terms. Democracy does not mean the erasure of
individuality in the man, the family, or the race. Its
unity is truer and richer because not run in one color
or expressed in monotony of form. Like all vital
unities, it is composite. It is consistent with the individuality of the man, it is consistent with the full individuality and the separate integrity of the races. No
one has ever asserted that the racial individuality of
the Jew, preserved for sixty centuries and through
more than sixty civilizations, by conviction from within
and by pressure from without, was a contradiction of
democratic life. Democracy does not involve the
fusion of races any more than it involves the fusion
of creeds or the fusion of arts. It does not imply
that the finality of civilization is in the man who is
white or in the man who is black, but in the man —
white or black — who is a man. Manhood, in a
democracy, is the essential basis of participation.

We hear upon every hand that the South has
refused its recognition to this principle. As a matter
of fact, and under their amended constitutions, tens
of thousands of black men are to-day registered voters
in the Southern States, voters registered not against
the consent of the South, but by the South's free and
deliberate will.[1] In view of the brief period of time
since the negro's emancipation and in the light of the

---

[1] See also footnote to p. 198 of this volume.

negro's political history, this voluntary registration of
black men in the South, this partial but increasing acceptance by the South of the qualified negro as a participant in the functions of government, is of far greater
significance in the essential history of democracy than
any temporary record of exclusion or injustice.   The
negro common school—nearly one million six hundred
thousand negro children are enrolled in public schools
supported by the Southern States [1]—this negro common school, with its industrial and political significance, is of greater import in the history of our
institutions than any temporary or partial denial of
political privilege.   With the suffrage question, in
detail, I shall deal hereafter.   I pause here only to
protest against that crudity of impatience with which
the world has so largely observed the development of
Southern life.   Expecting within the brief period of
a generation the entire re-creation of our industrial
fortunes and of our political institutions, men have
waited to see the whole character of a civilization
doffed like an outer garment; the fabric of a new
order—involving the deepest issues of memory, of
passion, of pride, of racial and social habit—instantly
re-created upon a strange loom and woven forthwith
after a pattern commended by that strenuous dilet-
tanteism which deals daily, with impartial ease, moral-
ity to presidents, reminders to empires, and a reserved
approval to the solar system.   Are not the real achievements of democracy at the South of far more significance than its failures?

Yet the gains of the past are not to be the occa-

[1] See Report of the U.S. Commissioner of Education for 1902, Vol.
II, p. 2063.

sions of surrender, but the ground of constructive effort. They are ours, not to excuse, but to inspire us. Out of those gains and out of the history which they have brought us, I think the cardinal considerations have come forth. The first is that, whatever Mr. Huxley may have read into the policy of emancipation, that policy meant to North and South, to the Nation as a whole, only a deeper acceptance of obligation. The second consideration is that this sense of responsibility, deepened rather than destroyed by the burden of slavery, was the noble and fruitful gift of the old South to the new, a gift brought out of the conditions of an aristocracy, but responsive and operative under every challenge in the changing conditions of the later order. It was personified in Lee. It spoke in Curry, in Wade Hampton, in L. Q. C. Lamar, in William L. Wilson. It has continued to speak through men like John B. Gordon and Henry Grady in Georgia, like Thomas G. Jones and Hilary A. Herbert of Alabama, like Fenner and Blanchard of Louisiana, like Montague in Virginia, like Aycock and Heyward in the Carolinas. It lies also at the heart of the future South, the South of younger men and more varied forces, and it is to this sense of responsibility, to this local and resident consciousness of power and right that—for every real and permanent enlargement of democracy—the appeal must be addressed.

That the South will do justice to the negro and to the more helpless elements of her industrial life, I have no manner of doubt. Certain current proposals of political policy at the South, certain passing phases of industrial oppression, receive direct and frequent criticism in the pages which are to follow. But this criticism is the criticism of a vigorous confidence, not the criticism of distrust. It is a criticism which assumes, before all things, the presence in Southern life of that quick sense of social obligation — always the deepest virtue of the nobler aristocracy — which has come over to us from the past. It is a criticism which represents the conviction that now, as ever, the appeal to the local conscience, to the resident forces of Southern character, — this and only this is the real hope of the future of democracy in our Southern States.

But — the reader asks — shall the Nation have nothing to say? Is not the South too sensitive to criticism from without? True, this sensitiveness is here. Is it a thing to be regretted? Is it not better than indifference? Is it not a more wholesome social asset than the leaden torpor of certain other localities of the Nation? Is it not a force of constructive good as compared with the temper of that self-satisfaction which is so conscious of its own attainment that it is wholly and placidly unconscious of the world's vaster hope, the century's ideal, the broader expectations of society? Is not this sensitiveness of the South a patent evidence of that very sense of responsibility to which reference has been made? Those only are sensitive to criticism who are conscious of failures because they are peculiarly conscious of great, commanding, haunting responsibilities.

But is not this larger and more sympathetic recognition of the sense of local obligation but another phase of the old cry to "Let the South alone"? In one sense, No; for in one sense that cry has been clearly wrong. There is such a thing

as a national citizenship, and the rights of all its
elements, however humble, must be the subjects of
national discussion. But what is a national discussion? Is it a criticism assuming that the Nation in
its righteousness is on one side and that the South is
sitting in darkness on the other? If the Nation must
include the South in the partnership of responsibility,
the Nation recognizes and includes the South in the
partnership of rectification. There is no federal
law which is not dependent for its efficiency upon
the action of Southern juries and upon the effective
sentiment of Southern communities. If this is one
country in the sense that there is no conceivable way
for men in the South to commit wrongs outside of the
Nation, it is also one country in the sense that there
is no conceivable way for the Nation permanently to
correct these wrongs except through the moral forces
of the South.

It is forgetfulness of this fact, it is the petulant
depreciation of the South as a whole, which has called
forth the cry, "Let us alone." And, as thus interpreted, this cry reflects no desire to ignore the
national interest and the national responsibilities
created by the rights of a national citizenship. Thus
understood, it is not so much a declaration of sectionalism as a protest against it.

Too often we find that when our Northern journalism discusses wrongs at the North or at the West,
it criticises the *wrongs*, but when it discusses wrongs
at the South it criticises the *South*. Such a criticism
tends to make evils arising in the Southern States
issues not between Americans everywhere and the
foes everywhere of a true Americanism, but crude

and bitter issues between the North and the South.
It is a temper reflecting a Pharisaism which is the
very soul of sectionalism — a Northern sectionalism
as offensive as any sectionalism in our Southern
States. The North, as the North, has nothing to do
with wrongs at the South. The North, as the North,
is, in the affairs of the South, a meddler pure and
simple. The Nation, including the South as well as
the North, and the West as well as the South and the
North, has to do with every issue in the South that
touches any national right of the humblest of its
citizens. Too long it has been assumed, both at the
North and at the South, that the North is the Nation.
The North is not the Nation. The Nation is the life,
the thought, the conscience, the authority, of all the
land. The South desires from every quarter — as
every section should desire — a true national participation in her interests. She wishes from every
spokesman of the Nation, whether in journalism or
elsewhere, a criticism national in the exacting nobility
of its ideals, national in its moral vigor, but national
also in its intelligent and constructive sympathy.

The development at the South of a larger sense
of nationality will be coincident with the development
of democracy. It is a consummation which a truly
national journalism and the forces of a truly national
criticism will advance. Such discussion is inevitable.
It is therefore the part of the South both to welcome it
and to inform it. This criticism may well speak frankly
and accurately of evils, of the misdirections of growth,
of failures both in purpose and in accomplishment.
But its effect will be corrective in proportion as its
temper is fraternal and its animus is coöperative.

Its dominant note may well be the note of a discriminating but sincere appreciation. The record of the Civil War, upon its Southern side, closes with a chapter of defeat; but it is a record of triumphs also, the triumphs of military genius, of industrial resourcefulness, of heroic if not unparalleled sacrifices. Yet the historian will record that the victories which have followed Appomattox are perhaps greater than the victories which preceded it. Indeed, one is reminded of that suggestive and moving passage in which J. R. Green has presented the dramatic moment in the passing of Puritan England : —

"A declaration from Breda, in which Charles promised a general pardon, religious toleration, and satisfaction to the army was received with a burst of national enthusiasm; and the old Constitution was restored by a solemn vote of the Convention, that 'according to the ancient and fundamental laws of this Kingdom the government is, and ought to be, by King, Lords, and Commons.' The King was at once invited to hasten to his realm; and on the 25th of May, Charles landed at Dover and made his way amidst the shouts of a great multitude to Whitehall.

"In his progress to the capital Charles passed in review the soldiers assembled on Blackheath. . . . Surrounded as they were by a nation in arms, the gloomy silence of their ranks awed even the careless King with a sense of danger. But none of the victories of the New Model were so glorious as the victory which it won over itself. Quietly and without a struggle, as men who bowed to the inscrutable will of God, the farmers and traders who had dashed Rupert's chivalry to pieces on Naseby field, who had scattered at Worcester the 'army of the aliens,' and driven into helpless flight the sovereign that now came 'to enjoy his own again,' who had renewed beyond sea the glories of Cressy and Agincourt, had mastered the parliament, had brought a King to justice and the block, had given laws to England, and held even Cromwell in awe, became farmers and traders again, and were known among their fellow-men by no other sign than their greater soberness and industry." [1]

Such was the victory of Puritanism over itself. It was indeed a triumph of self-conquest. And yet there is, perhaps, a victory even more striking, in the story of the men who turned their faces homeward from Appomattox. These went back, not as trades-men to their trading, but as men unused to the harder offices of industry, to take up, with unfamiliar labor, a grim and desperate struggle for life and bread. These went back to no waiting opportunities, to no world of appointed tasks, but to a saddened and desolated land in which tasks must be found and opportunities created. Before them was no prospective enjoyment of a successful compact with former foes, but the torturing vision of long years in which, through the consequences of their defeat, their homes and their meagre fortunes were to be the scene of administrative " occupation." They were to work out their task, not as members of a homogeneous population, heirs of a single civic fate, but confronted by the vast multitude of their former bondmen, — dark, vague, uncertain masses, — half-

[1] "History of the English People," J. R. Green, Vol. III, Chap. XII, p. 321; Harper & Brothers.

pitiful, half-terrifying, free forever from the white man's mastery, yet never free from the brooding and unyielding heritage of the black man's barbaric past. Under such conditions it was no easy thing to win the temper of confidence, to achieve the victories of patience, to find and actualize an industrial efficiency, a civic hopefulness, which might yield again an ordered and happy world.

The South, still possessing much of the fine genius of the old aristocracy, stood thus upon the threshold of a democratic age. We can hardly say that her entrance was unimpeded. She has brought little with her except her native resources, her historic and habitual faith in American institutions, her memories, her instinctive love of order and culture and beauty, her sense of civic responsibility. But she has crossed the threshold; and she has closed the door behind her.

THE SCHOOLS OF THE PEOPLE

CHAPTER II

THE SCHOOLS OF THE PEOPLE [1]

ᶠ Any description of the conditions of public education at the South must involve certain confessions of inadequacy and certain hearty celebrations of substantial progress.

It is not unnatural that there should still be left among us a large margin of the undone. That margin still remains — partly through the personalness with which the South has always conceived the training of the child, partly because of the class distinctions of the past, partly because of the poverty which followed war, partly because of the methods of spoliation which followed peace. The programmes of public expenditure which were made difficult by poverty were made odious by spoliation. Thus the domestic temper of Southern life, wrought upon by the moral distrust of appropriations for public purposes, and strengthened by the self-absorption of private industry, resulted in an exaggerated individualism which became half a dogma of politics and half a philosophy of self-reliance. It is therefore inevitable that democracy should have become, with many, a

[1] An address delivered, in part, before the General Session of the National Educational Association, Boston, Massachusetts, July 10, 1903.

mere creed of public economies ; and that self-reliance should have become, with some, but a doctrine of neglect.

It may be said in general terms that the present public school system of the South dates from 1870.[1]

In the period, however, which immediately followed the Civil War, the dissatisfaction of Southern life with the political organization of the State drew the life of the South with increasing earnestness into the denominational organizations of the Church.   These, at least, were loyally and securely Southern.   It is natural, therefore, that the actual educational organization of the Southern States should have first been denominational rather than civil, — an organization which left primary education to the home, which threw its influences into academic and sometimes narrow forms, but which has developed some of the noblest as well as some of the most characteristic forces of Southern life.

But the institutions of the Church represented largely, though not exclusively, the education of the aristocracy.   Following the period of reconstruction there arose a demand, increasingly self-conscious and increasingly imperative, from the great masses of an awakening democracy.   As the sense of democracy is aroused education must be democratized.   As the multitudes of our Southern citizenship came into the consciousness of power they turned instinctively to

[1] A State system of free public education was in partial existence in certain of the Southern States before 1860. In Alabama, the Act of February 15, 1854, may be regarded as the beginning of the State system ; but here, as elsewhere throughout the South, the issue of the Civil War involved a reorganization of the system with the inclusion of the children of the colored population.

put their citizenship to school.   It is the way men do. The beginnings of a real democracy, a democracy no longer bewildered by the older aristocracy which had been based upon slavery, no longer embarrassed by the later bureaucracy which had been based upon plunder, drew all men more closely together under the forms of the State, made men seek in the unity of their civic heritage and in response to the needs of a common citizenship what we call to-day the common school. The public school came in response to a more largely distributed consciousness of public life, a larger life of public interests and of public responsibilities. As the masses of men came to share the powers of the State, as men came to *be* the State, they wanted to do the thing well. We find in all lands and with all peoples that as democracy becomes a reality the school becomes a necessity.

And yet, while our public school system at the South has been necessary as an attempt, — an attempt which has had the consecrated intelligence and the heroic industry of our noblest souls, — we cannot say that it has thus far been wholly possible as an achievement. Its aspiration, however, is one of the great unifying and constructive forces in the life of the South to-day, an aspiration which, already expressed in the deliberate and official policy of every Southern State, would include within the opportunities of a free school at the public charge all the children of its citizenship, rich and poor, white and black. And that aspiration in its generosity and its justice, is itself, I submit to you, an achievement of ennobling and splendid augury.

For this policy of public education at the South

has called us to no holiday emprise. The way is thronged with difficulties. The task has first involved a problem of population. Ours is a double population, a population divided by the felt and instinctive diversities of race. The land is occupied by two families of men between whom the difference in color is, perhaps, the least of the distinctions which divide them. The differences in racial character are accentuated by the differences of social heritage — one is the population of the free-born, one has been the population of the slave-born.

The doctrine of race integrity, the rejection of the policy of racial fusion, is, perhaps, the fundamental dogma of Southern life. It is true that the animalism of both races has at times attacked it. The formative dogmas of a civilization are reflected, however, not in the vices of the few, but in the instincts, the laws, the institutions, the habits, of the many. This dogma of the social segregation of the races, challenged sometimes by fault of the black man, challenged sometimes by fault of the white man, is accepted and approved and sustained by the great masses of our people, white and black, as the elementary working hypothesis of civilization in our Southern States.

The great masses of our colored people have themselves desired it. It has made our public school system, however, a double system; and it is inevitable that it should have often made the negro schools inferior to the white schools. But the social and educational separation of these races has created the opportunity and the vocation of the negro teacher, the negro physician, the negro lawyer, the negro leader of whatever sort. It has not only preserved the colored leader to the negro masses by preventing the absorption of the best negro life into the life of the stronger race; it has actually created, within thirty years, a representation of negro leadership in commerce, in the professions, in Church, and School, and State, which is worthy of signal honor and of sincere and generous applause. The segregation of the race has thrown its members upon their own powers and has developed the qualities of resourcefulness. The discriminations which they have borne in a measure by reason of their slavery, and which have established the apartness of their group-life, are the discriminations which are curing the curse of slavery — an undeveloped initiative — and are creating the noblest of the gifts of freedom, the power of personal and social self-dependence. The very process which may have seemed to some like a policy of oppression has in fact resulted in a process of development.

Our problem of population has thus involved a double system of public education. If the duality of the system has been of advantage to the weaker race, it has been more than an advantage to the children of the stronger. It has been indispensable and imperative. In social as in personal achievement the necessities must precede the charities. The primary necessity of life in its every stratum of development is the preservation of its own genius and its own gains. The matured manhood of a more developed race may have something to give, should have something to give, through helpful contact, to the life of the undeveloped. But the more highly developed race must not make this contact through its children. In the interest of our own further development and

of our own larger achievement, in the interest of all
that our achievement and development may mean in
a nobler, juster, and more generous guidance of a
lowlier people, the point of helpful contact must not
be placed among the masses of the young, and the
leverage of interracial coöperation must not seek its
fulcrum upon the tender receptivities and the un-
guarded immaturities of childhood.

It is not merely that the marked differences of
race suggest marked differences of method.   We,
at the South, are dealing with the negro, not as an
individual, but as a multitude.   In hundreds of our
Southern counties the negro population is greater
than the white.   In my own home county, the
county of the capital of the State of Alabama, our
colored people outnumber our white people almost
three to one.   In an adjoining county the proportion of the colored population to the white population is six to one.   Under such conditions the
abandonment of the dual system of public education
and the enforcement of a scheme of coeducation
for the races would involve, not the occasional sending of a few negro children to a white school — as
is your custom here — but the sending of a few
white children to the negro school.   It would not
mean — as some would mistakenly advise — the training of the children of the weaker race in the atmosphere and under the associations of the stronger,
but the attempted training of the children of the
stronger race in the atmosphere and under the associations of the weaker.   Such a policy would not
give either promise or advantage to the stronger
race, to the weaker race, or to any far-reaching and

constructive interest of civilization. A double system
of public education is, with all its burdens and with
its varied difficulties, an inevitable and unchangeable
issue of our problem of population at the South.[1]

But our problem of population — turning now with
more especial consideration to the white population
of the South — includes a formidable problem of distribution. It is not only predominantly rural; it is
relatively more meagre in its numbers than many
have yet attempted to realize. There are almost as
many cities of twenty-five thousand people in the one
small State of Massachusetts as in all the States of
the secession put together. Taking our figures —
as throughout this address — from the twelfth and
latest census of the United States, we find, in the
single State of Massachusetts, twenty cities having a
white population of more than twenty-five thousand
— nearly twice as many as the total number of such
cities in all the States of the late Confederacy. There
are, including the State of Texas, in all the States of
the secession but *twelve* cities having a white population of over twenty-five thousand.

The one State of Massachusetts alone has forty-
seven cities with a white population of over ten
thousand. All the States of the Confederacy together have but thirty-eight such cities.

Moreover, the total aggregate white population of

[1] Even where the negro children are in a minority, as a negro
writer has pointed out in the *Congregationalist*, Boston, May 30,
1903, — it is an injury to the children of the weaker race to be educated in an environment which is constantly subjecting them to adverse
feeling and opinion. The result must be the development of a morbid
race consciousness without any compensating increase in racial self-
respect.

all the cities in Alabama, South Carolina, North Carolina, and Tennessee, having a population of ten thousand inhabitants and over, does not equal in number the population of the city of Buffalo or the city of Pittsburg.

The total aggregate white population of the States of Alabama and South Carolina does not equal the white population of the city of Chicago; and the white population of the present city of New York exceeds the aggregate white population of the States of Alabama, Florida, Louisiana, Mississippi, and South Carolina.

I have dwelt thus upon the relative meagreness of the numbers of the white population of the South because it is inevitable that that population will have to bear for many years the larger share of the responsibilities of education and of government. The burdens and the peculiar difficulties of the South are thus greater, I believe, than the world at large has yet appreciated. Of direct taxation the negro contributes little. Of indirect taxation he contributes an honorable and increasing share. The rents pay the taxes and the negro tenant helps to pay the rents. In a press telegram of the current week I am therefore glad to find the following characteristic illustration of the temper of the South in reference to the common schools of our colored people. The message appears in the columns of one of the daily journals of New York City under date of July 7 : —

" *Atlanta, Georgia, July 6.* — Advocates of schemes to block negro education by State aid are in a bad minority in the House of Representatives of the General Assembly of Georgia. To-day after a sharp debate the House, by an overwhelming vote, rejected a resolution providing that in the distribution of money to common schools the county authorities should apportion the money among white and colored schools according to the taxable property of the two races. This would have meant the death of negro education in Georgia, as the blacks pay only one-fifteenth of the taxes, although receiving about one-third of the State appropriation for public schools. To-day's debate showed that the sentiment of the Georgia legislators is that the State should contribute to the limit of its ability to the common school education of its colored people."

Georgia's action is not unique. The vote of her legislature reflects the settled and established policy of every Southern State.[1]

Returning to the fact that the white population of New York City exceeds the aggregate white population of Alabama, Florida, Louisiana, Mississippi and South Carolina, you will observe that our problem of population has thus brought clearly into view some of the difficulties of isolation. Ours is not only a rural population; in many sections it is a population so small in numbers as to be but thinly distributed over large areas, with poor roads, with inadequate recourse, therefore, to strong centres of organization, and without that consequent social efficiency which easily secures the creation and the administration of the efficient school.

In the United States at large 20 per cent of the

[1] See an effective criticism of the above proposal by Charles B. Aycock, Governor of North Carolina, in his biennial message to the General Assembly, 1903, Raleigh, N.C.; Edwards and Broughton.

school population live in cities of twenty-five thousand population or over; at the South our cities of twenty-five thousand contain but 6 per cent of the children of our public schools. Our city schools, however, are usually adequate and efficient.

The East has suffered, perhaps, from an over-municipalization of life, from the tendency of population cityward. The South has suffered from the under-municipalization of life, from that too general dependence upon agriculture which has kept almost 85 per cent of our population in the country, and has given us cities few and small. The building of good roads, the development of manufactures, the method of school consolidation, the increasing tendency to apply the educational qualifications of the suffrage to white men as well as black, the policy of our legislatures reënforced by the educational patriotism of all our people, will at length give us Southern schools adapted to Southern needs.

Those needs will slowly but surely have more adequate response. Our people are resolved to have their schools, despite the difficulties presented by our problems of population, — a population which is, as we have seen, biracial in character, comparatively small in number, comparatively rural in its distribution, — and despite the fact that our task of public education involves not only these grave problems of population but as grave a problem of resources.

The figures of our national census show that from 1860 to 1870 there was a fall of $2,100,000,000 in the assessed value of Southern property and that the period of reconstruction added, in the years from 1870 to 1880, another $67,000,000 to the loss.

In 1860 the assessed value of property in Massachusetts was $777,000,000, as contrasted with $5,200,000,000[1] for the whole South; but at the close of the war period Massachusetts had, in 1870, $1,590,000,000 in taxable property, as contrasted with but $3,000,000,000 for the whole South. The standards of assessment are probably much more exacting at the East than at the South, yet this consideration does not operate wholly to erase the contrast which remains. Such had been the shrinkage in values at the South, such had been the relative increase in values in New England, that the one small State of Massachusetts had more than one-half as much of taxable property as the combined wealth of all our Southern States.

The very theory of emancipation was that the fate of the black man was the responsibility of the Nation, yet the issue of war left the negro in his helplessness at the threshold of the South; and the South, with the gravest problems of our civilization challenging her existence and her peace, was expected to assume the task of the education of two populations out of the poverty of one. I confess that I think the conscience of the South has something to say to the conscience and the opulence of the Nation, when, with millions for battleships, tens of millions for armaments, millions for public buildings, and tens of millions for rivers and harbors, the Nation allows the academic fabric of paper theories to stand between the vast resources of its wealth and the human

---

[1] The fact that slaves were included in such estimates does not lessen the economic catastrophe represented in the loss of a form of property in which so much of energy and wealth had become involved.

appeal, North or South or East or West, of the children of its citizenship.

A democracy which imposes an equal distribution of political obligation must find some way to afford a more equal distribution of educational opportunity. To a national philanthropy or to our national legislation there should be an appealing significance in the fact that the annual expenditure for public education in the United States at large is — per capita of the pupils in average attendance — $21.38, that in the great States of the West the average expenditure is $31.59, while for such States as Alabama and the Carolinas this expenditure is approximately but $4.50. Let us not, in contrasting these figures, forget the educational heroism of the South. Unquestionably the South must call more freely and more generously into play the policy of local taxation by the school district or by the county, but of the State revenues for general purposes 50 per cent, in Alabama and the Carolinas, are appropriated to the support of public education.[1]

It is inevitable, however, that our problems of population, our problem of an isolated rural life, and our problem of resources should have resulted in the illiteracy of the present. If I dwell for a few 'minutes upon the figures as to the illiterate, I do so with the reminder that there are worse things in a democracy than illiteracy, and with the passing assurance that I

[1] It is interesting to note that in 1890 there was " expended for public schools on each $100 of true valuation of all real and personal property " 22.3 cents in Arkansas and 24.4 cents in Mississippi, as compared with 20.5 cents in New York and 20.9 cents in Pennsylvania. See Report of the U. S. Commissioner of Education, 1902, Vol. I. p. xci.

shall soon be able to turn to the brighter side. But remedies and congratulations will not avail us save as we frankly and resolutely face the facts.

There are in our Southern States more than 3,500,000 souls ten years of age and over, who cannot read and write; nearly 50 per cent of the colored population, and 12.7 per cent of the white.[1] Of the native white population of our whole country, ten years of age and over, the South has 24 per cent; but of the native white illiteracy of our country, the South has 64 per cent.

There are in the United States 231 counties in which 20 per cent and over of the *white* men of voting age cannot read and write. Of these 231 counties, 210 are in our Southern States.[2]

Taking a few of our States individually, we find that — among the white population ten years of age and over — there are 54,000 illiterates in South Carolina. That is, for South Carolina or for any other Southern State, a very large number of white people. It is only 13.5 per cent of the total white population

---

[1] The illiteracy of the native white population of the Southern States ranges from 8.6 per cent in Florida, 8 per cent in Mississippi, and 6.1 per cent in Texas, to 17.3 per cent in Louisiana, and 19.5 per cent in North Carolina; as contrasted with 0.8 per cent in Nebraska, 1.3 per cent in Kansas, 2.1 per cent in Illinois, 1.2 per cent in New York, and 0.8 per cent in Massachusetts. A far juster comparison, however, is that which indicates the contrast, not between the South and the rest of the country in 1900, but between the South of 1880 and the South of to-day. This progress is indicated in Table V of the Appendix, p. 300.

[2] See Appendix A, Table VIII. It will be noted that a number of the counties classified as in the South, and a number outside the South, include in the "white" population — on the border of Mexico and on the Canadian frontier — an appreciable foreign element.

over the age of nine. Yet this is a company of white people greater in number than the aggregate white population of the five largest cities of the State, — Charleston, Columbia, Spartanburg, Greenville, and Sumter.

The white illiterates of Georgia are but 11.9 per cent of the white population ten years of age and over, but their number exceeded in 1900 the number of the aggregate white population of Georgia's three largest cities, — Atlanta, Savannah, and Augusta.

The white illiterates of Tennessee, 14.1 per cent of the white population ten years of age and over, exceeded in 1900 the number of the total white population of her six largest cities, — Nashville, Memphis, Knoxville, Chattanooga, Clarksville, and Jackson.

The white illiterates of Alabama, nearly 15 per cent of the white population of ten years of age and over, exceeded in 1900 the number of the aggregate white population of her fifteen largest cities; and in 1900 the number of the white illiterates of North Carolina, 19.4 per cent, was more than double the number of the combined white population of her sixteen largest cities.[1]

The possible surprise occasioned by these contrasted totals should suggest to us that such figures teach much more than the relative magnitude of the number of the illiterate. The figures indicate, not only the number of the white illiterates in the State, but the relatively small proportion of the white population now found within the *cities*. Such comparisons indicate the presence of many colored people in our

[1] See Twelfth Census of the U.S. (1900), Vol. I, Table 23, and Report of the U.S. Commissioner of Education, 1902, Vol. II, p. 2316.

Southern cities, but they especially indicate a fact upon which I have already dwelt as of cardinal and conspicuous importance, the fact that the population of the South is still characteristically and preponderantly rural.

It is not as a prophet of calamity that I have dwelt upon some of the facts as to our illiteracy. The problem is formidable, but no problem need be the occasion of discouragement so long as that problem is apparently yielding to the forces of its reduction. Relatively and actually, illiteracy is not gaining upon the schools. The schools, in spite of all our difficulties, are gaining upon our illiteracy. Taking our population of prospective or possible voters, the male population, white and black, ten years of age and over, we find that there is not a State in the South which has not largely reduced its illiteracy within the twenty years from 1880 to 1900.

Upon the other hand, as I take some kindly satisfaction in reminding you, there is but one State in New England — Rhode Island — which has not added both to the percentage and to the aggregate of its *male* illiteracy since 1880.[1] Your percentages of general male illiteracy are very much lower than our own, but they are a little greater to-day than they were twenty years ago. If your figures must include the foreigner, ours must include the negro. New York had over forty-seven thousand more of male illiterates in 1900 than in 1880; Pennsylvania had in 1900 over sixty-two thousand more such illiterates than in 1880; Massachusetts, over twenty-three thousand more than in 1880; and the percentages have grown

[1] See Twelfth Census of the U.S., Vol. II, Table LV, p. ci.

with the aggregates. Totals have grown a little in some of the States of the South, but including even the colored population, the percentage of male illiterates has been reduced in Alabama from 49 to 32 per cent; in Tennessee from 36 to 20 per cent; in Georgia from 48 to 29 per cent; in North Carolina from 46 to 27 per cent; in Arkansas from 35 to 19 per cent. In the Southern States our public schools, with all their embarrassments, are overtaking our illiteracy; in some of the Eastern States the illiteracy of future voters has gained just a little upon the range and contact of the public schools. Illiteracy is, in fact, not a sectional, but a national, problem; and I think that we must everywhere declare that a democracy which still comprises more than six millions of people who cannot even read and write has not yet adequately solved the problem of popular education.

I find, however, no hopelessness in the illiteracy of the South, because, as I have suggested, we are now making decisive reductions in its volume. I find no hopelessness in it, because it is the illiteracy, not of the degenerate, but simply of the unstarted. Our unlettered white people are native American in stock, virile in faculty and capacity, free in spirit, unbroken, uncorrupted, fitted to learn, and worthy of the best that their country and their century may bring them.

To speak hopefully of the taught is to speak even more hopefully, even more confidently, of the teacher. The relative poverty of the South has its compensations. It places at the command of the public school system of the Southern States a teaching force of broad ambitions, of real culture, and of generous refinement. The high social standard of our teaching

personnel is our assurance that the training of the
children of the South is in the hands of worthy representatives of its thought and feeling. We know that
in its public school system the South of to-day is
touching through its *best* the life and the institutions
of to-morrow.

The crowning argument of our hopefulness lies, however, in the educational enthusiasm of all our people.
Alabama, within five years, has doubled her general
appropriations for public education. The masses of
a sincere people are taught the great realities of
order, liberty, and culture, not merely by what they
have, but by what they long to have. The things
that a whole people, in the passions of their sacrifice,
have *resolved* to do are of more significance and of
more importance in the history of a democracy than
anything that they may have failed to do.

But the Nation must be considerate of the South
and the South must be patient with herself. The
burden of responsibility among us must long fall
heavily upon the few. We have seen that there are
in our Southern States 210 counties in which 20
per cent, or over, of the white men of voting age cannot read and write. Place to one side the great unlettered masses of our colored population, add to these
the unlettered numbers of our white population, and you
will at once see that the number which remains has a
part to play which is so serious in its responsibilities
and so far-reaching in its moral and civic significance
that the South may well receive the large-tempered
understanding of all the lovers of mankind, and of
all the wise befrienders of the State.

A final and happy element of hopefulness lies in

the thought that if our system of public education is largely uncompleted, we can build, in completing it, by the light of the gains and the errors of older commonwealths. Tardiness should save from false starts and should protect us from traditional mistakes. I trust that we shall build in such a manner as more largely to practicalize and moralize the general system of public education. I trust that our consciousness of the problem of illiteracy will not lead us to the mistaken conclusion that the supreme task of any system of schools is the mere removal of illiteracy. The school must stand, rather, for a larger and larger measure of trained intelligence, of controlled and sobered will, of sound, resourceful, and efficient life.

I trust that we shall realize, moreover, that the fullest duty of the modern school, of the public school in a democracy, is a duty not only to culture, but to citizenship. The State-supported school must give the State support, — support as it teaches with a healing wisdom and an impartial patriotism the history of the past; support as it looks out into the track of an over-freighted destiny and clears and steadies the vision of the future; but first of all, support to the Nation in this day — in this day because this day is not supremely our fathers' or our children's, but uniquely and supremely ours.

The schools of a people, the schools of a *real* people, must be, primarily, not the moral gymnasia of reminiscence or the transcendent platforms of future outlook. They must touch this day's earth and this day's men through the truths and the perils of to-day. They must be instructors of the contemporary civic conscience. And in this hour, I take it, they must

help the State to bring to men a profounder and
therefore a simpler reverence for the institutions and
the processes of public order. For a long time we
have heard that democracy is an institution of liberty; but if democracy be not also an institution of
public order, liberty will not long be an institution
of democracy. Where minorities — mob minorities,
North or South or East or West — presume to administer the laws of the majority, the elementary compact
of democracy is dissolved. The mob which abandons
the processes of social self-control weakens the personal self-control which stays and conquers crime,
and increases by its ferocities the very animalism it
has attempted to destroy. Its instructions in horror
touch the minds of tens of thousands, its barbarities
burn to-day the guilty and set aflame the hates and
humors which to-morrow burn the innocent.

Such spectacles are national phenomena, challenging everywhere the national forces of American good
sense, and demanding of us whether the mere gravity
of the crime or the mere weakness of the constabulary is enough to excuse any American community in
abandoning the safeguards of justice and the solemn
processes of trial for the processes of a social hysteria
which divides its noisome interest between the details
of the crime and the souvenirs of the execution. Are
these the august and reverend trappings of Justice in
a democracy?

Our schools must teach our children what their
country is. Our schools, North and South, must
help men to see that liberty of government means
that there is no liberty except through being governed, that being governed and being governable are

largely the measure of our distance from the jungle;
that a governed and governable people, when challenged by the sickening atrocities of crime, by the
torturing spectacles of lust and hate, first have a
sober recourse to the thought, not of what is due to
the criminal, but of what is due to their civilization,
their country, and their children.

For we may be well assured that, whether we teach
through the school or not, the teaching is being done;
for society itself is the final educational institution of
our human life.   Not only through school and home
and Church, but through the habits of our commerce,
through books, through each day's press, through our
posters on the streets, the music in our parks, our
amusements and our recreations, — above all, through
that great enfolding, effectual instrument of our social
self-projection, the public opinion of our day, our
children are being put to. school.

I pray that within these varied orbits the people's
schools may do their schooling well, not as detached
or isolated shops of truths and notions, but as deliberate
and conscious factors of a sounder social equilibrium.
I pray that they, North and South and East and
West, may take their places as the organs of that
force of social gravity, that moral dynamic which in
the University of the World keeps the poise of factions and classes, upholds the authority of institutions, the majesty and the happiness of government,
the worth of laws, the high securities of freedom —
that moral dynamic which wise men have called the
fear of God, the force of affection and sobriety which
holds life to reverence and reverence to reason, — as,
through their uncrossing pathways, the stars flash,
star-lighted, round their suns.

A CONSTRUCTIVE STATESMANSHIP

CHAPTER III

A CONSTRUCTIVE STATESMANSHIP

I

THE movement of democracy at the South presents, essentially, a task of constructive statesmanship. If the representatives of political and party action are earnestly concerning themselves with the problems of popular education, it is because such problems are the reflection, not only of the desire of the people, but of the need of the State. It is understood that universal education is, in the broadest sense, no mere topic of the educator. It is the interest of the citizen.

Illiteracy is being recognized with admirable candor and increasing courage. Here and there a voice is heard which speaks with depreciation of its significance. There is an occasional note of denial and resentment. But with increasing knowledge denial is abandoned, and with increasing reflection resentment passes into concern, and concern into a deepening solicitude both for the unfortunate and for the South. Men recognize that the greater reproach is not illiteracy, but indifference to it. They perceive that its significance cannot be offset by dwelling upon the admitted and often darker evils of other sections. When the life of the State is burdened or imperilled by unfortunate conditions, the word of a true patriotism is that which recognizes these conditions in order to remove them. It is never that word of superficial partisanship which, lulling to sleep the consciousness of need, gives permanence and increase to the need itself. If States do not grow wise by forgetting their knowledge, it is equally true that they do not add to their knowledge by forgetting their ignorance.

The South has been moved, however, by the fate of the unfortunate as well as by the need of the State. Her interest in the unlettered masses of her white people is due to no motive of condescension or contempt. Most of them are a people of pure and vigorous stock — our " contemporary ancestors," as the president of Berea has described them. Many of them are distinguished by peculiar intelligence and force. Some of them are people of property. An occasional reactionary spirit declares that because he esteems and loves them, and because they are better than many of the literate population of other sections, the movement which reveals their ignorance and insists upon their education is to be resisted. The answer of the South, as a whole, is that — because she esteems and loves them — their children are entitled to the broadest opportunities and the best advantages which life may offer; that any movement which reveals their ignorance in order to bring them knowledge, which would increase their knowledge not upon the ground of their incapacity, but upon the ground of their value to society, which asserts their right to the world's best, and the world's right to their best, is a movement to be commended and reënforced.

There was a time when illiteracy was a normal

factor in society. That time has passed. Illiteracy
is abnormal; literacy is the normal assumption of
civilization. When practically all men — all of the
general masses of mankind — were illiterate, literacy
was hardly an element in the movement of popular progress or in the play of industrial competition. Such conditions have passed forever. Literacy
in the greater fraction and illiteracy in the smaller
fraction of population means that the smaller fraction is subjected to a relative disadvantage in
every movement of experience, whether religious,
social, political, or industrial. It is shut out, reli-
giously, from the broader outlook upon that word
of God which is daily uttered in the increasing
freedom and fulness of human life; it is shut out,
socially, from that wholesome largeness of temper
which results from the knowledge of a more varied
world of men and things; it is shut out, politically,
from the educative influence of those great national
debates which form the instruction of the plain man
in economic truth and democratic policies, thus helping to make of citizenship no mere local perquisite,
but a national privilege. The fraction of the illiterate is shut off, industrially, from that confidence which
results from being able to read what others read, to
know what others know, and so to do, to the freest
and best advantage, the business of life. The farmer
or the laborer who can read and write finds in that
power the enlargement of his market. He is not
only more fitted to work or to produce, he can be
informed in a broader sense as to the conditions of
industry, and can sell to more intelligent advantage
his product or his labor. It is evident that, here and

there, the individual member of society may rise by sheer force of some peculiarity of character, or some chance of opportunity, out of many of the limitations which illiteracy imposes. But it is true, upon the whole, that for the great masses of men in the civilization of our world to-day, illiteracy is the symbol of non-participation.

II

Thus, in relation to the fuller life of our civilization, there are in our Southern States two classes of non-participants, — the masses of our negroes and the illiterates of our white population. There is now little question at the South as to the nature of her policy toward the latter. Their freest education and equipment is almost everywhere recognized as the supreme interest of society and the State. The nature of the policy of the South toward the former, the task of the education of the negro, presents a problem upon which there has been much of serious and explicit difference. Writing from within the South, and as a part of the South, I may wish the negro were not here, but my wishing so would not provide him either with adequate transportation or another destiny. He is here among us. We are face to face with him. We must take him as we find him, and talk about him as he is. The problem he presents is one which silence has not dissipated, nor indifference answered; which bitterness may always intensify, but which bitterness has never solved. There are those who tell us that the negro is to go to Africa. How long will it take to persuade the negro he should go? Then how long will it take to persuade

the white man to let him go? Then how long will
the going take? If he fails, he will return; if he
succeeds, the white man will follow him upon his
lands, as he has followed the Indian here and the
Filipino across the seas, and, competing with him
upon his new soil, will create the same difficulties
which were here abandoned. The great problems
of civilization, for individuals or for races, are not
solved by deserting them.

In the meanwhile nine millions of them are here.
What are we to do with them?

There are some who tell us that "as a matter of
scientific fact" the negro death-rate is a little greater
than the negro birth-rate, and that therefore the negro
is to become extinct. But a busy world cannot count
so much on "sociological data" as to pause to calcu-
late the proper estimates of extinction for a race which
does its dying by doubling its numbers within forty
years.

And in the long generations through which the race
is dying, what are we to do?

If education as a power of real and constructive
good is of value to a living race, to a race achieving
and succeeding, it is of still greater value to a failing
race. If society needs the corrective and upbuilding
force of education to protect it against ignorance in
the wholly capable, the ignorance of the partially
incapable requires — for the protection and upbuilding of society — not less education, but more, an education practical in its forms but human and liberal in
its spirit.

And yet it were folly to ignore the fact that the
policy of negro education has been often and seriously

questioned. One may well write of it, however, not as an alien policy, but as a policy of the South, inasmuch as negro education has been for thirty years — under local administrations elected by the people — the official and authoritative policy of every Southern State. If, therefore, I speak here at length of the schooling and the training of this backward race, I do so, not because it is a duty which the South has ignored, but because the South, with generous foresight and incalculable patience, has so largely attempted to discharge it.

Three objections, however, have partially attended and embarrassed the maintenance of this policy of our Southern States.

I. There has been opposition to the policy upon the ground that the education of the schools would lead to vanity in life; that the supposed tendencies of the negro would increasingly draw his ambition in the direction of the higher education, and that the higher education of the negro would imperil the interests of race integrity.

II. There has been opposition to the negro common school, — first, upon the ground that it has done too little, inasmuch as it has left the general life of the race so largely unaffected; secondly, upon the ground that it has done too much, and has " spoiled good field hands by teaching books."

III. There has been opposition, not only to lower education and to higher education, but also to industrial education, — to industrial education upon the ground that this form of negro training must result in industrial friction and competitive warfare between the races.

It would be strange indeed if education — a policy of God long before it was a policy of man, a policy of the universe long before it was a policy of society — were to find its first defeat at the negro's hands.[1] And yet in each of these objections there lies the force of a half-truth, a half-truth to be frankly recognized, and to be fully understood before it can be fully met. I believe, however, that the long-standing policy of the South has been fully justified, and that such mis-apprehensions as have existed have arisen partly from the misunderstanding of the facts and partly from certain evident errors in our traditional educational methods.

1. In dealing with the familiar question as to the "increasing perils of the negro's higher education," let us see, first of all, if these perils are increasing; then we may inquire as to how far they exist at all. Let us see how much higher education the negro is getting, not merely at the South, but from anybody anywhere.

Let me say at once, however, that the South can-not well be opposed to the higher education of those who are fitted for it.[2]   Where individual capacity exists, the only thing, the only right and wise thing

---

[1] See Report of the Superintendent of Public Instruction of North Carolina, 1902, p. viii. Superintendent Joyner's report should be care-fully read in forming any adequate estimate of the real temper of the South in reference to negro education.

[2] See also an admirable paper on " Negro Education," by W. B. Hill, Chancellor of the University of Georgia, in the Proceedings of the Sixth Conference for Education in the South, 1903, p. 206, published by The Committee on Publication, Room 607, 54 William Street, New York City.

in the world, to do with it is to equip it and direct it. The repression of it will result, not in its extinction, but in its perversion. A thwarted and perverted capacity is a peril both to the individual and to the State. Repression is not a remedy for anything. The repression and perversion of the capacities of our greatest negro would have made him the most dangerous factor in Southern life. Such capacities may be seldom found. Where, however, these capacities exist, there is neither joy nor safety nor right nor common sense in the belittling of a thing which God has given, or in the attempted destruction of a power which has entered into the experience of the world as one of the nobler assets of the Nation and of humanity.

But higher education is, it seems, not a broadening pathway of negro progress. The dread that our colored people, in increasing multitudes, would thus clutch at the vanities of culture in order to leave behind the homelier interests of useful labor has not been realized. Let us note the facts. Says Commissioner Harris : —

"In 1880, the population of the entire country had 4362 persons in each 1,000,000 enrolled in schools of secondary and higher grade, but in that year, 1880, the colored people had only 1289 out of each 1,000,000 enrolled in secondary and higher education. This means that the general average of the whole country showed three and one-half times as many pupils in schools of secondary and higher education as the general average for the colored people.

"In 1890, the number of colored persons in high schools and colleges had increased slightly, namely, from 1289 to 2061 in each 1,000,000 of the colored

population, and in the year 1900 they had reached
2517 in each 1,000,000. But in the meantime the
general average for the United States had increased
from 4362 to 10,743 per 1,000,000. While the number in colored high schools and colleges had increased
somewhat faster than the population, it had not kept
pace with the general average of the whole country,
for it had fallen from 30 per cent to 24 per cent of
the average quota.

"Of all the colored pupils only 1 in 100 was engaged in secondary and higher work, and that ratio
has continued substantially for the past twenty years.
If the ratio of colored population in secondary and
higher education is to be equal to the average for the
whole country, it must be increased to five times its
present average."[1]

If the figures of the commissioner could take into
account the number of negroes who are classed as
pursuing the courses of "colleges" which are colleges
only in name, the figures would show a still larger
percentage of negro pupils in strictly primary work.
The statistics indicate, as compared with the white
race, no relative increase in the number who are
taking a so-called higher education, and the record of
all the facts would indicate that truth still more clearly
than the figures quoted.

It is true that higher education possesses its
"perils." All education possesses its perils. They
are apparent among any white population as well as
among any negro population. There is always present the danger of superficiality, the danger of self-

[1] See Report of United States Commissioner of Education for 1899–
1900, Vol. I, pp. lviii and lix of the Preface.

glorification, the insistent temptation to substitute show for reality and cleverness for work. Education, on its most elementary side, involves risk. Many a life, among our white people, has been educated out of contentment without being educated into efficiency. Many a blind heart which was at peace in its blindness has gained only enough light to lose its peace without the gain of full and accurate sight. These are but the familiar risks of liberty. Many a man would have been prevented from being a murderer if he had been kept always in a prison. But society has realized that while the lifelong prison might have prevented murder, it would also have prevented manhood, and that it is well to give men freedom, upon the broad and familiar ground that the smaller risk of murder is of slight concern as compared with the larger chance of gaining manhood.

Education brings its dangers. But the risk of making fools is of smaller import than the larger chance of making men. Through long experience society has also found that the dangers of ignorance are greater than the dangers of knowledge. In the case of the negro it is evident that the educational process has a larger record of failure than in the case of the Caucasian. | This was inevitable. The kind of education which has been tried by the negro in the mass has not been adapted to his racial need; it has been the Caucasian's kind. But as the Caucasian's kind is the only kind which the Caucasian has been largely active in giving, the faults of misadaptation can hardly be charged against the negro.

Undoubtedly our negroes in the mass need, chiefly, an education through industrial forms. Of this I shall speak hereafter. It is, however, in the interest of the race as well as in the interest of the South that the exceptional negro should be given a broad and generous measure of exceptional advantage.

That every race is a wiser, safer, and better social force for having a leadership — wise, well-informed, and true — is axiomatic. No race can succeed, as one of their number has wisely said, "by allowing another race to do all its thinking for it." The South has insisted, and has insisted wisely, on maintaining the absolute distinctness of racial life. The wisdom of this insistence, the deep sociological value of what has been called "race prejudice," — despite its sometimes brutal and excuseless manifestations in every section, — will have, I believe, an ever widening recognition. But if human society is to establish its distinctions of racial life, it will find that it can base these distinctions upon intelligence more securely than upon ignorance. Ignorance will be blind to them, will hate them and attack them. Intelligence will perceive them, and, if they are reasonably and soundly fixed, will understand them and coöperate with them. The "troublesome" negro at the South is not the negro of real intelligence, of sound and generous training, but the negro possessing, or possessed by, the distorted fancies of an untrained will and a crude *mis*education.

The very segregation of the negro race seems thus to establish the necessity for the real training of their abler minds,— for those differentiations of negro ability which will give to the race a sane and instructed leadership from within.

The development of this leadership, the opportunities of freer and larger growth, are more important to the race, to the South, and to the interests of racial separation than can easily be realized. Racial distinctness is chiefly threatened at two levels, the lowest and the highest; at the lowest, where vice obliterates the safeguards of domestic purity; at the highest, where the occasional refusal of the broadest development sometimes obliterates the safeguards of liberty. The true and permanent way to lead the negro race to keep wisely to itself is to make it sufficient within itself. The race which is to be forever forced to go outside of itself to touch the broadest and richest life of its generation will never be consciously and finally anchored in the doctrine of race integrity. The true basis of race individuality is not in race degradation nor in race repression, but in race sufficiency.

II. In discussing the questions arising from the negro common school, it is perhaps too often assumed that the policy of general education has been really tested. If the results are unsatisfactory, is it not largely due to the inadequacy of the experiment? Almost half of our colored people in the Southern States — after forty years of freedom — are wholly illiterate. Large numbers of them are indeed the despair of statesmanship. But they are not worthless because they have gone to the school. Rather, they are worthless because they left it, or they have left it because they were worthless. Shall the worthlessness of these negroes condemn the school? Shall we condemn the education of the negro, shall we condemn the education of any people, on the evidence presented by those who, through poverty or weakness or wilfulness, have touched the system of education only to desert it?

Nor in bringing an impeachment against negro education are we merely impeaching the negro; we should also be impeaching the only remedial, corrective, and constructive policy of a democracy. If we are not going to educate them, what are we going to do with them?

At least, let us not condemn the policy of negro education until we have established it and until the negro has tried it. One who will carefully and accurately investigate the real conditions of negro life may well maintain that those among them who have really tried it, who really know something and who can really do something, are, on the whole, a credit to themselves, to the South, and to their country. The great overwhelming masses of them, however, have as yet come about as near to illustrating the results of education as though education were the scourge, rather than the sceptre of broad, efficient, and resourceful living.

Great numbers of them can read a little and write a little. But is that education? Who will presume to test the high policies and to dispute the imperative validity of education in a democracy, because, forsooth, thousands of witless and idle blacks, after a prolonged and convulsive labor of aspiration and perspiration, can just manage to put some kind of a vague scrawl upon a piece of soiled paper with a lead pencil? Yet these people are supposed to show the evil result of negro education. Now, it would be hard to say just what that much education proves, except perhaps that there would be less folly if there were

F

more knowledge.[1] But a constructive statesmanship may well protest against the insistent and preposterous assumption that one can ever judge any sort of education, negro, Caucasian, or Malay, by seizing a random conclusion from the general mob of the uneducated. There is no test, there can be no test, of the policy of the school except in the number and quality of those who have at least seriously attempted the sacred experiment for which it stands.

We may well continue to be tolerant of the policy of negro education until we ourselves have applied it, and until the negro has practised it.

We may condemn him for his failure to practise it. Yet the fault is not wholly his nor ours. The fault is not his alone, inasmuch as the public resources of the South have been utterly insufficient for the double burden placed upon them. As we are told by the United States Commissioner of Education, it is estimated that the South, since the year 1870, has expended $109,000,000 upon the education of our colored people.[2] And yet it also appears that, for these thirty-odd years, the annual school term afforded to the negro child has averaged less than seventy

[1] The general social and economic conditions presented by large numbers of the colored population render it obviously impossible to establish any close relation between mere literacy and crime; yet Mr. Clarence A. Poe, of Raleigh, N.C., clearly shows that even under the more adverse conditions the literate negroes are the least criminal (*The Atlantic Monthly*, February, 1904). There is also a clear distinction to be made between literacy and "education." The greater criminality of the negro at the North is due, not to his partial emancipation from illiteracy, but to industrial discrimination and to the unwholesome conditions of city life. See p. 186, and note on p. 173.

[2] Report of the United States Commissioner of Education, 1899–1900, Vol. II, p. 2501.

days. Indeed, the school term for our white children in our rural districts has averaged little more. If the negro child has had upon the average less than three months in which he could go to school, he has thus had more than nine months of every year in which to forget what he learned. It is hardly wise to condemn the policy of negro education, to condemn any policy of religion or culture or statesmanship, upon the basis of so inadequate a trial.

If the less fortunate results cannot be wholly charged against the negro, neither can they be charged against the dominant people of the South. Theirs has been a task of baffling difficulty and of torturing confusion. They have had to re-create their properties before they could hope to create those institutions which represent, through the resources of taxation, the active participation of property in the tasks of government and of education. The South has had to get something before it could give anything. Yet out of its poverty it has given much. The negro, too, has given — directly or indirectly. As has already been suggested, the rents pay the taxes, and the negro helps to pay the rents.

The negro primary school is the result.

Before dealing more explicitly with its merits and its defects, let me dwell, in passing, upon the argument of those — a decreasing number — who oppose the negro school, not because it has done too little, but because it has done too much. We are told that "it has spoiled good field hands by teaching books."

The charge is in part well founded. It is a charge which at one time or another has been brought, in every nation in the modern world, against the education of the agricultural laborer. It has been used so long against the training of white men that one need not be surprised to hear it made against the training of black men.

Those who are inclined to attribute the animus of this objection wholly to what they may call the "race prejudice of the South" have too readily forgotten the arguments which, within less than half a century, have everywhere opposed the education of the industrial classes. There are those who are always tempted to believe that it is the chief business of the poor man to remain poor, and of the cheap man or the cheap woman to remain cheap. The leisure classes — and the employing classes — both North and South are too often opposed to any broad realization of an industrial or political democracy, and the basis of this opposition is a class feeling as well as an economic fear. The wonder is, not that such opposition still exists, but that it now exists under so many evident modifications.

As a mere class prejudice, one is indeed under no constraint to argue with it. There are those, both in England and in America, who have accepted as one of the finalities of thought that "shopkeepers," "tradespeople," and "working-people" must never be anything else. There are those, North as well as South, who are confirmed in the opinion that the negro should remain a field hand, a field hand only, and that the nine millions of the negro population in our democracy are forever to find their industrial function solely in menial service or unskilled employments. So impossible a contention it is unnecessary to discuss.

But there is also an economic objection to the education of the agricultural laborer at the South. It is true

that certain special interests feel that their fortunes
are involved in the preservation of a labor uninstructed and therefore cheap. These interests are instinctively averse to " the spoiling of field hands," and
it is altogether probable that where too many establishments are doing business upon the basis of the lowest
living wage some of them will have to suffer through
any differentiation in the mass of their unskilled labor.
But in any normal diversification of interests there
will always be enough labor of the cheaper type.
There is little danger, at the South especially, that
there will soon be any serious dearth of labor commanding but the lowest wage. Is not this precisely
the economic difficulty of the South at large ? A few
interests may see a peril in the fact that a few of the
negroes are ceasing to be field hands ; but the South
as a whole finds a greater peril in the fact that so few
of them are fit to be anything else.

For the broader welfare of democracy, involving
not merely one class but all classes, is not injured by
the " spoiling of field hands," if in that process the
man who was worth but fifty cents a day is changed
into a man worth a dollar and fifty cents. The process of change has manifestly helped the man himself :
it has helped the employer, unless he is a victim still
to the old economic fallacy that the " cheapest " labor
is the most inexpensive. He will also find, as I have
suggested, that it is always less difficult to secure
dozens of men worth a low wage than to secure one
man who is really worth a higher wage. This indicates that society wants, because society values, the
higher wage, — values it not only as a measure of the
increased efficiency which life demands, but as an

effective part in the forming of the wage standard of every man who works. We have too long assumed that the negro in the fields at fifty cents a day is a non-competitor, and that he becomes a competitor only when he comes to town, or when he attempts to do what white men do. Every man who labors is a competitor with every other man who labors. If a considerable class in any civilization are on a fifty-cent basis, the tendency of the reward of all employments is affected in the direction of that basis. The annual salary of the cashier of the largest bank in one of the older cities of the South has been but $2400; near him, in the surrounding territory, are thousands of men on a fifty-cent basis. The man worth only the low wage in the fields holds down the wage of the unskilled laborer in the town, for if the town laborer reject his wage the laborer from the fields may be summoned to take his place. If the lower skilled labor of the town reject its wage, the more efficient of the unskilled may easily be substituted, and thus on through the ascending scale, rank pressing upon rank, the wage of each advancing or depressing the wage of all.

The remedy, of course, lies not in the crude device of paying the fifty-cent man more than he is worth. It lies in adding to his wage by first adding to his worth. If he is worth more, the employer can afford to pay him more. His increasing efficiency bears upward against the level of the labor just above him, compelling, not merely a higher wage, but a higher qualification for that wage; the ascending competition of efficiency is substituted — from level to level — for the depressing attraction of inefficiency at the base; and society, as a whole, moves with a freer sense of accomplishment and enters into a broader measure of welfare.

For the man on a fifty-cent basis holds down, not only the individual wage, but the collective profit of the community. He is upon a basis of mere existence, affording no surplus store for wants beyond the demands of animal necessity. He has no margin to spend. He is not a purchaser because he is hardly a producer. Yet commerce is carried on, banks are conducted, churches are extended, schools are supported, homes are maintained, governments are administered, upon the margin that remains between the bare limit of existence and the outer limit of the wage. Where great masses of men are worth no more than a mere existence they contribute little more than a mere existence to society.

How shall he be worth more, worth more to the farmer, worth more to the intimate and interwoven fortunes of all labor and all society, — worth more not only to himself but to the State, — worth more that he may contribute more? All the institutions of civilization are first to unite in that exacting and supremely difficult process by which he is to be transferred from the ranks of the incapable to the number of the capable. The home, the Church, the press, — the play and challenge of the forces of industry, — all are to have their part; but evidently one of the institutions upon which society must most largely depend for the conduct of this complex and stupendous task is that simple, familiar, but much neglected institution, the rural common school.

In the course of this change, many a field hand

will be "spoiled," spoiled, not by being made more useful, but by being made less useful. This fact cannot be forgotten or denied. In every such process of transformation there is a fraction of failure. A human being is taken out of one economic setting and is not transferred successfully to another. It is the tragedy of all education, but it is a tragedy of education only because it is one of the inevitable tragedies of all experience. Surgery saves life, but surgery has sacrificed lives in trying to save them. The Church labors divinely for belief, but the Church has sometimes made men doubters in trying to make them Christians. Institutions are not perfect; men are not perfect. Of all men, — when we especially consider the exacting demand with which the negro in his weakness is confronted in a modern democracy, — the negro may be expected perhaps to furnish the largest percentage of failures, of failures in that process by which society transforms the masses of the inefficient into the efficient. This would be true under the best conditions. It is all the more naturally and inevitably true when we consider the limitations of the chief instrument of this transformation, the negro common school.

Let me dwell first, however, upon some of its contributions to this process. It has its manifest weaknesses. It may represent strange, grotesque misadaptations of theory and method. I often suspect that the last thing it does is really to educate — educate, that is to say, in the word's usual and familiar sense. But there is one thing which this school does. It represents the first contact, the first constraining, upbuilding contact, of the life of civilization with the life of the uncivilized. It serves in at least four definite ways (aside from any knowledge it may impart) as an institution of moral power in the life of every child within its walls.

(1) It represents the discipline of *punctuality*. When the untutored child first gets into his mind the notion of going to a particular place and of doing a particular thing at a particular time, he has begun to get into line with conscious, intelligent, efficient human life. In other words, he has got hold of one of the rudimentary assumptions of civilization. Is it not of importance to realize what a difference lies just here between the state of the savage and the state of the citizen? There is a moral idea and a moral achievement in the notion of punctuality, and the rural primary school stands for that.

(2) It stands, also, for the discipline of *order*. The child finds not only that there is a time to come and a time to go, but that there is a place to sit and a place not to sit. He finds that there is a place for everything, that everything has its place, and that even standing and sitting, as well as the whole task of *behaving*, are to be performed under the control and direction of another.

(3) The primary school stands also for the discipline of *silence*. For a group of chattering children — negro children, any children — there is a moral value in the discipline of silence. To learn how to keep still, to learn the lesson of self-containment and self-command, to get hold of the power of that personal calm which is half modesty and half courage, to learn a little of the meaning of quiet and some-

thing of the secret of listening, — this is an element in that supremacy of will which is the faculty and privilege of the civilized.

(4) Finally, the primary school stands for the discipline of *association*. It represents the idea of getting together. Getting together is a civilizing exercise. Ten people, old or young, cannot get together in a common room for a common purpose without every one's yielding something for the sake of others — some whim, some impulse of restlessness, some specific convenience, or some personal comfort. Human society is a moral achievement. Associated effort, however slight the sphere of its exercise, represents part of the discipline of civilization. The more ignorant the company, the greater is the effort represented, and the more significant the lesson. In the primary school, the children learn something not only from getting together, but from one another. As the teacher, however lowly in attainment, is usually at least one rank above the pupils, the personality of the teacher makes the contribution of its influence. No negro school, however humble, fails to represent something of this discipline of association.

Now, these things are worth while. The discipline of punctuality, the discipline of order, the discipline of silence, the discipline of concerted action, — these are elements of merit in the influence of our primary educational system which in the training of a child-race are worth, of themselves and irrespective of the nature and amount of the instruction, all the cost of this system to the country and to the South.

When, however, we touch this system on the side of its more positive contribution as an *education*, its faults are conspicuous and formidable. We have been giving the negro an educational system which is but ill adapted even to ourselves. It has been too academic, too much unrelated to practical life, for the children of the Caucasian. Yet if this system is ill adapted to the children of the most progressive and the most efficient of the races of mankind, who shall measure the folly of that scholastic traditionalism which would persist in applying this system to the children of the negro, — and which would then charge the partial failure of the application upon those very tendencies of the negro which a true educational statesmanship might have foreseen, and which a wise educational system should have attempted to correct? If the weaknesses of the negro have made him run to the bookish and the decorative in knowledge, we must remember that the schooling we have provided for him has at least been bookish, even if it has not been decorative.

The South, I think, will face this question and will deal with it. We must incorporate into our public school system a larger recognition of the practical and industrial elements in educational training. Ours is an agricultural population. The school must be brought more closely to the soil. The teaching of history, for example, is all very well; but nobody can really know anything of history unless he has been taught to see things grow — has so seen things, not only with the outward eye, but with the eyes of his intelligence and his conscience. The actual things of the present are more important, however, than the institutions of the past. Even to young children can be shown the simpler conditions and processes of growth, — how corn is put into the ground; how cotton and potatoes should be planted; how to choose the soil best adapted to a particular plant, how to improve that soil, how to care for the plant while it grows, how to get the most value out of it, how to use the elements of waste for the fertilization of other crops; how, through the alternation of crops, the land may be made to increase the annual value of its product; — these things, upon their elementary side, are absolutely vital to the worth and the success of hundreds of thousands of these people of the negro race, and yet our whole educational system has practically ignored them. The system which the negro has, let us remember, is the system which we ourselves have given him.

I make no adverse criticism of our educational authorities. The South's indebtedness to them is beyond expression. They are, for the most part, in sympathy with such suggestions. The question can be reached at last only through the wiser training of the teachers; and, with the teachers actively ranged upon the side of such amendments to our educational policy, the change will come. Such work will mean, not only an education in agriculture, but an education *through* agriculture, an education, through natural symbols and practical forms, which will educate as deeply, as broadly, and as truly as any other system which the world has known. Such changes will bring far greater results than the mere improvement of our negroes. They will give us an agricultural class, a class of tenants or small landowners, trained

not away from the soil, but in relation to the soil and
in intelligent dependence upon its resources. Thus
the "spoiling of the field hand" will never mean a
real loss to the lands of the State, but an added force
of intelligent and productive industry.

In a number of the fertile agricultural counties of
the South there has been for twenty years a slight
but gradual decrease in the per capita wealth of the
county. The best negroes have been moving away.
Progress for the negro has come to mean emancipation from the soil. The State becomes poorer when
the lands of the State are left in the care of the idle
and incapable. This error can be corrected only by
identifying the negro's progress with his labor, by increasing his value as a farmer through teaching him
to farm intelligently and successfully, — by linking
his interest and his hope directly to the land. As he
prospers, the larger owner will not have to waive his
rents. As the tenant comes up, the land comes up
with him. The successful farmer raises the value
and the productive power of the soil upon which he
stands.

We can get the wealth out of the soil only by putting into the soil the intelligence and the skill of the
man who works it. When our tenants and our farm
labor can mix in their ideas with the land, and can
put thinking and planning into their ploughing, sow-
ing, and harvesting, the whole earth begins to lift up
its head like a pasturage of wealth, happiness, and
dignity. We must sow something more than seed.
We must put ideas into the ground if we are to get
more money out of it. A pound of ideas and another
pound of hard work will go further than ten pounds

of any fertilizer that was ever made. And what is the fertilizer but the practical product of an idea?

Let me repeat. If the South is to advance the wealth of the land, we must advance the practical intelligence of the labor which works it. If we are to advance the intelligent usefulness of our labor, we must go straight to the children. If we are to reach the children, we must get hold of them through the school.

If the school is to represent saner methods and a wiser educational system, we must begin with the training of the teacher. The teacher who teaches must be in sympathy with the soil, with honest work, with intelligent and fruitful industry, and must be so in love with the practical bearing of a practical education upon the concrete life of his people that the drift and direction of his training will be toward thrift rather than toward idleness. Education, under such a teacher, will represent, as has been said, "not a means of escaping labor, but a means of making it more effective." This is where we touch upon the contribution of Hampton and Tuskegee.

These are industrial normal schools, schools for the finding and equipment of just such teachers. They are, primarily, institutions for teacher-training. They are not, primarily, institutions for the training of domestic servants. Schools for instruction in domestic service might well be founded by their graduates in some of the larger cities of the South. I hope that that may be. But the white race is providing few teachers for our population of nearly eight millions of negroes. The teaching of their countless children — through the policy and the preference of

the South herself — is left to negroes. Hampton and
Tuskegee are trying to better the quality and to
increase the technical and practical value of these
teachers. If these two schools could *double* the out-
put of their work, they would be touching but the
remoter limits of this stupendous task. Theirs is the
work of the education of these teachers through practical methods and industrial forms, in order that they
may go forth to this backward people in our rural
South, and there may train the children in the intelligent use of the soil, of concrete objects, and of
natural forces, so that, as there comes about the rising of this race, the whole land may rise with it, —
the true progress of the negro thus representing, not
the fattening of the industrial parasite, but that wholesome and creative growth which will capitalize the
life of the State with the skilled hands and the productive capacity of its masses.

III. Is there any danger in the coincident industrial
development of our two races? There are those who
tell us so. Many of the same men who assured us,
ten years ago, that industrial education is the only
education the negro should have, are now ready with
the assurance that for fear the industrial development
of the negro will clash with that of the white man,
this form of negro training is the most dangerous
contribution that has thus far been made to the solution of our Southern problems. The poor negro!
The man who would keep him in ignorance and then
would disfranchise him because he is ignorant must
seem to him as a paragon of erect and radiant consistency, when compared with the man who first tells

him he must work, and then tells him he must not
learn how.

He tells the negro he must make shoes, but that
he must not make shoes which people can wear; that
he may be a wheelwright, but that he must make
neither good wheels nor salable wagons; that he
must be a farmer, but that he must not farm well.
According to this fatuous philosophy of our situation,
we are to find the true ground of interracial harmony
when we have proved to the negro that it is useless
for him to be useful, and only after we have consistently sought the negro's industrial contentment on
the basis of his industrial despair.

The South had no trouble with her slaves before
the war; we had no trouble with them during the
war, even when our women were left largely at their
mercy. We had no trouble with them after the war,
till the carpet-bagger from the North came down
upon them. They were a peaceful and helpful people because slavery had at least taught them how to
do something and how to do it well. The industrial
education of the negro is intended to supply, under
the conditions of freedom, those elements of skill,
those conditions of industrial peace, which our fathers
supplied under the conditions of slavery. It is not
without significance that no graduate of Hampton or
Tuskegee has ever been charged with assault upon
a woman.

We must not forget, however, that the critic of our
negroes still further arraigns them because, in Alabama, for example, while constituting over 45 per
cent of the population, they pay perhaps less than 5
per cent of the direct taxes; yet, strangely enough, the

same man declaims in the next breath on the peril of the
negro's industrial rivalry. For thirty years this type of
the arraignment of the negro has paid the negro the
tribute of its fear, and has insulted the white man by
its assumption of his industrial impotence. Certainly
it should seem conspicuously evident that if there is
one thing the South need not fear at present, it is
any general or too rapid increase in the productive
efficiency of the masses of her negroes. Her peril,
as has already been suggested, lies in precisely the
opposite direction. It is certainly no tribute to the
Caucasian to assume that his own proud and historic
race, with its centuries of start and the funded culture
of all civilization at its command, cannot keep ahead
of the negro, no matter what the negro can know or
do. The only real peril of our situation lies, not in
any aspect of the negro's wise and legitimate progress, but rather in the danger that the negro will
know so little, will do so little, and will increasingly
care so little about either knowing or doing, that the
great black mass of his numbers, his ignorance, his
idleness, and his lethargy will drag forever like a
cancerous and suffocating burden at the heart of our
Southern life. And yet, were the industrial development of the negro tenfold as rapid and twentyfold as
general in its scope, should we then be compelled to
witness the predicted annihilation of the weaker race
at the hands of our industrial mob? I think not.

The native qualities of the negro persist as his
protective genius. Whenever the negro has looked
down the lane of annihilation, he has always had the
good sense to go around the other way. "The
negro," says Mr. Dooley, "has many fine qualities;

he is joyous, light-hearted, and aisily lynched." But
the last of these qualities is individual, not collective.
He avoids its expression by avoiding the occasion for
its exercise. If Burke was right in saying that we
cannot indict a whole people, it is also true that we
cannot lynch a whole race, especially when this race
has a preference for amnesty, will accept in the
white man's country the place assigned him by the
white man, will do his work, not by stress of rivalry,
but by genial coöperation with the white man's interests, will take the job allotted him in that division of
the world's work which is made by the white man's
powers, and will do that work so well that the white
man can make more from it by leaving it with the
negro than by doing it himself. Such has been the
working principle of the industrial coördination of
these races, North as well as South. It is a principle
which I have here stated in its crudest form. It is
often modified by especial consideration on the one
side, and by especial efficiency on the other. But
the principle itself runs back into the nature of men
and the nature of things.

A weaker race dwelling in the land of a stronger
race makes no war upon the stronger, creates no
critical social or industrial issues, takes the place assigned it in the political, social, and industrial economy
of the land. The negro will prove himself so useful,
so valuable to the country, to humanity, that the
world will want him to live. He will not invite extinction through industrial exasperations, through
self-assertive competitions. He gives way. He
comes back upon another track. He fits into his
own niche. The increase of his efficiency increases

the possible points of his adaptation to the world's work. The world holds more of work than of workers, and the more varied the opportunities for work, the more chance for all the workers. Industrial conflicts are found in their acutest form, not in the complex fields which only the few can occupy and where the principle of the division of labor is most fully recognized, but in the elementary tasks which almost every man can perform, and in which all the unfitted are fitted for competition.

The field of competition is narrowed as the field for differentiation is broadened. As we touch the tasks of skill, we touch the keys of industrial harmony. The negro comes with his skill to our industrial organization; the world gives him his place. He takes it. He demands, he can demand, no more than the world gives him. Whatever it may be, it is his lot; and he accepts it. This is not cowardice. Our negroes have fought well in war. It is something deeper than cowardice. It is something deeper than self-preservation. It is a profounder, a more constructive impulse. It is self-conservation. It is life.

And we need not dwell too much upon the theories of alarm. There is nothing more weakly theoretic than a theoretic fear. The apprehensions which have attended the progress of the negro have usually come to nothing with the arrival of the facts. Just as it was " conclusively established," before the general use of the locomotive, that passengers going faster than twenty miles an hour would certainly perish " from lack of breath," so it was confidently argued that the negroes when emancipated would rise and slay the women and children of their absent masters. Some of the Nation's wisest men thought that emancipation would lead to slaughter. Later, it was contended that the immediate and universal bestowal of the ballot — an act of unpardonable folly — would lead to interracial war. But the oft-predicted "negro rising" has never come. It is always well in dealing with the negro, or with any factor of experience, to determine one's policy, not from the possible results which one fears it *may* produce, but from the actual results which one may see it *does* produce.

Here are the negroes of our representative Southern communities. Does the South have serious difficulty with those who really know something and who can really do something? Which class of negroes is the greater menace to our peace, — the negroes who have the scores of little homes through the better negro districts of our Southern cities, who are increasing their earnings, sending their children to school, buying clothes, furniture, carpets, groceries, chiefly from the white man's stores and to the white man's profit; or those negroes whose industry is indeed no competitive menace to the most sensitive, who, if they are without ambitions, are equally without excellences, who are unskilled enough to satisfy the most timorous, who work three days that they may loaf four, who may be responsible for several families, but who are without a sense of responsibility for even one, who are without pride except the pride of the indolent and the insolent? Which class of negroes chiefly figures in the police records and makes the chief burden upon our courts? Which class of negroes constitutes, therefore, the real peril

of our situation, the efficient or the inefficient?
— the negro who is making real progress, or the
negro who is making none? The one class adds
little to the wealth and much to the burdens and
perplexities of the State; the other is the most
adaptable and tractable element in the race, and it
adds by everything it produces, by everything it
buys or sells, to the volume of business and to the
wealth of the community.

We are sometimes tempted to go off upon a false
and hopeless quest. We at times imagine that the
two classes of negroes between which the South may
choose are the old-time darky and the present-day
negro. But practically there is no such alternative
for us to-day. We must clearly see, many of us with
sorrow, that the old-time darky is forever gone.
He was the product of the conditions of slavery, conditions which no man at the South could or would
restore. We cannot choose between the old-time
darky and the new. The South, in the exercise of
a practical responsibility, must necessarily make its
choice between the two classes of the new: the
class of quiet, sensible, industrious men and women
(as yet a minority, but a minority steadily increasing)
who seek through intelligence and skill to be useful
to themselves and to their country; and the class,
upon the other hand, which is backward, thriftless,
profitless — which draws from the land or the community only what it may consume — which creates no
wealth because it has no needs, which furnishes the
murderer, the rapist, the loafer, the incendiary —
which presents no theoretic competition for the job
of our skilled laborer largely because this class of

negroes is not much possessed of any skill nor much enamored of any conceivable job. There are just two classes of negroes in our land to-day, those who are going forward and those who are going backward. I have little doubt as to the choice which the South will make.

The somewhat morbid fear of the negro's industrial education would never have arisen but for the prevalence of the economic error that the volume of the world's work is fixed in quantity, and that if the negro does a part of it, there will be less of it for the white man. But one man's work does not reduce the volume of the work open to other men. Every man's work produces work for all. Every laborer who is really a producer represents a force which is enlarging the market for labor. The man who makes a table broadens the opportunities of industry behind him and before him. He helps to make work for the man who fells the trees, for the man who hauls the trees to the sawmill, for those in the mills who dress the timber for his use, for those who dig and shape the iron which goes into the nails he drives; he makes work for the man who provides the glue, the stains, and the varnish, for the man who owns the table at the shop, for the drummer who tells about it, for the men who sell food and apparel to those who handle it and who profit by its repeated sales from the factory to the wholesaler, from the wholesaler to the retailer, and from the retailer to the final purchaser. The man who makes a table makes business. The man who makes shoes or harness or tools or wagons makes business. The work of the trained producer does not restrict the market of labor. It enlarges that market. The friction sometimes due to the negro's possession of a lower standard of living passes away as the negro advances in real education and genuine skill. As he begins to work productively, he begins to live better. He is not like the myriad labor of the Orient which never accepts American standards. As the negro goes up, his standard of living goes up. There will never be any question about the negro being a consumer. He is ever a free spender. To strengthen him, upon wise lines, as an American producer will add not only to his capacity to work, but to his capacity to buy, and both what he produces and what he purchases will directly contribute to the wealth and peace of the community and the State.

And what, let us ask, is the alternative? If, in dealing with these people, we are not to seek the results of stability and harmony in the conditions of intelligence and industry, where and how may we seek them? Is there a sound basis for stability and harmony in these great black masses of ignorance and idleness that we find about us? Have prosperity, peace, happiness, ever been successfully and permanently based upon indolence, inefficiency, and hopelessness? Since time began, has any human thing that God has made taken damage to itself or brought damage to the world through knowledge, truth, hope, and honest toil? Industrial activity is the best security for industrial harmony. The world at work is the world at peace.

The negro has his weaknesses. He has his virtues. He is not here because he chose this land of ours. The land chose him. We can abandon this task, but it cannot abandon us. It is the grave but unescapable privilege of our Southern States to take it and to work out through it, as the stewards of our country's power and our country's will, one of the greatest national obligations of American life.

What trait among the negro's weaknesses is made better by idleness, hopelessness, and industrial helplessness? What trait among his virtues is destroyed by right thinking, by real knowledge, by the capacity to see clearly and to work successfully? God made him a man. We cannot and we dare not make him less. But we may not be self-deceived. If we are to make him all he may become, we have before us a task of immeasurable and appalling difficulty, a task more difficult than that attempted by the armies of the North when they moved against the South, a task more difficult than that of those heroic armies of the South which withstood the North, but a task which the higher and holier purpose of the North and of the South, in response to the challenge of our children and of humanity, will yet perform. Its difficulty is not a reason why we shall fail. It is the reason why we shall succeed. The sore strain and trial of such a task will touch, not merely the chords of our compassion, but the metal of our manhood, and the thing will be done — done wisely, justly, courageously, and with the patience of a great country's love — just because it was so hard to do.

III

I have dwelt thus long upon the subject of negro education partly because many of the principles involved are to a degree identical with the principles involved in the education of the unprivileged masses of our white people, partly because the Southern policy of negro education invites a fuller discussion than any policy of white education can require.

What is true, however, of the negro masses is largely true of the white masses. With the few necessary qualifications, everything that has here been said in behalf of a more practical educational system for the negro school may be said in behalf of similar changes in the rural schools of our white people. The differences in racial heritage should be recognized. Certain forms of industrial training may be emphasized the more clearly with the masses of our negroes; certain forms of scholastic training may be emphasized the more clearly with our white children. The two races are not the same, and they will not respond in the same way to precisely similar influences. The average negro child starts much farther back than the average white child. To recognize that fact and to educate as though we recognized it is not cruelty to the negro, but the fairest and tenderest kindness. Nor does this mean that the negro is always to have a poorer quality of education. A difference in form, in the interest of a closer adaptability to need, should represent, not the reduction, but the preservation of the wisest and truest educational standards.

The racial heritage of the white man must be clearly accepted and recognized in the form of his educational system; and yet a white population so largely dependent on its agricultural resources and its productive industry must bring its public education into more articulate relations with the soil and with its work. If the South needs to secure the sounder industrial progress of her negroes, she must be sure that the industrial progress of the great masses of her white people is given a support which shall be even more resourceful in its enthusiasm and even more aggressive in its activities.

The relation of the system of public education to the needs of an agricultural people is a subject which has engaged the consideration of the great States of the West just as it must engage the attention of the South.[1] But there is this significant and striking difference. The West, since 1870, has received an efficient foreign white population of more than 5,000,000 souls. The South is gaining comparatively little from white immigration. In 1900 the

[1] There is much of practical value in the Report for the year ending June 30, 1900, of the State Superintendent of Education for Wisconsin. Those who may be interested in the general methods already adopted in Ireland, France, Sweden, Denmark, Belgium, Switzerland, and Germany may well turn, among the documents of the same State, to the Report of the Commissioner appointed by the Legislature of Wisconsin in 1899 "to investigate and report upon the methods of procedure in this and other States and countries in giving instruction in manual training and in the theory and art of agriculture in the public schools." Among practical elementary manuals on the subject of agriculture may be mentioned: "Principles of Agriculture," by L. H. Bailey; "Agriculture for Beginners," by Burket, Stevens, and Hill of Raleigh, N.C. (Ginn & Co.); and "Rural School Agriculture," by W. M. Hays.

five Southern States — Alabama, Georgia, Mississippi, North Carolina, and South Carolina — had, in a total population of over 8,800,000 souls, only 44,996 of the foreign-born. In the small State of Vermont, with a total population of only 343,641, there were 44,747. In the single State of Kansas there were 126,685 of the foreign-born; in the one State of Nebraska there were 177,347; in the State of Ohio there were 458,734.[1]

It is from the ranks of the masses of our own people (if we are to have a sound and vigorous economic development) that we must largely secure, not only the populations of the market and the professions, but the more intelligent populations of our shops and fields. We must put at the command of our humbler white people — perhaps I had best say our prouder white people — an educational system freed from the follies of inadequacy upon the one hand and of misadaptation upon the other. The stores of our fields and our mines will be of small avail unless the skill and equipment which shall transmute them into wealth are exercised within the borders of the South, in loyal and affectionate attachment to her interests and her happiness.

Upon the necessity and the policy of white education, we are practically agreed. And yet the possibility of neglect is also present here. It is not that danger of neglect which comes from bitter and definite aversion, but the more subtle peril of vaguely assuming that a work upon which everybody is agreed is somehow going to be performed just because we are agreed upon it. There is in mere

[1] See also Table VII of the Appendix, p. 304, columns 4 and 5.

agreement no real dynamic of social progress. There is little moral power in the universal affirmation that two and two make four. Our need to-day in behalf of the unprivileged masses of the rural South is not that we shall agree upon education, but that we shall educate.

The task before the South is one of conspicuous magnitude. Striking an average for the eleven States of the secession, we have found that of the native white population ten years old and over 12.2 per cent cannot read and write; while in North Carolina and Louisiana — and Alabama is not far ahead, — one white person in every six is recorded as illiterate. No other eleven States in the Union anywhere nearly approximate this condition. In all the States outside of the South, taken together as a group, the average rate of illiteracy among the native white population is only 2.8 per cent as against 12.2 per cent of native white illiteracy in the South. The negroes are not here included. These figures deal with none other than the native white population. If we add to these figures the number of our white people who can just pass the test of literacy, who perhaps can barely sign their names, but who are practically illiterate, our conditions are seen to be still more serious.

And yet the hope of democracy in the life of the South to-day lies in the fact, as we have seen, that among increasing multitudes of men the agreement to educate is passing into conviction. The percentage of white illiteracy is large, but it is to-day decreasing. From 1880 to 1890, according to the United States census, the percentage of illiteracy in the native white population ten years of age and over was reduced from 22.7 per cent to 15.9 per cent. From 1890 to 1900 it was reduced from 15.9 to 12.2 per cent. The reduction of this percentage within the next ten years will be even more striking. The great host of the non-participants is entering into its own.

A political statesmanship is recognizing that the desire of the people is the education of all the people, and that the political influence of the South is to be advanced by no merely negative devices of resistance, but by the South's intelligent and positive contribution to the great national decisions upon economic and party issues. Quality, as well as quantity, must always enter into the subtle influence of constituencies. An educational statesmanship is perceiving that, as the people come to know, the opportunity of the university is enlarged. And the common schools contribute to the university something more than an increasing practical support. The university in the South is beginning to appreciate the vital relation between a sympathetic culture and common need, realizing as never before that the ideals of the higher learning cannot flourish in freedom or in fruitfulness save in the responsive atmosphere of a popular faith in ideas and a popular kinship with the scholar's spirit. A religious statesmanship perceives that the mission of Christ was to the largeness as well as to the rectitude of life, that breadth and sweetness of temper find a deeper security in the inheritance of the educated man, and that what every citizen claims in his heart for his own children he must desire as instinctively for the children of another. The statesmanship of our public press is perceiving that in the existence of a generally educated public opinion there reside some of the secrets of editorial independence, of adequate circulation, of broader journalistic power. An industrial statesmanship is declaring that the South's largest undeveloped wealth lies in its undeveloped populations.

Public education, as the primary policy of the South, is thus presenting, not merely an opportunity and a duty; it presents a policy of investment — wise and sacred and secure. A constructive statesmanship — a statesmanship of educational and religious insight, of political sagacity, of economic validity — is informing and renewing the life of the land; and not alone in the heritage of the past or in the wealth of fields and forests and mines, but in the promise of the forgotten child of the people, the enlarging democracy finds its charter.

THE INDUSTRIAL REVIVAL AND
CHILD LABOR

CHAPTER IV

I

THE present industrial development of the South is not a new creation. It is chiefly a revival. Because the labor system of the old South was so largely attended by the economic disadvantages of slavery, and because the predominant classes of the white population were so largely affected by social and political interests, it has often been assumed that the old order was an order without industrial ambitions. The assumption is not well founded. Instead of industrial inaction, we find from the beginnings of Southern history an industrial movement, characteristic and sometimes even provincial in its methods, but presenting a consistent and creditable development up to the very hour of the Civil War. The issue of this war meant no mere economic reversal. It meant economic catastrophe, drastic, desolate, without respect of persons, classes, or localities. And yet through all the phases of catastrophe there still remained the essential factors of the old prosperity — the land and its peoples. Thus the later story of the industrial South is but a story of reëmergence.

Without some conception of the industrial interests of the old South, the story of the later South is, how-

ever, not easily understood. It is, for example, to
Colonel William Byrd of Westover, known more
recently in the pages of fiction, that we are indebted
for some of the interesting particulars as to the
early development of the iron properties of Virginia.
Writing in 1732, he tells us, among others, of "England's iron mines, called so from the chief manager
of them, though the land belongs to Mr. Washington."
These mines were about twelve miles from Fred-
ericksburg. A furnace was not far away. "Mr.
Washington," says Colonel Byrd, "raises the ore and
carts it thither for twenty shillings the ton of iron
that it yields. Besides Mr. Washington and Mr.
England, there are several other persons concerned
in these works. Matters are very well managed there,
and no expense is spared to make them profitable."
This "Mr. Washington," thus one of the earliest
factors in the iron industry of the South, was the
father of our first President.[1]

Before 1720 Governor Spottswood of Virginia had
established several iron-making enterprises, and the
General Assembly of Virginia had passed, in 1727,
"an act for encouraging adventurers in iron-works."
Not only in Virginia, but in North Carolina and

---

[1] Quoted in " Facts About the South," by R. H. Edmonds, Baltimore, 1902, from Swank's " History of Iron in all Ages." To Mr.
Edmonds's interesting brochure and to the columns of the *Tradesman*
of Chattanooga, as well as to the several issues of the United States
census, I am indebted for many of the statements in the first section
of this chapter. I especially wish to express my obligations to Mr.
Edmonds. It should be said, however, that the figures as to the
assessed value of Southern property in 1860 include the wealth which
existed in the form of slaves. This should be borne in mind in noting
the contrasts here quoted on p. 101. See also the footnote to p. 41.

South Carolina as well, there continued — until the close of the century — much interest in the development of this phase of manufacturing, and the colonial forces made frequent requisitions upon its product.

In 1795, however, there had been developed an invention which began to transform the conditions of Southern life. Eli Whitney — a native of Massachusetts then living in Georgia — gave to the world the cotton-gin. With its introduction, cotton became the dominant interest of the South. Other enterprises suffered by comparison, as men came to realize the increased availability given by Whitney to the cotton product, and the increased value thus contributed to the cotton lands. From 2,000,000 pounds in 1790, the cotton crop rose to 10,000,000 pounds in 1796, and to 40,000,000 pounds in 1800. Ten years later, the crop amounted to 80,000,000 pounds, and by 1820 it had reached the enormous total — as contrasted with the yield of 1790 — of 160,000,000 pounds.

Nor was this astonishing increase of thirty years coincident with " four-cent cotton." For nearly forty years, beginning with 1800 and closing with 1839, the average price per pound was over seventeen cents — forty-four cents per pound being the maximum price attained, and thirteen cents the minimum.

During this period it was inevitable that the cotton interest should have become the all-absorbing occupation of the South. Beginning, however, with 1840 we may note a sharp decline in prices — reaching in 1845 a point slightly lower than six cents — and while from time to time the price rallied feverishly for brief and uncertain periods, there was no general recovery. The average price for the ten years, from 1840 to

1850, was the lowest average maintained throughout any decade in the history of the American trade.

The same causes, therefore, which had drawn the energy of the South in so conspicuous a degree to cotton, were now operating partially to detach the South from cotton and to secure the direction of Southern effort upon other enterprises. Accordingly in the decade from 1850 to 1860 — the ten years immediately preceding the Civil War — we find a marked and rapid development in the South's general agricultural and manufacturing interests. According to the United States census of 1860, — as Mr. Edmonds has pointed out, — the South, with one-third of the country's population and less than one-fourth of the white population, had raised more than one-half of the total agricultural products of the country. The total number of Southern factories in 1860 was 24,590, representing an aggregate capital of $175,100,000. In 1850 the South had but 2335 miles of railroad as contrasted with a combined total of 4798 miles for New England and the Middle States; but by 1860 the South had quadrupled the mileage of 1850, and, while the total for New England and the Middle States now reached 9510 miles, the South had achieved a total of 9897 miles. In 1850 the combined mileage of the two Northern sections had exceeded that of the South by 2463 miles. In 1860 these conditions were reversed, and the South had a margin of 387 miles to her credit. The railroad development of the decade at the South represented an expenditure, largely from Southern sources, of over $220,000,000.

Then came war and the more bitter years that followed war. In 1860 the wealth of the South had exceeded the combined wealth of the New England and Middle States by $750,000,000, but in 1870 we find the conditions reversed and the wealth of these States exceeding the wealth of the South by $10,-800,000,000.

" The assessed value of property in New York and Pennsylvania in 1870 was greater than in the whole South. South Carolina, which, in 1860, had been third in rank in wealth, in proportion to the number of her inhabitants, had dropped to be the thirtieth; Georgia had dropped from seventh to the thirty-ninth; Mississippi, from the fourth place to the thirty-fourth; Alabama, from the eleventh to the forty-fourth; Kentucky, from tenth to twenty-eighth."

The decrease in values at the South had been coincident with an increase in values at the North. In 1860 the value of assessed property in South Carolina exceeded by $68,000,000 the combined totals for Rhode Island and New Jersey. But in 1870 the assessed property of Rhode Island and New Jersey exceeded by more than $685,000,000 the assessed value of the properties of South Carolina.

Beneath these cold and unresponsive figures there lie what tragedies of suffering, what deep-hidden recurrent pulses of despair, of self-repression, of patience, of silent and solemn will, of self-conquest, of ultimate emancipation!

About the year 1880 the long-waited change begins. By 1890 the industrial revival is in evident progress. By 1900 the South has entered upon one of the most remarkable periods of economic development to be found in the history of the modern indus-

trial world.   This is not over-statement.   It is fair
and accurate characterization.

The agricultural progress of these twenty years has
been more than creditable as compared with the totals
for the country at large.   But the most distinctive element in the economic movement of this period is the
increasingly dominant position of manufactures as
contrasted with agriculture.   This industrial revival
is but the reëmergence of the tendency which we
found so manifest in the statistics of 1860.   It is but
one reassertion of the genius of the old South.

In 1880 the value of the manufactured products
of the South was $200,000,000 less than the value
of her agricultural products.   But in 1900 all this is
changed.   The value of Southern manufactures then
exceeded the value of Southern agricultural products
by $190,000,000, and "if mining interests be in-
cluded, by nearly $300,000,000."

In 1880 the products of Southern factories had not
reached a valuation of $458,000,000.   By 1900, such
had been the progress of twenty years, their value
had reached a total of more than $1,463,000,000 —
an increase of $1,200,000,000, or more than 220 per
cent.   To realize the deep and far-reaching significance of such figures, one must be able to see through
them — by the faculties of an intelligent and sympathetic insight — the vast industrial and social changes
which they represent.   They mean that the industrial
centre of gravity at the South is shifting, however
slowly, from the field to the factory; and that the
factory is to take its place beside the church, the schoolhouse, the home, as one of the effectual and characteristic forces of civilization in our Southern States.

II

By "the factory" the average Southern community understands the cotton factory. To the eye, in the new industrial scene, it is the most conspicuous representative of the South's industrial transformation. In the twenty years from 1880 to 1900, the capital invested in cotton manufacturing at the South increased from nearly $22,000,000 to nearly $113,000,000, and the number of establishments had increased from 180 to 412. So rapid, however, has been the growth of this especial interest of the South, that since the taking of the census for 1900 the number of cotton mill establishments has reached, in January, 1904, a total of over 900, — has already more than doubled.

This astonishing development has been due to many causes, — to the South's possession of the raw material, and thus to the partial truth of the adage that "the mills must come to the cotton;" to the South's vast store of available and inexpensive fuels, her ample water-powers, her attractive and "easy" climate; but chiefly to her supplies of tractable and cheap labor. It is this last factor, rather than the possession of the raw material, which has contributed to the rapid development of cotton manufacture in our Southern States.

What is the source of this labor? It lies in the unlettered masses of the white population. The negro population forms but an infinitesimal fraction of it. Their practical omission from the labor of the cotton mills is attributed to a number of causes, — to the inadaptability of the negro to the long hours and the sustained labor of the factory system; to the desire of the Southern captains of industry to favor, upon the grounds of sentiment, the training and employment of white labor; to the fact that, inasmuch as it is often difficult to employ the two classes of labor together, and as white labor — by reason of its teachableness, endurance, and skill — is the more valuable of the two, the preference is naturally given to the stronger race. It is probable that all these considerations, in greater or less degree, have entered as determining factors into the situation as we find it, although it is to the last that I should be inclined to attribute the chief measure of importance. But the situation, whatever the explanations, is what it is. Men may not agree as to the alleged causes, or as to their respective validity, but the fact remains, that thus far the characteristic labor of the cotton factory has been almost wholly white.

Upon a personal investigation of a large number of mills, one will find, among managers, superintendents, and foremen, the representatives of almost every social class. Although the mill can hardly be called the instrument of an industrial democracy, there will sometimes be found men in the ranks of factory administration who have worked themselves forward from the vague multitude of the unlettered and unskilled. It is from this multitude, however, — from the great army of the non-participants, — that the population of the factory is chiefly drawn. From their little homes in the "hill-country" of the Piedmont, where for years they have maintained a precarious existence upon a difficult and forbidding soil, thousands of them have been drawn within the precincts of the new industrial life. Some of them have come from the heavier lands in the malarial sections of the "Black Belt."   Whether from the hills or from the valleys, — and most of them are a "hill-people," — they have sometimes found in the factory an instrument of industrial rescue. In many instances, however, the change from agriculture — however hard the old life — has represented a loss of freedom without a compensating gain of ease.   I have known cases where the bright promises of the factory's labor agent have lured families from their little holdings of poor land to a fate even more dreary and more pitiless. In other cases the change has represented more of gain than of loss. The family has found in the opportunity presented by the mill a new chance for a real foothold in the struggle for existence. Having failed under the conditions of agriculture, it has found under the conditions of manufacture at least the possibility of another world.

On the farm the whole family has usually worked together, and so the family still remains, under the changed conditions, the working unit. Often at the week's end they will find themselves in possession of more real money than they have seen in months before, and, not clearly perceiving that more of money does not always mean more of life, — an error not unusual among more favored classes, — and feeling the magic spell of fellowship, of closer social contact with other human souls and other human forces, they soon forget whatever of advantage the old life may have contained.

Nor is the promise of the new world always vain. With some the possibilities of promotion are perceived, and steadily and sometimes successfully pursued. The more important factories are now seldom found without the factory school, where — in spite of the many calls to the mill, to meet the exigencies of "rush orders" — the children, or a fraction of them, are given an elementary training in "the three R's." When the more ambitious boy or the more capable girl is advanced to " piece-work," the result of an active day is often a gratifying wage. But the period of satisfactory earning power reaches its maximum at about the eighteenth or nineteenth year, and the operative is held by the rewards of the industry at the only time when another career might seem possible and practicable. When it is clearly perceived that the strain of the long factory hours does not bring a really satisfactory adult wage, it is too late to change; and the few who pass upward in the mill are but a small proportion of the mass. These, under the pressure of the economic situation just suggested, yield to that class tendency which is just as active among the poor as among the rich. The forces of a common origin, of neighborhood life, of a social experience shut in by the factory enclosure, — with no opportunity for the home, that best basis of social differentiation, — all conspire to emphasize the distinctions and the barriers of caste, and we find in process of creation a "factory people." They are marked by certain characteristic excellences and by certain characteristic evils. I would not forget the first in dwelling here upon the latter. There will be found among them, in frequent and appalling evidence, two symbols of a low industrial life, — the idle father and the working child.

Neither could exist without the partial complicity of the mills. The adult men among the new recruits have untrained hands and awkward fingers. The younger children are taken at first as the " pupils of the industry," but the mills have clung to them with a tenacity which indicates that while their immediate labor may be profitless, the net rewards of their "instruction" do not fall exclusively to the children. Upon the little farm among the hills the family worked and lived close to the very limit of existence. The father, there, had often done the hunting and the fishing while the women and the children labored. The family earnings in the new environment at the mill present a small but appreciable margin. As there has rarely been a thought or a plan beyond a little fuller measure of subsistence, — subsistence of the same kind and according to the same standards, — it is now obviously possible when this measure is attained for some one in the number of the workers to " fall out." The father does not seem to be seriously in demand, the children are. The member of the family who ceases work is thus not the youngest, but the oldest. If the father has never entered the mill, — as is sometimes the case, — and if there still appears a little margin in the family wage beyond the limit of subsistence, the one who falls out is the mother. The children work on.

Have they not always worked upon the farm, and upon the farm have not their fathers and forefathers worked before them ? Wrought upon at first more by ignorance and apparent need than by avarice, though avarice follows fast — the father and mother do not easily perceive the difference for the child between factory labor and farm labor. It is true that the work of the factory — especially for the younger children — is often lighter than the work brought to the child upon the farm. But the benumbing power of factory labor lies not so much in its hardness as in its monotony. Picking up toothpicks from a pile, one by one, and depositing them in another, may be light work, but when continued for twelve hours a day it is a work to break the will and nerve of a strong man. The work of the factory means usually the doing of the same small task over and over again — moment in and moment out, hour after hour, day after day. Its reactive effect upon the mind is dulness, apathy, a mechanical and stolid spirit, without vivacity or hope. The labor of the farm is often hard, but it is full of the play and challenge of variety. It is labor in the open air. It is labor, not under the deadening and deafening clatter of machinery, but under the wide spaces of the sky, where sound comes up to you from free and living things, from things that may mean companionship, and where the silence — brooding — passes and repasses as a power of peace and healing. Upon the farm the child labors, as it labors in the home, under the eye of a guardianship which is usually that of the parent, which is full of a personal solicitude even if it be not full of intelligent affection. In the factory the child works as an industrial unit, a little member of an industrial aggregate, under an oversight which must, of necessity, be administrative rather than personal. Letting your own child work for you is a wholly different thing from letting another man work your child.

And the evil has its quantitative side. The child

is not alone. The child is a part of that vague and pathetic industrial force which the world calls, and ought to call, "child labor." No man would be permitted to operate his farm with that labor for ten days. A distinguished Southern expert has testified that 60 per cent of the operatives in the spinning departments of the cotton mills throughout the Piedmont district were under sixteen years of age.[1] The United States census for 1900 discloses the fact that of the total number of operatives in the cotton mills of Alabama nearly 30 per cent were under sixteen; and that in the Southern States as a whole the proportion of the cotton-mill operatives under sixteen years amounted to 25.1 per cent. What farmer, operating a large farm and employing large numbers of hands, would presume to conduct his farm upon the basis presented by such conditions?[2]

Just how many of the workers of the mills are under fourteen years and just how many are under twelve it is difficult to say. The census of the

[1] See Report of the Testimony in the Hearing of April 29, 1902, before Subcommittee No. VII of the Committee on the Judiciary of the House of Representatives, on House Joint Resolution No. 20, p. 16.

[2] The gross number of cotton-mill operatives at the South under the age of sixteen was, in 1900, 24,459 out of a total of 97,559 operatives. See Twelfth Census of the U. S., Cotton Manufactures, Bulletin 215. By the month of August, 1902, the number of establishments had doubled, and therefore, if the same proportion was maintained, the number under sixteen was approximately 50,000. Since the passage of the child-labor laws of 1903, there has probably been a reduction in the proportionate number of child operatives. The United States census places the line of the division between the child operative and the adult operative at sixteen years. If some operatives under sixteen are a little old to be classed as "children," it is hardly less obvious that there are many over fifteen who are a little young to be classed as "adults."

United States makes no distinction in the ages of those who are under sixteen.   Only one Southern State — North Carolina — makes any provision for the collection of the statistics of labor, and in North Carolina we are provided with the data for only those who are under fourteen.   In the last available report for this State,[1] 18 per cent of its textile operatives were under this age.   As the conditions in North Carolina were probably not worse than in the South at large, the total under fourteen in the whole South was approximately 30,000 at the beginning of the year 1903.   The number of children under the age of twelve in Southern factories — basing the estimate upon definite figures from certain representative localities—was, at the beinning of 1903, about 20,000.   The passage of the North Carolina child-labor law — in March, 1903 — has probably resulted in a marked reduction in the number of the younger children in that State.   A similar reduction has probably taken place in other States, for in the year 1903 — in addition to Kentucky, Louisiana, and Tennessee, which had already acted — child-labor laws were passed for the first time, not only in North Carolina, but also in Alabama, South Carolina, Virginia, and Texas.   There is thus but one manufacturing State in the South which is now without such legislation.

Even here, however, the legislature of Georgia has passed a bill visiting heavy penalties upon the able-bodied parent who is guilty of living in idleness while his younger children are at labor for his support.   The demand for such a law and the

[1] See p. 187 of the North Carolina Report of the Department of Labor and Printing, 1901.

passage of such a law are manifestly a confession that a child-labor law is needed. Even the less progressive mills naturally rallied with righteous unction to the passage of any legislation which would seem to shift the responsibility for present conditions from the factories to the parents. Yet it is evident that, although the parents have been part offenders, the factories have been the principals. The parents have often been too ignorant to be responsive to higher industrial standards. The factories, however, are controlled and administered by men of intelligence and property. Neither ignorance nor poverty can be urged as an excuse for the persistent activity with which so many of their representatives have thronged the lobbies of Southern legislatures in the effort to defeat such an elementary law as the prohibiting of factory labor for children under twelve. By the advocates of protective legislation such an age limit was felt to be inadequate. But in view of the vigor and power of the opposition a twelve-year limit was regarded as the best obtainable result. Indeed it is cause for congratulation that such a measure of success should have been secured, and that within so short a period, in localities in which the problems presented by the factory were of such recent growth, eight States of the South should once for all have abandoned the old *laissez-faire* conception of industrial evils, and should have accepted, at least in its negative application, the principle of social responsibility in reference to the industrial status of the child.[1]

---

[1] While many of the younger children are being excluded from the mills by legislation, many more are being excluded and aided through the moral pressure created by the agitation for protective laws.

In Georgia, legislation has been delayed, but a rapidly maturing public sentiment will soon secure the needed law.

Here, as in the States which have already acted, there is occasion, however, for clear and insistent reply to the pleas by which some of the representatives of the factories are still attempting to lull the social conscience. Even where legislation has taken place, the old objections still arise, partly as a criticism of existing laws and partly as a protest against their full enforcement.

III

Still we hear the contention, sometimes upon the lips of well-meaning men, that legislation restricting the labor of the child is " paternalism," is usurpation of the functions of the parent. But the right of the parent is not the only truth of our democratic institutions; these institutions rest also upon the right of the child. The right of the child to live is only a part of its right to be a child. The State which prevents a parent from killing a child by poison or from maiming a child by a blow, may also prevent a parent from killing or injuring the child by enforced and unnatural labor. The lighter duties of the home and the farm, duties which are half play, may often constitute no injury to children of tender years. And yet we must remember that among the most distinctive of the rights of the little child is the divine right to do nothing. An abnormal tension upon muscles and nerves, in the period of immaturity, is an injury to all life, whether animal or human. To the human organism, with its greater delicacy, the peril is of course the greater. Immunity from such a burden is, for the young, a physical and natural right. All nature and all society are organized upon the basis of the recognition of this right. It is a right which is much more important to the home and to society than the right of the parent to shift the burdens of the breadwinner to the shoulders of his defenceless children. The State's protection of such a right involves, not the restriction, but the enlargement of liberty. It means the extension rather than the negation of freedom, and its enforcement is not paternalism, but democracy.

The democratic doctrine of the freedom of contract is a good doctrine. But no wise democrat will try to make this doctrine both iniquitous and absurd by giving it as an instrument of domestic constraint, into the hands of ignorant or idle or unscrupulous parents. As was declared long ago, by such an individualist as John Stuart Mill, "the doctrine of freedom of contract in relation to the child can mean little more than freedom of coercion."

The advocate of industrial liberty may well ask, How many of our younger children are clamoring for the "right" to labor in the mills? I know of one little girl who, tempted by a few pennies, cried to go in. The next week she cried to come out. But those sturdy foes of "paternalism" who so loudly asserted her right to go in had nothing to say about her right to come out. The real befrienders of her liberty, and of liberty in the State, may well be chiefly concerned as to her right to come out.

There is no essential conflict between the right of

the parent and the right of the child, for the guarding of the child's liberty will, through the increase of its permanent efficiency, redound to the distinct advantage of the parent; but if such a conflict of rights should arise, society must find its primary interest in the assertion of the right of the child to its childhood — for the child constitutes both the heritage of the past and the promise of the future.

The movement of a population from industrial dependence to industrial competence, from distress and poverty to comfort and property, is not a process of ease for any of its elements. Above all, the industrial readjustment of a population, moving from the conditions of agriculture to the conditions of manufacture, must bear with severity upon every form and aspect of the family life. But this process, however painful, must be adjusted with the maximum of compassion to the lives of the helpless and defenceless. The chief burden of this readjustment should not be laid upon the child. The life of the child should be, not the point of the severest pressure and the acutest suffering, but the point of chief protection. And yet I have knowledge, and every close observer of our factory conditions has knowledge, of dozens of grown men who pass their days and nights in idleness and dissipation, while they live upon the wages of their tender children.

This is partly due to the inhumanity of the man. It is also due, however, to the indirect operation of the system of child labor. A well-known observer tells us that "a pathetic feature of the movement which is turning the mountaineer farmers into mill-hands is the fact that no regular employment is fur-

nished to the men by the mills. The women and
children all find places in the factories, but the men
are left with nothing to do but to care for the little
kitchen garden and carry the lunch pail to the family
at the mill at noontime. The mills could employ
them, but they seem content with their self-imposed
tasks." [1] While the statement that "no regular employment is furnished to the men by the mills " is not
wholly true of the mills in many of the sections of
the South, yet, as the statistics would indicate, the
tendency to put the economic burden partly upon the
defenceless members of the family naturally operates,
among the ignorant, as a temptation to the father to
shift that burden entirely to the woman and the children.

This tendency represents a lowering of the standard of parenthood which the State cannot well ignore.
Aside from the direct benefits of legislation, the expression of the interest of the State in the freedom
and the welfare of the child must react upon the
sentiment and practice of the family. Just as the
concern of the State for the welfare of the child,
expressed in the provisions for public education, has
actually deepened the interest in private education,
so the pressure of a higher ideal of solicitude, through
a considerate measure looking to the relief of the conditions of child labor, must react upon the standard
of parenthood, will lend a new and sweeter dignity to
childhood in the homes of the ignorant, and will bring
to the aid of the conscience of the father the wholesome forces of legal exaction and of social expecta-

[1] See an address by Frank Leake (1900) before the Manufacturers'
Club of Philadelphia, Pa. (p. 14).

tion. The humblest home will come to reflect that
ideal of the value and promise of the child which has
become articulate in the judgment of society.

We may still expect to hear, at times, the reiterated
claim that child labor is "necessary" to the family.
It involves, however, so serious a confession that it is
now expressed with much less confidence than of old.
There will be fewer and fewer mills which will wish
to admit, explicitly, that they in fact pay an adult
wage so low as to force the economic burden of the
family upon the frailest and the youngest. It does
not sound well, and it is not true.

A well-known expert has declared that he has had
direct knowledge of numbers of mills "making profits of 35 to 40 per cent, and some close to 100 per
cent, per annum on the capital invested." [1] Making
every allowance for any possible element of exaggeration, can so profitable an industry for one moment
present the plea that it must fix its adult wage at
so low a point as to force the family, in the mere
struggle for existence, to throw the burdens of employment upon its children under twelve? Is such
an enterprise the instrument of our industrial awaken-

---

[1] Address by Mr. Frank Leake (1900) before the Manufacturers'
Club of Philadelphia, p. 15. The year to which Mr. Leake refers was
one of exceptional prosperity, and later years would not show so large
a margin of profit, — but the rapid and continuous development of
cotton mills at the South is ample evidence that the business is not a
"failing venture," and that if there exists among the operatives an
economic necessity for the labor of little children, the responsibility for
that need rests squarely upon the mills. The profits of the mills, the
profits of any legitimate industry in America, easily justify an adult
wage which — under any normal conditions — will relieve the younger
children of the family from the burdens of sustained and confining
labor.

ing? Our factories cannot long oppose the protection of our children upon the ground that the children, and that the very standards of our industrial life, are in need of protection from the factories.

There has been little plea that the mills have been seriously dependent upon the younger children. Certain factories have looked upon their employment as an advantage, but by the greater number of experienced operators their labor has been regarded as peculiarly unreliable and expensive. Yet the mills, as a whole, have clung to the younger children as long as it was possible to do so, partly for the purpose of training the child for the work, and partly for the purpose of "holding the family." Both these arguments seem to be gradually yielding, however, to the argument for conservative legislation. It is true that the child's fingers gain a certain added dexterity from early work; but this advantage at one end is more than offset by the dulling effect of exacting labor upon the immature; by the increase, at the other end, of premature senility and the consequent shortening, not only of productive capacity, but sometimes of life itself. Even where life lasts on — and there are observers who claim that child labor has no effect upon the mere period of expectation — the victim of the child-labor system is early counted among the relatively incapable.

I say the "relatively incapable," because, while he may continue to do the labor of the child, he usually fails to advance very far into the activities of the man. There are exceptions to this rule. But the canons of social security cannot be based upon exceptions. The abnormal strain of premature labor induces premature development, and, as a rule, premature development results in arrested development. To the industry itself, dependent in all its higher and more profitable forms upon the skill and efficiency of its operative class, there is neither wisdom nor security in a policy which contributes to such conditions.

Nor will it serve, as an objection to a child-labor law, to maintain that the mill must grant employment to the younger children in order to hold the family. Incredible as it may seem, the demand for the using of the children has come in many instances from the mills rather than from the parents. But there have also been cases in which the "good mill" has been placed under pressure from the parents, the parents threatening to go to other mills unless their younger children were admitted to labor. Such an instance, however, instead of proving an objection to a law excluding the younger children from employment, is in itself an argument for the enactment of the law. The passage of the law has a tendency to put every mill under the same economic standard, makes futile and impossible the threat of the parents to go to other mills (inasmuch as the "other mills" would also be subject to the law), and upholds the juster regulations and the more wholesome conditions of the progressive factory.

One of the most serious phases of the Southern factory system, especially as that system touches the life and fate of the child, lies in the habit of "long hours." I have known mills in which for ten and twelve days at a time the factory hands — children and all — were called to work before sunrise and were dismissed from work only after sunset, laboring from dark to dark. I have repeatedly seen them at labor for twelve, thirteen, and even fourteen hours per day. In the period of the holidays or at other "rush times" I have seen children of eight and nine years of age leaving the factory as late as 9.30 o'clock at night, and finding their way with their own little lanterns, through the unlighted streets of the mill village, to their squalid homes. It was for the correction of the evil of night work quite as much as for the establishment of an age limit that Southern sentiment has recently been aroused.

In Alabama the campaign for a child-labor law was organized under the leadership of a voluntary State committee, including within its personnel representatives of the Church, the press, the judiciary, the labor unions, and the mercantile and banking interests of the State. The effort for the passage of a child-labor law was defeated before the legislature of 1900, largely through the skilful and aggressive opposition of the representative of one of the New England factories in Alabama.[1] The defeat of the bill served, however, only to increase the activity of its advocates.[2] The organization of the committee

[1] A correspondence in reference to the partial responsibility of New England for the opposition to child-labor laws at the South will be found in the Appendix (B) to this volume, p. 309.

[2] Explicit acknowledgment should be made of the work performed at this time by the special agent of the American Federation of Labor, Irene Ashby Macfadyen. Mrs. Macfadyen (then Miss Ashby) was subjected — as an outsider and as a "labor representative" — to some criticism, but her single-hearted devotion to her cause was supreme; and while she left the State in 1901, her able and conscientious work contributed in no small degree to the ultimate success of the bill.

was strengthened and enlarged. An aggressive effort was made to create a literature of the subject, a literature which might be available not only in Alabama but throughout the South, a number of pamphlets were prepared upon the several phases of the argument, and nearly thirty thousand copies were freely circulated. The press of the South, almost without exception, responded to the emergency. The women's clubs, the Christian clergy, the labor unions, and the representatives of a few of the mills, united with earnest men and women of almost every class in the demand for a conservative measure of legislation. When the legislature of 1903 assembled at Montgomery, the manufacturers met at the capital, appointed a committee to represent them, and agreed, through their committee, to enter into a discussion of terms. The method of personal conference was at once accepted in the hope that a bill might be decided upon which would command — before the legislature — the support of all the parties in interest. A bill was agreed upon, signed by the representatives of both sides, and passed by the General Assembly. It did not satisfy either of the contestants, but the advocates of legislation accepted it as the best measure then obtainable. It prohibits child labor in factories — save under a few exceptional conditions — to children under twelve, prohibits any night work for those under thirteen, limits the night work of those under sixteen to forty-eight hours per week, provides for the registration of the names and ages of all minors in employment, and affixes penalties upon the parents for false registration of ages, and upon employers for violations of the law. It is to be noted that it totally prohibits night work only for those under thirteen and that the law provides no special system of inspection. Upon these phases of the bill the Chairman of the Child-labor Committee expressed himself as follows:—

"The Alabama bill was a compromise. For example, the original measure totally prohibited night work for all the children under sixteen years of age. The representatives of the manufacturers, in the conference between the committee of the manufacturers and the representatives of the Child-labor Committee, refused to accept this provision, and even declined to allow the prohibition of night work for children as young as fourteen. They insisted that the limit should be put down to thirteen years. I think that the insistence of the manufacturers upon this point clearly indicates that there is a fallacy somewhere in the claim that our manufacturers have been exclusively the representatives of the tenderest philanthropy.

"Many of our factories are opposed to night work. Many of the strongest men among the manufacturers have never worked a little child after six or seven o'clock at night. One must confess, however, to a certain amount of disappointment that the strongest and best men should so far yield to the influence of the men representing lower standards that a committee representing the manufacturing interests of the whole State should demand as an inexorable condition of legislation that the proposed law should permit the continuation of night work for children of thirteen, fourteen, and fifteen years.

"As to the plans for the future, and as to whether

or not we will ask for a system of state inspection, these things depend upon the course of the mill men. A committee of gentlemen, formally appointed to represent the factories, have agreed in writing to the terms of the law. I shall not assume that they are going to go back on the word which they have thus solemnly given, given not to me especially or to our committee, but to the whole people of the State. I shall assume that the law will be obeyed until I learn that it is violated." [1]

In Tennessee, Kentucky, and North Carolina there are partial — though inadequate — provisions for inspection. As the evidences of non-compliance arise and are accumulated, the system of State inspection will be introduced throughout the South where it does not exist, and will be strengthened where it does exist, — for the people of the Southern States, whatever their limitations, are not given over to indifference or to commercialism. The very name of "reform," under the exploitations of the reconstruction period, was made odious to them. They have not been familiar with the social problems presented by manufacturing enterprises, and they have been without legislative precedents for the correction of industrial wrongs; but the South has been aroused upon this issue, and the people of the Southern States — if they are in earnest about anything — are to-day in earnest about the liberties and the opportunities of the child.

The South cannot and will not provide millions of revenue at one end of her social system in order to give her children schools, and permit any industry,

1 See the issue of *Charities*, New York, May 2, 1903, pp. 454, 455.

however important, to stand at the other end of that system and shut up her children in the factory. Those who have contended for industrial reforms have conceived these reforms as an integral element of educational progress, and they have conceived both these aspects of advancement, the movement for industrial liberty and the movement for the "schools of the people," as but two phases of the one underlying, essential direction of Southern life, the movement toward a truly democratic order.

The system of child labor, especially at the South, is at war, not only with the welfare of the child, the parent, the industry, but with democracy itself. It stands, not only for arrested development in the individual, for ignorance and industrial helplessness, but for arrested development in the social class to which the child belongs. These have been the white non-participants of the older civilization. The greater number of them, as indicated in the opening chapter of this volume, are now being incorporated within the general body of democratic life. They are becoming conscious participants in the fulness and freedom of their century. Those who have become involved in the industrial movement represented by the mill might well find through the mill, — as a few have done, — not only more to eat and more to wear, but more to live for. The mill might well be to all, as it has been to some, the instrument of their transplanting, — out of a life of barren and isolated non-participation into a life of fruitful and generous relationship with men, with work, with the rewarding world. But it has too often seemed to be the policy of the factory to save only in order that it might consume.

The isolated family is called in from the barren lands about its rural cabin, but too often it is redeemed from isolation only that its helplessness may bring profit to the instrument of its redemption. It is put to dwell within the factory enclosure; its instinctive desire to live somewhat to itself, to own a little land, to have a home, is denied; it must be "the company's" tenant, it must — usually — trade at "the company's store," its children are to go upon "the company's roll." The child is trained almost from infancy into a certain human and economic dependence upon one particular industry. If it have a few months, now and then, for schooling, it must go to "the company's school." If the family go to worship, there is at the larger mills "the company's church," a chapel in which the salary of the minister and his helpers is defrayed by the same resourceful and generous "company" — the company, by the way, which has charged that the enactment of a child-labor law would be paternalism!

Here and there the exceptional child, through an exceptional virility, rises out of the enfolding powers of the system; here and there a life escapes. But as a rule the system is effective; and the familiar saying, "once an operative, always an operative," rings all too seriously true. The operatives remain a fixed and semi-dependent class. One manufacturer bluntly informed me that he wished them to remain so, upon the double ground that they would then "never organize and would never want or get high wages." "My business," said he, "is a low-wages business." I will not charge that his temper is representative. Many of the manufacturers honestly and

earnestly desire the progress of their people.   But
the fact remains that the factory system, as a system,
betrays a tendency to hold its humbler industrial
forces in a state of arrested development; which,
from the broader social standpoint and in relation
to the larger life of democracy, means an arrested
participation.   Here is an eddy in the fuller and
freer current of democratic life; here, in the industrial imprisonment of the child, is a contradiction —
however temporary — of those juster and deeper
forces which are claiming the human possibilities
of the individual — however lowly — as elements in
the power and happiness of the State.

CHILD LABOR AND THE INDUSTRIAL SOUTH

CHAPTER V

CHILD LABOR AND THE INDUSTRIAL SOUTH [1]

OUR subject brings to us a national question. And yet I must begin what I shall try to say to you this evening with a disclaimer and an explanation. As my disclaimer, I would say that I use the word "national" in no political or federal sense. The conditions of industry vary so greatly and so decisively from State to State and from locality to locality that the enactment of a federal child-labor law, applicable to all conditions and under all circumstances, would be inadequate if not unfortunate.

As my explanation, I would say that I use the word "national" in that geographical sense in which we must all say, and with all emphasis, that the problem of child labor is a national problem. North and South, it belongs to all of us. If the proportionate number of child workers is greatest at the South, the actual number of child workers, in the year 1900, was greater in the one State of Pennsylvania than in all of the States of the South together. Wherever we find the factory and the child, we find the working of those economic and human forces which draw the

[1] An address delivered before the National Conference of Charities and Correction, at Atlanta, Ga., May 9, 1903. Reported stenographically, and revised for publication.

child into the processes of industrial production. The factory, like every instrumentality of progress, brings its blessings and its evils. Let us recognize its blessings. Let us yield to those blessings, potent and far-reaching as they are, an intelligent and generous measure of appreciation and applause. But let us also have an intelligent perception of the evils of the factory, and let us resolutely bring to those evils — in the name of our children, our country, and our industries — such remedies as we may be able to secure.

While it may be somewhat depressing for us to realize that the industrial development of our country bears its curse, it is inspiring to remember that the realization of this curse has revealed the essential soundness of the national heart. If child labor is a general evil, the general recognition of this evil has brought — in the recent successive victories of child-labor legislation — the most conspicuous evidence of the inherent right-mindedness of American life with which I am familiar. In Texas, in Alabama, in South Carolina, in North Carolina, in Virginia, Illinois, New Hampshire, New York, — in State after State, in locality after locality, — the common conscience of the land has pierced the sophistries by which men would bind the children to the drudgery of factory and mine, and has written its solicitude and its compassions in the terms of law.[1]

Much of this legislation has been inadequate. In

[1] See an admirable summary of the child-labor legislation of the United States in the Hand Book for 1904, compiled by Madeleine W. Sykes and Josephine Goldmark ; National Consumers' League, 105 East Twenty-second Street, New York City. See also Report of the U.S. Commissioner of Education, 1902, Vol. II, p. 2347.

some States it has represented the effort to reaffirm
and to reënforce the intention of older statutes; in
other States it has represented the first explicit recognition of the State's responsibility toward the more
defenceless elements of an industrial society, toward
the potential citizenship of the industrial child.   In
all cases, however, — whether in response to the
demand for law enactment or for law enforcement, —
the heart of our country, North and South, has shown
itself to be a sound heart, and the soul of the Republic
has kept watch above its children.   When we contrast
the recent victories of child-labor legislation, victories
so speedily secured, with the long struggle of the
heroic Shaftesbury, we gather an evidence, a signal
and gracious evidence, of one of the ennobling distinctions between his generation and our own.

In speaking to you this evening, I wish, however,
to deal as concretely and as definitely as I can with
certain phases of the struggle for legislation in our
Southern States.   I have consented to do so, not because I would ignore the evils of the North or would
exaggerate the difficulties of the South, but because an
account of the controversial experience of one section
in relation to a great and vital industrial issue may
be of some possible value to the experience of other
sections.

At a very early period in the history of our movement for legislation, our proposal of a child-labor law
was met by a counter proposal.   There were manufacturers who admitted the existence of evils, who
lamented the prevalence of conditions which they
protested that they were anxious to rectify, but who
assured us that the real remedy was not the prohibi-

tion of child labor, but the enforcement of compulsory
education.   The suggestion possessed an engaging
plausibility.   And yet I confess that I believe it to be
well to survey with a watchful interest and a somewhat exacting analysis the remedies offered by those
who have permitted, and who may have profited by,
the very evils to be remedied.   Under such conditions, the counter proposal is sometimes only the
most deceptive element in a neat and effective
machinery of estoppel.   This impression was not
abated by an examination of the terms in which the
proposal was conveyed.   One of the most aggressive
of its advocates was a representative of New England
who has been largely interested in cotton-mill properties at the South.[1]   In the columns of the *Evening
Transcript* of Boston he declared that the thing for
Alabama to do was simply to follow the example of
Massachusetts, pass a law for compulsory education,
and, presto, the problem would be solved.   We found,
however, that the physician was not ready for his
remedy.   He was careful to add that any compulsory
education law which might be passed in Alabama
should "of course" not become operative till after
the passage of similar laws in the States of North
Carolina, South Carolina, and Georgia.   This enthusiasm for reform, only on condition that all the rest
of the world will reform too, is somewhat familiar to
the students of the history of economic progress.

I do not quite know why the representative of
Massachusetts investments at the South should have
opposed a child-labor law, why he should have felt
compelled to reject one method of reform because

[1] See Appendix B, p. 320.

Alabama would not accept another; but men have been known to attempt the blocking of a reform which is clearly possible by the safe and vigorous proposal of a reform which is impossible. That a child-labor law was practicable, and that under our local conditions a compulsory education law was impracticable and impossible, was evident to the vast majority of the friends of progress in Alabama.

The counter proposal was as inadequate as it was impracticable. What would compulsory education mean in our Southern States ? Would such a provision mean at the South what a similar measure would mean in the States of the North ? It has been so assumed, and as the proposal has been urged upon us, our Northern friends have naturally made their mental pictures, pictures constructed from the materials of their local experience, in which they have seen the children freed from the mills by the simple operation of a nine months' compulsory attendance upon the schools. But at the time when that suggestion — with such commendable fervor — was urged upon the friends of protective legislation, the public school term of the Carolinas was but seventy-six days and the public school term of Alabama was but seventy-eight days. Those terms are somewhat longer now. And yet you can easily see that with so inadequate a school term this counter proposal of compulsory education could hardly have been regarded as a counter remedy. Even if adopted, it would have left the children of our humbler classes, for the greater part of the year, entirely available for the factories. The programme made possible by this counter proposal could have been expressed within a sentence, — " For the little children of the poor, three months in the school, nine months in the mill."

Whatever the advantages of a policy of compulsory education, I think you will at once agree with me that such a measure could be no adequate substitute for a child-labor law. It is obviously true that we cannot reach a comprehensive bettering of conditions by the mere enactment of an age limit for employment, nor by any of the expedients of a purely negative and corrective legislation. All this we have not failed to realize. But we have thought it best to do for the children of the factories the one best possible thing now obtainable in our Southern States; for if we cannot yet secure for every child a fixed attendance upon the school, we can at least secure for the younger children that industrial freedom which will afford them the possibility of the school. If we cannot compel them to be educated, we can at least permit them to be educated. And how men who claim to be in favor of compulsory education can at the same time oppose the prohibition of child labor is somewhat difficult for the uninstructed intelligence to understand, — inasmuch as the present factory system of our country with its low wages and its long hours obviously represents, as it touches the lives of the children, a system of compulsory ignorance.

The movement for the prohibition of the labor in factories of our children under twelve has also been opposed by what I have regarded as a mistaken commercial prejudice. A few representatives of our "business interests," under the leadership of some of the narrower trade journals of the South, have disputed the wisdom of protective legislation. Such

opposition was inevitable. It has made plausible
appeals to familiar forces. " Business " is everywhere
a word of mighty omen. It is altogether natural that
it should be so. At the South, especially, we have
come to look with peculiar appreciation upon those
practical and material forces which have wrought
the rehabilitation of the land. After the desolation
of war, and after the more bitter desolation of the
period which followed war, it is inevitable that the
question of bread-winning should have become with
many of our people a question of absorbing and
paramount importance. "Prosperity," commercial
and industrial "prosperity," has been a name of
mystic and constraining force. To invite " prosperity " has been a form of patriotism. To alienate
" prosperity " has seemed almost like apostasy.

When, therefore, we offered the proposals of
protective legislation for the children, we were met
with protests. We were greeted with indignant
questions : " Do you not see that this legislation
will touch the cotton factories ? " — " Do you not
know that the cotton factories are the agents of
prosperity ? " — " Do you want to compromise or to
arrest the prosperity of the South ? " — " Do you not
know that this child-labor law is an attack upon business ? " It was thus that we were questioned ; and yet
such questions, I submit to you, were in themselves
as gross and as insidious an insult as was ever offered
to the " business " and the " prosperity " of our
Southern States. For what do they imply ? They
imply, if they mean anything whatever, that there is
some inherent and essential connection between the
prosperity of the South and the labor of little children

under twelve years of age. They imply that the business success of the South is in some way involved in the right to throw the burdens of employment upon the immature. They carry the suggestion that our material progress is dependent upon unwholesome economic and humanitarian conditions, and that the development of the South is possibly contingent upon the prolonged, enforced, and unnatural labor of the defenceless and the helpless. I resent that imputation. I resent that suggestion not only in the name of the South at large but in the name of the business interests and the conservative commercial forces of our Southern States ; and I contend that from these laws to protect our children under twelve no damage can result to our business interests, — no damage comparable to the damage which would result from the general acceptance of the impression that child labor is the basis of our success, and that with the restriction of child labor there would follow a restriction of our industrial development. I solemnly declare that the forces which are injuring the prosperity and compromising the industrial repute of the South are the agencies, political or journalistic, which have tended to give currency to that assumption, and which, by their opposition to protective legislation for the younger children, have made our progress synonymous, in many minds, with the baser methods and the retrogressive policies of production. These are the agencies which, despite their lavish zeal, are injuring the standing of Southern investments and Southern properties. And I as solemnly declare that the men who are to-day befriending the industrial South are the men, men in commerce, in the trades, in the professions, men of every phase of contemporary Southern experience, who in eight States of the South have rejected this leadership, have welcomed the prohibition of the labor of the younger children, have resolved to free their properties from any occasion for prejudicial discussion and oblique advertisement, and have given notice to the world that the prosperity of the South is based, not on the labor of the immature, but on the fertility of her fields, the advantages of her climate, her cotton, her ores, her forests, her waters, and — above all — upon the character and the capacities of her manhood.

We have also been met by the manifestation of what I must not hesitate to call a false humanitarian prejudice. We have been assured that "these children are much better off in the mills than they were out of the mills." And indeed I confess it to be somewhat hard to deal with the arguments of those who end by defending as a benefit what they have begun by denying as an evil. We were first assured that there were practically no little children in the mills. The reports of the Twelfth Census of the United States[1] show that in the States outside the South the relative number of the cotton-mill employees under sixteen years of age had, in twenty years, been reduced from 15.6 per cent to 7.7 per cent; but that in the cotton mills of the South, during this period from 1880 to 1900, the relative number of the operatives under sixteen years of age had remained at approximately 25 per cent. Yet we were assured that few of these were under twelve. Just how many, as a matter of fact, were under

[1] See Bulletin No. 215, on Cotton Manufactures.

twelve, no man can accurately say. We began our movement for reforms with every effort to secure the definite data of exact conditions. Weeks were spent in laborious investigation, only to find that the evidence was contradicted as rapidly as it was collected. The most notorious facts were subjected to solemn and peremptory denial. We soon found that our best recourse in debate, a recourse abundantly convincing, was simply to assume what our opponents were on every hand compelled, conspicuously, to admit. On one day we might find the representatives of the factories declaring that the mills contained practically no children under twelve; but on the next day we found them thronging the lobby of the legislature to prevent the passage of a law which might take those under twelve out of the factories. "Why," we asked, "do you oppose a law prohibiting something which nobody wishes to do; why object to the abridgment of a liberty which nobody wishes to exercise?" Under such persuasions it was hard to believe that there were no factories employing, or desiring the employment of, many of the younger children. And yet these protestations have become an interesting evidence of sensitiveness. It is interesting to discover that the employment of the younger children, the children for whom legislation had been invoked, was thus denied, emphatically, as an evil.

Yet strangely enough we straightway find that their employment is admitted and defended as a benefit. We are told that "these children are much better off in the mills than they were in the places where they came from." I question whether it is ever fair to estimate our duty to the child by the disadvantages

of its past.   But is the contention true?   Is the labor
of the mills a philanthropic provision for the children
under twelve?   To hear some of our opponents dwell
upon the mill as a philanthropy, you would suppose
the average child could find in the average cotton
mill a comprehensive educational equipment — a sort
of institutional civilizer: — kindergarten, grammar
school, high school, university, — and a trip to
Europe, all in one.   Do not believe one word of it!
It is true, in some instances, that the general condition of the child at the mills is better and happier
than the condition of the same child before coming
to the mills.   I say, "in some instances," because in
many cases the child is less fortunate than before.
But, in the cases in which the change is a change to
better things, is the bettering of the fortune of the
child the result of child labor, or the result of the
general bettering of the condition of the family?
Let us be clear about this.

It is true that the outward lot of the child of the
mill family is sometimes better than that of the poor
white child of the country.   But where this is true,
it is true not because of child labor, but in spite of it.
There are men at the East who claim that the condition of the child in the sweat-shop is a "vast improvement" on the condition of the child in the crowded
foreign city where it once lived.   Does that prove
that the sweat-shop labor of its tiny hands is responsible for the change?   No.   Is child labor responsible
for the better condition of the factory child?   Its life
may share in the general improvement of conditions,
but the child, instead of receiving, as childhood
should, the maximum of immunity from distress, and

the largest freedom which the new environment
affords, is bearing in its tender strength the greatest
burden and the heaviest curse of the new prosperity.
Let us not be guilty of mental confusion.   Let us not
credit the good fortune of the family to the misfortune
of the child.

The cotton mills, indeed our factories of every sort,
are bringing their blessings to the South.   They are
touching with inspiring and creative power the fate
of some of the poorer people of our isolated localities, are enabling them to shift the industrial basis of
their lives from the conditions of agriculture, in which
they may have failed, to the conditions of manufacture, in which I trust they will at length succeed.
Let us grant, not reluctantly but gladly, the possible
blessings of the factory.   But let us stick, resolutely
and persistently, to the question now at issue.   That
question is not the economic and social advantage of
the factory.   Upon that we may be all agreed.   The
question now at issue is not the question as to whether
the factory is an advantage, but the question as to
whether the advantages and the blessings of the factory, to the community or to the child, are based upon
the labor of our children under twelve.   That is our
question.

I yield all legitimate credit to our factories.   I
yield instant and explicit tribute to those men among
us — no matter how greatly they may differ from me
upon the question of child labor — who have given of
their abilities and their fortunes to the upbuilding of
the industrial South.   But I protest that the economic
and social advantage of the factory has nothing whatever to do with this question in debate, and I further

protest that when these questions are confused, when men assume that the advantages of the factory to the community and to the child are based upon the monotonous and confining labor of our younger children, they are wronging not merely the community and the children but our factories as well.

In the course of this discussion at the South, there has also been much appeal to the interests of an undiscriminating industrial policy. There is much prejudice against labor unionism. The South, upon economic and social issues, is intensely and overwhelmingly conservative. Because, therefore, the child-labor bills have had the sympathy of the labor unions, there have been men who have attacked them as labor measures. They have opposed a child-labor law because the labor unions have approved it. Such men, if they followed the logic of their argument, would go back on the Ten Commandments if the labor unions should make a declaration of sympathy with the Decalogue. Now, I hold no brief for the labor unions. I am free to say, however, that when the capitalist opposes protective legislation for our children on the ground that the labor union has approved it, he injures the interests of capital far more than he injures the interests of the union. I can tell our friend the capitalist — and he is my friend — that just now the most striking and the most general encouragement of labor unionism in this section of our country is the fact that upon the one most vital, most practical, most popular industrial issue before the South to-day labor unionism has got upon the right side, and "capital" has too often been upon the wrong side. Strictly from the selfish standpoint of the capitalistic

interest, what is the inevitable result of the joining of
such an issue? That result might easily have been
predicted. The popular sympathy, the public opinion
of the South, has been drawn as never before to the
side of labor unionism, and it has come to question, as
never before, some of the too familiar methods and
policies of organized capital. In a conflict between
the organized forces of labor and the organized forces
of the employers, it is absolutely inevitable, as the
whole history of civilization might have informed us,
that the great common, fundamental instincts of
humanity were bound to go to the side which has
represented the need and the appeal of the defenceless. I am glad to say that thousands of the business
men of the South have recognized this fact, have
recognized it not only in justice to themselves but in
justice to our children of the mills, and have labored
in season and out of season for wise and righteous
measures of reform.

These are the men who have represented the wiser
and higher conscience of our industrial development.
For we touch at this point certain profounder issues
in the industrial policy of the South than the mere
issue between unionism and capitalism. One is an
issue which touches the ethical assumptions, the
moral standards of our economic progress; the other
touches the old, old issue between sagacity and
stupidity, between wisdom and folly, between justice
and selfishness, as we deal with the human factors
of industrial greatness.

The South has one great characteristic natural
product — her cotton. In its possession she is without a rival. Her monopoly may be challenged, but

her preëminence will remain.   Upon the basis of
this great and characteristic natural product we are
creating a great, characteristic, and commanding industry.— cotton manufacture.   Its successes and its victories are as inevitable as they are desirable.   It can
have no enemies unless we constitute ourselves its
enemies.   It can have no perils unless we ourselves
found it in embarrassment and league it with disaster.   Its growth, its triumphs, its opportunities, its
rewards, its infamy or its glory are a part of the distinctive heritage of our children and of our children's
children.   What is the basis of this industry ?   What
shall be its economic and moral character ?   How are
we settling it and founding it ?   This is the issue, the
intimate and inclusive issue, of this question of child
labor at the South.   I am interested, therefore, in
the question of child labor, not merely for the sake
of our children of the mills, not merely because I
have seen and photographed children of six and
seven years who were at labor in our factories for
twelve and thirteen hours a day, not merely because
I have seen them with their little fingers mangled by
machinery and their little bodies numb and listless
with exhaustion, but because I am not willing that
our whole economic progress should be involved in
such conditions; and because as a Southern man,
born, reared, and educated in the South, I am
resolved to take my part, however humbly, in the
settling of the industrial character of this our greatest industry.   Because I belong to the South and
because I love the South, I do not want its most
important and distinctive industry to stand under any
sort of odium, moral or economic.   I believe that an

intelligent moral interest in the conditions of the factory, and the jealous guarding of its ethical assumptions, will minister not merely to the humanity of its standards and the happiness of its operatives, but to the dignity, currency, and value of its properties. In the interest of its success as well as in the interest of its renown, I wish its repute to be as fair as the white fields of our cotton. Commanding the economic and moral confidence of the investors in our securities, of the spectators of our progress, of the enlightened and approving opinion of mankind, I wish this industry to take its place among us as one of the noblest as well as one of the greatest of the productive forces of our century and our civilization.

We must, moreover, settle once for all the industrial policy of the South as that policy touches the human factors of industrial greatness. In thinking so much about sociology, let us not forget to think a little about childhood, — nor about childhood only, but also about the children. The two things are not synonymous. Such are the academic hypocrisies of humanity that the "age of chivalry," the age which talked so nobly and so inordinately of womanhood, did comparatively little for its women. And our age, which talks very beautifully of childhood and the child, is finding in its entrancing preoccupations much opportunity to neglect its children.

To this neglect the South cannot and — I thank God — will not yield. If the cotton, the crude material of our industries, is peculiarly the South's, so the human factors of our industry are also ours. The children of our Northern mills — as Miss

Addams [1] could inform you — are largely the children of the foreigner. If the Northern States can legislate to protect the children of the foreigner, surely we can legislate to protect the children of the South. I speak not in jealousy of the foreigner — God forbid! — but I dare not speak in forgetfulness of our own, of the children of these humbler people of our Southern soil — a people native to our section and our interests; of our own race and blood, slowly preparing for their share in the advancing largeness of our life, and worthy through their children of to-day to constitute an ever increasing factor in the broader and happier citizenship of our future years.

They are called a " poor " white people; but from that knowledge of them which has come through a long experience of affectionate and familiar contact, I can say that their poverty is not the essential poverty of inward resources, but rather the temporary and incidental poverty of unfortunate conditions. They are rich in capacities and aptitudes. The exploitation of their children, though their own ignorance may sometimes make them a party to its processes, is a crime not only against the rights of the defenceless, but a crime against the economic progress and the industrial future of the South. Why, the man upon the farm does not put the burden of sustained employment upon the immature among his cattle. Shall we be less solicitous of our children? If cotton manufacture is to continue to thrive at the South, it can do so only upon the basis of the intelligence and efficiency of its operatives.

[1] The preceding speaker, Miss Jane Addams, of Hull House, Chicago.

Ignorance and helplessness may make the profits of
an hour, but the increasing and abiding wealth of
a great industry lies only in the hands of knowledge,
capacity, and skill.   Sustained labor in the factory
has always tended to arrest the mental and physical
development of the child, and so to lower the productive power of the operative.   An industrial State
which throws the burdens of employment upon its
children of tender years burns its candle at both
ends.   The South makes comparatively small gains
from immigration.   The sacrifice of the childhood of
our poorer people, the exhaustion of their best skill
and of their fullest vigor and intelligence means
nothing less than the exploitation of our one indigenous industrial population, the real hope of the textile future of our Southern States.

The potential industrial and moral wealth represented by the child belongs, moreover, not to the
eager avarice of a single industry, but to the growing
body of social opportunities and needs.   Society has
need of the children, for it has need of the fullest
womanhood and manhood.   Its right to protect the
child is based upon this need as well as upon the
need of the child.   A human life is a continuous
and expanding asset of social promise and fulfilment.
Stooping over the tiny spring, a single man might
drain it at the moment of its first leap into the sun-
light.   But Nature hides the spring away; keeps it
within the kindly and secret protection of the cool
forest or the unyielding granite.   Thus she nurses it
into charm and fulness.   As it flows, it grows.   Its
freedom gathers an access of volume and motion as
it runs.   Out of its fulness and its freedom, receiv-

ing tribute from earth and sky and flower, yielding
tribute to every thirsting thing, the brook leaps at
last, as a tiny pulse, into the river's arm, that it may
lift somewhat of the burden of the world. So all
charm and all power have come out of a hidden
place. So all life is first enfolded within the protection of a tender and secret hand, that, with every
potential force, it may belong at length to the labor
and welfare of the years. If the spring had been
given in its earliest moment to the thirst of one devouring avarice, the valleys would have lost their
noblest and fairest wealth. And yet there are those
who would build the factory, so often the symbol of
our ruthless industrial impatience, over the heart-
springs of the childhood of the South.

The world cannot permit a single industry, or a
half-dozen industries, to hold the child in an economic status which is out of touch with the assumptions that underlie the industrial, educational, and
humanitarian organization of our human life. Under
these assumptions the function of the child is not
productive but receptive. Upon the preservation of
this function depends the child's future productive
power. Its protection constitutes one of the strongest as well as one of the holiest interests of civilization. The reversal of this function, upon a universal
scale, would mean the degradation and extinction of
the race. Within the heart of the child lie the well-
springs of the future. Its freedom means the freedom of our country. Its power, knit through the
slow years of free and happy growth, means the
power of our armies. Its play, its joy, its growing
knowledge, its simple and radiant courage, the smil-

ing, teasing challenge of its irresponsibilities and
immunities, constitute (if we will preserve them in
their unspoiled freshness) the indestructible sources
of the power, the dignity, the culture, the laughter,
the freedom, of a great people.

For, my friends, these children are no mere factors
of industry. They are vital and personal factors of
our country and of our humanity. They are heirs
with us of this immediate and present day, this day
of vivid human interests, — of imperious reciprocities,
of ever enlarging fidelities between land and land, between class and class, between life and life. They
are the heirs with us of a deeper and more compelling patriotism. Back of the patriotism of arms, back
of the patriotism of our political and civic life, there
lies, like a new and commanding social motive, the
patriotism of efficiency. Every interest, every institution, every activity of our day must reckon with it.
It is not merely the patriotism of industrial power.
It is the patriotism of social fitness and of economic
value. It is the passion of usefulness. It is the love
of being useful, and, therefore, the love of helping
others into usefulness. The man must be worth
something to his country; his country must be worth
something to the world. In the interest of our country and of our world, it covets for every human life
that emancipation which means the freeing of capacity.

It is this patriotism which we shall invoke, North
and South, in behalf of every wounded, helpless,
defenceless element of our industrial society. It
realizes that the good of one life comes only out of
the fulness of all life; that no power is safe which
reposes solely upon the weakness of another; that

no liberty is safe which depends upon the slavery of another; that no knowledge is safe or sound which bases itself upon the ignorance of another; and that no wealth has reached the fulness of its distinction and its happiness which depends for its existence solely upon the poverty of others. It is to the immediate interest of every man, that every other man should have something to give. In so far as every life becomes a producer and a contributor, every other life becomes a beneficiary. Thus the meaning of patriotism is but the nerve and instinct of society. To bring others into their own believing, hoping, and loving, — this is religion; to share with others the powers of acquiring, and thriving, and rejoicing, — this is wealth; to open to others the liberties of thinking, and knowing, and achieving, — this is education; to enlarge for others the glory of living, — this is life; to behold the great thronging masses of men alive and radiant with those capacities and efficiencies which redeem the waste and silence of the world, — this is indeed the supreme efficiency, and this I believe to be the supreme patriotism.

THE SOUTH AND THE NEGRO

CHAPTER VI

I

POLITICALLY, there still exists "the solid South";
yet, for the more intimate phases of Southern opinion
in relation to the most serious of Southern problems,
no one may speak as a representative authority. In
the presence of the negro, we may say truly that the
mind of the South is of many minds. Just as the
negro divides the sentiment of the North, he divides
the sentiment of the South.

Under the different conditions obtaining to-day in
our industrial and political life, from year to year
and from place to place, the negro is different and
the white man is different. In each locality of the
South, the problem is, therefore, a different problem.
Ultimately, of course, the problem is one — is the
mutual social, industrial, and political adjustment
upon the same soil, of two races between whom the
difference in color is perhaps the most superficial of
the distinctions which divide them.

As this fundamental problem, however, is presented
under the concrete working conditions of Southern
life, it assumes a different phase in each State of
the South, in each county of the several States, and
even in the separate communities of each particular

county.[1] When studied in the city where the white
population slightly outnumbers the black, where
churches and schools are provided, and police protection is abundant, the racial conditions of such a
State as Alabama present one problem; in an adjoining county, where the negroes outnumber the white

[1] "The variety of conditions in different parts of a single State is
often greater than would be imagined. If one were to say that certain
counties of Virginia, North Carolina, Tennessee, and Alabama contain
fewer negroes than certain counties of New Jersey, Connecticut, Massachusetts, or Rhode Island, it might awaken surprise. But the figures
for a number of counties in the South are as follows: —

	Total	Negroes		Total	Negroes
Garrett, Md.	17,701	126	Unicoi, Tenn.	5,581	130
Buchanan, Va.	9,692	5	Union, Tenn.	12,894	79
Graham, N.C.	4,343	26	Van Buren, Tenn.	3,326	37
Fentress, Tenn.	6,106	25	Towns, Ga.	4,748	71
Pickett, Tenn.	5,366	11	Cullman, Ala.	9,554	21
Sequatchie, Tenn.	3,326	37	Winston, Ala.	17,849	7

"The twelve counties contain 90,756 people, of whom 575 are
negroes, a single negro to 175 of the population. Nantucket Island,
Mass., contains more negroes than most of these counties.

"But again it may cause surprise to find how small is the proportion
of white people in some counties. In Issaquena County, Mississippi,
only six people in every hundred are white, and there are five other
counties in which the per cent is less than ten. In fourteen counties
in the South, seven-eighths of the people are negroes; in fifty-four
counties, three-quarters; and in one hundred and eight counties, two-
thirds. The great difference in race proportions in different counties
is shown in Alabama, for example, where the proportion varies from
Winston County, in which there are only seven negroes, to Lowndes,
in which they number over thirty thousand.

"It needs no argument to show that the 'negro problem' is quite
a different thing in Winston from what it is in Lowndes." — GEORGE
S. DICKERMAN, in the *Southern Workman*, Hampton, Va., January,
1903.

people six to one, where both races are poor, where
schools and churches are not numerous or usually
impressive, where the constabulary is necessarily inadequate, our racial conditions present what may be
readily understood to be a very different problem
indeed.

Even in the rural South, the problem, as suggested
by one of my correspondents, varies from neighborhood to neighborhood. It is one thing in those
regions of light and sandy soil where the farms of
the white man and the negro adjoin, where the white
man's farm is cultivated by his own labor, where the
negro is not to any large extent a dependent class,
and where the relation of master and servant exists
but to a slight degree; it is another thing where the
negro exists in large numbers as a working class
upon the plantation of the white man. It assumes
still another phase in the regions of black and heavy
soil, where the white man who owns the land finds it
too unhealthful to work his own plantation, and the
large negro population comes into personal relations
only with boss, overseer, or superintendent. In our
mining regions, moreover, where the negro comes
into direct contact with the white man, not as a land-
owner or overseer, but as a fellow-laborer, often with
the foreign laborer, we find a different problem still.
The problem differs not only from locality to locality,
but from man to man. There is a personal equation
as well as a local equation.

And in addition to a personal and a local equation
there is a class equation. In certain sections of the
South the negroes themselves are different from those
in other sections. Those negroes of Virginia who

have been reared in proximity to the white population of the higher type, reflect in aspiration, in character, in manner, the better qualities of their environment. The negroes of other sections who are the descendants of those inferior slaves that were "weeded out" of the better plantations and "sold South," present a far more difficult situation.

And the white population, also, has its social classifications. Between the more intelligent negroes and the representatives of the planter-class — the old aristocracy — there is little if any friction. But between the negro of any class and the representative of the "plain people," the people whose energies are re-creating the fortunes of the land, whose prejudices are quite as vigorous as their industry, who have never known the negro at his best and have too often seen him at his worst, — between the new negro and the new white man, there is likely to be enmity and there is very sure to be suspicion. The Southern white man also presents those marked varieties of temperament and disposition which go everywhere with a greater complexity and a deeper refinement of social organization. He differs also under the changing and instructive forces of travel, of education, of experience. From class to class, from man to man, as well as from place to place, what has been called "the problem of the races" assumes a distinctive phase and becomes a different problem.

Dwelling upon still another aspect of our Southern situation, the writer addressed the following words, in March of 1900, to a representative audience in the city of Philadelphia: "Under wholly normal and natural conditions our race perplexities at the South

would have been serious enough.   You have found
them serious here.   Those of you who are familiar
with Du Bois's book [1] on the subject of 'The Philadelphia Negro' know the humiliating difficulties of
the problem in a city which is so resourceful in its
educational and humanitarian provisions that we, of
smaller and poorer communities, are wont to look
upon you as just one great organized compassion.
If here you have found the task one of such saddening perplexity, what will you say of the difficulties of
this task when presented under the conditions of
Southern life ?   If the negro in Philadelphia presents
a problem which you have not solved in justice either
to the negro or to yourselves, what would you do
with him under conditions which should multiply by
fifty fold his numbers in your midst, which should
multiply the burden of his illiteracy and should increase
his tendencies to indolence ; under conditions which
should make his freedom the legacy of a desolating
war, under changes which had torn him from one
place in the social organism and had not fitted him
to another, which had removed him as a slave without fitting him for freedom ?   What would you do
with him under conditions which, through the administrative policy of his liberators, had then placed him
in the care of those who, representing neither the
conscience of the victors nor the dignity of the vanquished, befriended him solely to despoil his truest
friends ; who, after using him for the humiliation of
his master, left him shorn indeed of his shackles, but

[1] "The Philadelphia Negro, A Sociological Study," by W. E. Burg-
hardt Du Bois ; Philadelphia, The American Academy of Political and
Social Science, 1899.

shorn also of that heritage of care which the weak should possess in the compassions of the strong? What could you have done with a problem, naturally so difficult, that had been left to you under the conditions of military defeat, with its prostrating influence upon social enthusiasm and civic hopefulness; under conditions of economic depression, of industrial exhaustion and personal poverty — compelling the worthier classes of the white population into so intense a struggle for rehabilitation that the very necessities of survival forced the superior race partly to ignore the weaker; under conditions of antagonistic legislation from an alien but dominant party government, and often under the provocations of harsh and self-sufficient criticism from those who judged where they could not know, and who advised where they had not suffered? You may not think as I think, but suppose these were the things you did think; suppose you had not only the negro in Philadelphia, but Philadelphia and the negro together under such conditions as I have named, conditions which you yourselves should really view as the great masses of our people have viewed our conditions at the South. I think you will see that there is to-day with us not the negro problem only, under its varied personal and local phases, but other problems with it, and I think you will understand me, therefore, if I say that when a man attempts to discuss the negro problem at the South, he may begin with the negro, but he really touches, with however light a hand, the whole bewildering problem of a civilization."

The difficulties of the situation are not simplified by the fact that this civilization is included within a

larger civilization and a more democratic order, and
that every problem of the one necessarily emerges
under its varying political and industrial forms as a
problem of the other. It is still true that there is
one sense in which the problem itself is profoundly
sectional. Locally as well as historically the negro
question is a Southern question. Seven-eighths of
the negro population are in the South, and they are
in the South to stay. There will be occasional movements northward. Long-established negro " colonies "
in cities like New York, Philadelphia, and Cincinnati
will continue to increase in numbers. But these people, in the mass, and because of the silent, unyielding
sway of climatic and industrial forces, will remain south
of an imaginary line connecting the cities of Washington and St. Louis. Even within this Southern territory, it is evident that it is the lower South, the South
within the South, which is receiving the largest relative increase in the number of its negroes.

And yet, while this is true, it is also true that there
are two aspects of our question under which it must
assume a national form. Although the larger proportion of the black population lies within the South,
the actual number of negroes at the North is steadily
increasing ; and the national distribution of the negro
as a factor of population involves the national
distribution of the negro as a problem of American
civilization.[1] From being a problem which was once

---

[1] The city in the United States having the largest number of negroes
in 1900 was Washington, D.C., with 86,702 ; then follow Baltimore
(79,258), New Orleans (77,714), Philadelphia (62,613), and New
York (60,666). It will be noted that only one city south of Washington has as large a negro population as the city of New York.

accorded a wrong solution in one section of our country, it has become, for every section of our country, a
problem which has received no adequate solution
whatever.

The issues presented by the negro in American life
are national, however, in no merely geographical sense.
They are national because of the principles, because
of the industrial and political assumptions, which they
involve. The national welfare is the larger context
of every local problem; and while the negro question
finds its locality in the South, it must find its ultimate
adjustment — if it ever receives adjustment — in the
conscience, the wisdom, the knowledge, the patience,
the courage of the Nation. The problem under its
older form was created by the complicity of the
Nation. The problem under its later forms has been
created by the deliberate enactments of the Nation.
The Nation, including the South, the West, the East,
the North, cannot be permitted to evade responsibilities which it has always been zealous to accept
but which it has not always been so zealous to discharge. Least of all can the South be a party to
that evasion. If national action could be really in-
spired by the wholesome and constructive spirit of a
truly national policy, could be pursued really in the
interest of the whole people, rather than in the interest of sectional bitterness or partisan advantage,
it would bring significant and lasting benefits. Too
often, however, the policies which have been proposed in the Nation's name have been so pursued
as to bring the negro into American life as an issue
of sectionalism rather than as an occasion for nationality, — nationality of temper, of sympathy, of pur-

pose. It is not enough to say that government by
parties is inevitable. There are some crimes of which
even parties ought to be incapable.

I have not hesitated to speak of the presence of
the negro in American life as a "problem." We
have been told that the negro should be regarded not
as a problem but as a man. There is truth in the
suggestion. And yet out of this truth there arises
the problem — he is a man, and yet a man unlike,
in history and in racial character, the men about him.
Every man, white or black, presents a problem. The
problem increases in perplexity when to the characteristics of the individual are added the characteristics
which distinguish and differentiate the group — social,
national, or racial — with which he is associated.
When this group is brought into contact with another
group, or with other groups, the elements of complexity are increased. The problem grows. Russia's
former serfs — struggling out of bondage in one form
and hardly attaining liberty in any form — present a
Russian problem. Her student-bodies — struggling
for the broadest realities of democracy under auto-
cratic conditions — present another problem. Where
the anomalous conditions are created not from within
but by forces and elements from without, the problem
is greater still. The Russian in China is a Chinese
problem. The Jew in Russia is a Russian problem.
The white man in Africa is an African problem.
The African in America is, and will be for centuries,
one of the problems of American life.

Nor can we say that the negro presents not a problem but a task. That would be to assume that the
supreme need is the need of resources, material and

moral, and that all could be well adjusted if there were sufficient power and sufficient patience. These, undoubtedly, are great needs. The task presents, however, not only the aspects of moral and physical difficulty but of intellectual confusion. If we all knew what to do and there were not the strength or the will to do it, the negro would present a task. Because there is much strength and some will, and yet because no ten men have ever yet agreed as to what we should all do, the negro presents something more than a task; he presents a problem.

Fortunately, there is increasing agreement upon the programme presented by such institutions as Hampton and Tuskegee. And yet this programme is rightly and obviously but a programme of beginnings. That is its supreme success; and that is its limitation. What lies beyond? What, politically and socially, is the *terminus ad quem*, the far-on result, of such wise and righteous training? Before that question men divide. It is altogether probable that large numbers of men, white and black, North and South, have united upon the support of this programme for wholly dissimilar or for antagonistic reasons. All are agreed that this is the next step. The next step to what? Before *that* question will rise all the ancient and lurid spectres of misapprehension and suspicion.

II

As the negro problem has been presented at the North and in the South — its more especial local home — it has apparently assumed, within the past five years, certain more acute and more serious forms.

To these unfortunate developments the whole situation has contributed, from the side of the negro and from the side of the white man. And yet, while it is true that there are grave evidences of loss, it is equally true that there are marked evidences of gain. Progress has been coincident with retrogression. Many of our difficulties are due to the delinquencies of the negro; quite as many, however, are due to his advancement. Nor do the difficulties of the problem lie wholly with the negro. At the South, the processes of social evolution which were accentuated, if not inaugurated, by the issue of the Civil War had their profound effect upon the life of the negro masses. They have also involved, however, the life of the white masses, and have set to work within it certain forces of transformation which, for many years, must bear with insistent pressure upon the fortunes both of the negro and of the South. Let us turn, first of all, to the consideration of some of the social changes wrought in the masses of negro life by the issue of emancipation.

Slavery was nothing if not a system of restraint. This restraint was sometimes expressed in ignoble and brutal forms. It was sometimes expressed in the forms of a kindly and not ungenerous paternalism. But, good or bad, it held the race in check. It imposed its traditional limitations, it exercised a directive and restrictive oversight. It was bondage.

This bondage fixed, instinctively, a limit beyond which the negro must not ascend; it fixed a limit below which the negro must not fall. It operated in both directions as a check. To the negro who was inclined to rise into the larger liberties of thought and

knowledge it opposed — it was compelled to oppose
— its barriers. To the negro who was inclined to
descend into the debilities of inefficiency and crime it
also opposed — it was compelled to oppose — its barriers. As the race had come to these shores from a
land of pitiless barbarism, the number of negroes
who tended to fall below the standard of slavery was
probably very much greater than the number who
tended to rise above it. It is evident, therefore, that
for some generations the net result of slavery was
not, in its practical operation, a disadvantage to the
masses of negro life. And yet the deep cry of the
few who would aspire will always possess — in God's
heart and in the heart of all our race — a more imperious validity than the dark longing of the many
who would descend.

Upon the two tendencies of the negro thus held
in check the effect of emancipation must be evident.
Restraint withdrawn, negro life is released in two
directions — the smaller number of better negroes is
permitted to rise, and many of them do rise; the
larger number of weaker negroes is permitted to fall,
and most of them do fall. It was inevitable.

The South, the country as a whole, is confronted,
therefore, with an upward and a downward tendency.
We are in the presence of two different, two oppos-
ing movements — the one serving at many points and
in many ways to check the other, but each distinct
and each representing the social momentum of
natural and spontaneous forces. The masses of the
race, released from the restraint which slavery imposed, and isolated, through the pressure of political
exigencies, from the sympathetic guidance of the bet-

ter South, have shown many of the tendencies of
moral and physical reversion.   At certain points
within the South, especially at points where the white
population has represented the highest average of
culture and character, these tendencies have been
arrested.   But it was to have been expected that,
upon the whole, the masses of the negroes would first
become worse before becoming better.

And yet the process upward — although the story
of a smaller number — must be borne clearly and
steadily in mind.   The failure of great masses of
men — in the total life of any race — must not obscure the achievements of the few.   Indeed, to the
historian of the great ventures and experiments of
civilization, the achievements of the few are of more
significance than the failures of the many.   For
achievement — even though upon a small scale — is
a demonstration of possibilities.   It gives a starting-
point for constructive theories and policies; it gives
authority to anticipation.

It is no small thing that the illiteracy of the negro
males of voting age has been reduced in the Southern States from 88 per cent in 1870 to 52 per cent
in 1900; and yet it is only when we turn to the more
intimate victories, here and there, of individual men
and women that we get the full measure of the
negro's promise.   Nor would I be disposed to seek
that promise in the rare and exceptional attainments
of the men of genius.   Neither in the marked reduction of the illiteracy of the masses nor in the marked
distinction of such artists as Tanner or Dunbar or
such leaders as Washington, Grant, and Walker can
we seek the sure evidences of a people's essential

progress. All promise and all attainment are worth while, but the only adequate measure of social efficiency and the only ultimate test of essential racial progress lies in the capacity to create the home; and it is in the successful achievement of the idea and the institution of the family, of the family as accepted and honored under the conditions of Western civilization, that we are to seek the real criterion of negro progress.

For the very reason that the test is so severe — and yet so instinctively American — the weaknesses of the race will seem conspicuous and formidable. American society, as a whole, stands not unscathed in the white light of its own ideal. The heritage of the negro — his heritage from slavery and from the darker age which preceded slavery — has given him but small equipment for the achievement of this task. And yet the negro home exists. That its existence is, in many cases, but a naïve pretence, that negro life often proceeds upon its way with a disregard — partly immoral, partly non-moral — of our accepted marital conditions, is evident enough. And yet those who would observe broadly and closely will find a patiently and persistently increasing number of true families and real homes, a number far in excess of the popular estimate, homes in which with intelligence, probity, industry, and an admirable simplicity, the man and the woman are creating our fundamental institution. Scores of such homes, in some cases hundreds, exist in numbers of our American communities — exist for those who will try to find them and will try, sympathetically, to know them. But one of the tragic elements of our situation lies in the fact that of this most honorable and most hopeful aspect of negro life the white community, North or South, knows practically nothing. Of the destructive factors in negro life the white community hears to the uttermost, hears through the press and police court; of the constructive factors of negro progress — the negro school, the saner negro church, the negro home — the white community is in ignorance. Until it does know this aspect of our negro problem it may know more or less accurately many things about the negro; but it cannot know the negro.

The white man, North as well as South, feels — and feels wisely — that the social barrier should remain. So long, however, as it remains it shuts out not only the negro from the white man but the white man from the negro. Seeing the negro loafer on the streets, the negro man or woman in domestic service, the negro laborer in the fields, is not seeing the negro. It is seeing the negro on one side. It is seeing the negro before achievement begins, often before achievement — the achievement which the world esteems — is possible. Knowing the white man only under those conditions would not be knowing the white man. Yet this side of the negro is usually the only side of which the white community has direct and accurate knowledge. It is the knowledge of industrial contact, and of industrial contact upon its lower plane. It is not the knowledge of reciprocal obligations, of social revelation. And at the point where this lower contact ceases, at the point where the negro's real efficiency begins, and he passes out of domestic service or unskilled employment into a larger world, the white community loses its personal and definite infor-

mation; the negro passes into the unknown. As the
negro attains progress, he, by the very fact of progress, removes the tangible evidence of progress from
the immediate observation of the white community.
Thus the composite idea, the social conception of the
negro which is beginning to obtain among us, is determined more largely by the evidences of negro
retrogression or negro stagnation than by the evidence, the real and increasing evidence, of negro
advancement.

Nor is the inadequacy of the composite picture of
the negro due only to the way in which the social
cleavage between the races imposes its limitation
upon the vision of the white community. The inadequacy of the picture is due to subjective as well
as to objective causes. A partly mistaken conception of the negro has resulted from the fact that
the white world does not see the negro at his best;
it has also resulted from the fact that the white world
which now sees the negro habitually, which judges
him and speaks of him most constantly, is not infrequently the white world at its worst. How large a
number of the white world, upon its educated side,
have ever really seen the life of a negro home, or the
life of the negro school, or the life of the saner negro
church? The conception of the old-time darky is a
national heritage, a heritage more sacred to the South
than those outside the South can always understand.
That conception, however, as it lives in the consciousness of our domestic and literary life, is due not to
one factor only but to two. It was the result, like
all conceptions, of the thing seen and the seeing eye.
It was not due alone to the negro of our older age.

It was due to the eye which looked upon him, which judged broadly his qualities of character, which had regard to his fidelities, and which understood, with the humor, the patience, the magnanimity of an educated class, the occasions of the negro's failure. The conception of the old-time darky is thus a double contribution, the contribution of the better negro as known and interpreted to us through the better heart of the older South.

But the mind of that older South no longer dominates the visual habits, the racial prepossessions of Southern life. The political and industrial reorganization of the South has formed a new democracy, a democracy which has brought into its fellowship the neglected masses of the white population, which has been forced to seek its basis of organization upon the one ground of the unity of race ; and within this larger white world — alert, vigorous, confident, assertive — many of the old attitudes of spirit have passed away. An educated minority may transfer to the crude multitudes of a new order a sense of power, a sense of freedom, a sense of responsibility, but not its more intimate phases of temper, of individuality — its urbanities, its genial humor, its share in those pervasive charities which spring from a sense of leisure and from an assured consciousness of power, quite as much as from a fertile earnestness of heart.

The old South does last on within the new, the old South with its magnanimity and its poise; and, here and there, in numberless men and women and in many establishments of city and country, one may still observe the persistence and charm of that amazing patience with which the South has served the

negro while the negro has served the South. And
yet these forces are no longer dominant. The new
world which has resulted from our political and industrial reorganization has brought into power vast
multitudes of the unlettered and the untrained, a
white population possessing all the pride, all the
energy, all the assertiveness of the older order, without its experience or its culture. It does not always
rule. It has usually been so wise and so sincere as to
choose its leaders from the ranks of trained and at least
educated men; but among these it has usually chosen
those who were fitted to understand it and to serve it
rather than those who would instruct it. Have Northern constituencies wrought otherwise? But when the
cruder forces of the South have found themselves in
the possession of nobler leaders, chosen by them or
chosen for them by the occasional influence of the
commercial and professional classes, the masses of the
people have been quick to respond to the appeal of
every free and upbuilding purpose; and here lies the
promise of the future. As yet, however, it is too soon
to expect that the new and untrained elements of the
white democracy will view the negro otherwise than
from their own personal and present and actual standpoint. In States where, in many localities, more than
20 per cent of the white men of voting age are illiterate; where the rural population which can read and
write does actually read and write but little; where
large numbers of the people have known nothing
of the slave except as the representative of a hated
competitive labor, and where the negro in freedom
has lost many of the virtues of his bondage, it is impossible to suppose that ignorant men will judge the

negro, or any other factor of experience, otherwise
than ignorantly.   Even where knowledge is greater
and experience broader, the popular conception of
the negro is largely determined by the impressions
that arise among the ignorant.   Almost every family
makes, in thought and expression, an " honorable exception " of the servants of its own household, the
negroes it really knows; but the collective conception, the composite picture of the negro, is too often
the negro as interpreted through the medium of an untrained public opinion, an opinion sometimes voiced in
the rant of the political hustings, in sensational press
reports, in the rumors of the street.   The mind of
the white world, as it sees and judges the negro, is
thus not the mind of the white world at its best.   It
is a mind now influenced by the presence within it
in abnormal proportions, of unsympathetic and untutored forces ; forces which are gaining daily, however,
in both sympathy and training ; forces which may
well be the occasion, therefore, of no inconsiderate
pessimism but of a reasonable and wholesome faith,
a faith which the true citizen of a democracy gives,
and is bound to give, to every social possibility of his
country's life.

III

We may be tempted to say, therefore, that the
kindlier conception of the old-time negro resulted
from the fact that the white world at its best was
looking upon the negro at his best; the harsher conception of the present negro resulting from the fact
that a white world which is not at its best is looking
upon the negro at his worst.   The generalization

thus expressed may be too clearly drawn, and yet
it is sufficiently evident that just at this period in the
history of the South the two races have entered
into new conditions, and that under these conditions
their relations to each other are at many points the
relations of disadvantage. The necessary social
cleavage between the races forces the negro — as he
rises — to rise out of the familiar view of the white
community. The race secures little credit for its
actual, its most significant, gains. The white world
has been influenced both in thought and in action,
not merely by the fact that negro progress has been
obscured, but by the fact that its own vision has been
affected by the rapid and overwhelming rise of a
great class — possessing the hereditary antipathies
of race, accentuated by the economic antipathies of
all free labor toward the labor of the slave. To the
resulting conception of negro life, to the inadequacy
of this composite picture of negro experience, — limitations due to the thing seen and to the seeing eye,
— we may attribute some of the serious signs of popular exasperation, and many of the more recent evidences of racial friction.

That these evidences have not been confined to the
Southern States is now one of the commonplaces of
current observation. And where racial irritation has
arisen at the North, it has been due largely to the same
causes, to the popular ignorance of the better phases
of negro life, and to the preponderance, in many of
our American cities, of uncontrolled and " difficult "
human masses. Yet there is present there another
factor which is also present in the South, and
which contributes its sinister and baffling element

to the composite picture upon which I have just dwelt. This factor is the "criminal" negro; numerically not a large proportion of the race, but as a factor of disturbance one of the baneful as well as one of the most formidable of social forces.[1] The number of such negroes is relatively small, and yet it has assumed a morbid and unfortunate importance. To this importance three influences have contributed.

First, the distinctively criminal negro is often guilty of unusual and abnormal crimes. He is associated in the public mind with one crime, particularly, which is unspeakable in its brutality and infamy. It is true that this crime has sometimes been charged against the innocent; that is true of all crimes. It is also true — as has been suggested — that the number of such crimes is relatively small; and yet it must not be forgotten that, in order to shield the victim, the suppression of the news of this crime is often as significant as its exaggeration. But the fact that the criminals of this class are so few in number, should make the attitude of the public mind in dealing with them a task of simplicity and ease. And yet, because of the deep forces of inter-racial suspicion, a crime which should be the very last crime to present any other than an essential human

---

[1] Negro crime seems to be proportionately greater at the North than at the South — due probably to the fact that at the North the negro is found under the conditions of the city, while at the South he lives chiefly under the simpler and more wholesome conditions of the country. The percentage of crime is, in both sections, much larger for the negro than for the white population, and the statement of the text as to the small proportion of criminal negroes refers only to the degenerate roving type, peculiarly irresponsible, and guilty of the more serious offences.

issue between good and evil, has been made one of
the most complex and difficult of "questions," the
occasion for some of the most irreducible points
in the discussion of racial issues. I think it must
be fairly said that the difficulties of the situation are
chargeable to false conditions in the public opinion
of both races. Negro opinion, organized and unorganized, has seemed to be too protective; white
opinion has too often been lawlessly retributive.

That negro opinion, unorganized and uninstructed,
should be inclined to protect even the more degraded
criminal may be easily explained though not excused.
A weaker race constantly subjected to indiscriminate
attack is likely to undertake an indiscriminate defence.
The very intensity of external criticism produces, in an
ignorant and untrained human mass, a morbid and
exaggerated solidarity. It is the blind moving of the
instinct of self-protection. The race, however mistakenly, feels that it must "stand together." A disposition upon the part of the white world — the
stronger race — to judge the negro with firm but
clear discrimination and to administer exact justice
under the law would probably result in a gradual but
effective counter movement within the negro masses,
a movement to yield the guilty up to the processes of
trial. It is not, however, to the interest of the negro
that this movement should await the arrival of millen-
nial conditions among the white race, and that the
development of a firmer attitude toward negro crime
should be delayed until the arrival of juster class
conceptions. The negro often assumes that he alone
is subjected to the prejudices of class, whereas almost
every element of society is compelled to face them

and to bear with them. The Jew has confronted them for centuries, in America the German faces them among the Irish, the Irishman faces them among the Germans, the Italian meets them at every point, and — long after national idiosyncrasies have been effaced — the poor man encounters them in the presence of the rich man, the rich man confronts them in the jury composed of poor men.

It is in the negro's own interest that the negro criminal should receive the penalty of his crime, for the protection of the criminal means the demoralization of every social standard. In rural sections of our country there is often the fear that the accused — if surrendered — will be ruthlessly punished without trial; but the tendency among the negro masses to protect the criminal is also operative in the cities — even in cities like New York or Boston or Philadelphia — where there is every assurance that trial will be accorded.

To negro opinion, as expressed in the formal declarations of representative assemblies, we must naturally look for a definite quality of leadership. Yet these declarations have left much to be desired. The denunciations of wrong usually place the word "alleged" before all direct reference to serious offences, and the deprecations of "alleged" crime are usually coupled with conspicuous counter charges against the similar crimes of white men. The dominant note, even to sympathetic observers, has seemed defensive, exculpatory, rather than decisively corrective; an appeal to the world rather than an honest, wholesome word at home. More recently these expressions have seemed to take a better tone, and under the rapidly broadening influence of the wiser and stronger negro leaders, I believe we shall soon find that the organized opinion of the race will reflect the standards of a sympathetic but effective self-correction.

And how has the white race — in its knowledge and pride and power — dealt with the problem of the negro criminal? Surely, not too well. The average criminal, the negro charged with commonplace or familiar crimes, is — in the South at least — at no unusual disadvantage. If brought before the court he is sometimes punished with undue severity; and he is sometimes punished with absurd leniency. Petty crimes are often forgiven him, and in countless instances the small offences for which white men are quickly apprehended are, in the negro, habitually ignored. The world hears broadly and repeatedly of the cases of injustice, it hears little of those more frequent instances in which the weaknesses of a child-race are accorded only an amused indifference or a patient tolerance by their stronger neighbors. That such an attitude has its disadvantages as well as its advantages for the negro need not be forgotten.

Dealing with the negro criminal of the baser type, white opinion has too often attempted to answer lawlessness with lawlessness and ferocity with ferocity. To the popular mind the crimes against women appear not only as attacks upon the individual but as attacks upon the integrity of race. They are occasions both of personal offence and of race humiliation.[1] They

---

[1] See a paper by the Hon. Alex C. King of Atlanta, Ga., in the Proceedings of the Conference on the Race Problems of the South, p. 160 ; the B. F. Johnson Publishing Co., Richmond, Virginia.

are often so intended by the criminal and are often so accepted by the white community. The peculiar horror of the crime, the morbid sense of race injury which it arouses, the tendency of innocent negroes to protect the guilty, all unite to produce a degree of emotional tension, a condition of social hysteria which few who have not endured the experience can understand. Add to the difficulties of the situation a wholly inadequate constabulary — inadequate because the South is not merely poor but so largely rural that efficient police organization is practically impossible — and the conditions for the rise of the mob are at once apparent.[1]

The mob, so far as it has had a conscious philosophy, has attempted the justification of its course upon these grounds: — It has insisted that its methods were necessary in order to prevent the crime; in order to avoid the procrastination of the courts; and in order to protect the victim of assault from the ordeal of presenting testimony at the trial of the offender.

---

[1] The inadequacy of a rural constabulary has not been sufficiently considered in accounting for the presence of lynch law at the South. That the mob tendencies are active in many Eastern localities is evident from the large number of "attempted" lynchings. A score of these have been noted in the limits of the city of New York within the period of a year. In some cases the accused was actually in the hands of the infuriated crowd. The lynching was prevented by an efficient constabulary. Given, however, the conditions of rural life in our Southern States, where farms are widely scattered, with poor roads, infrequent railway service, limited telegraph facilities, and few large centres of social organization, — and the "attempted" lynching has its intended issue. Within the cities of the South lynchings have been practically unknown. The cases of mob violence in the cities of such Northern States as Delaware, Indiana, Ohio, and Illinois have few, if any, recent Southern parallels.

It has become increasingly obvious, however, that
whatever the practice of lynching may or may not
be, it is not a remedy. It does not prevent crime.
Through the morbid interests which it arouses, and
through the publicity which it creates, it inflames to
the utmost the power of criminal suggestion and
aggravates all the conditions of racial suspicion and
antagonism. The so-called "remedy" has always
been followed by new outbreaks of the disease, the
most atrocious crimes coming at short intervals after
the previous exercise of the mob's philosophy of
"prevention."

It is true that the procrastination of the courts has
sometimes resulted in deep and pardonable irritation.
Where the nature of the offence is peculiarly ab-
horrent, where every circumstance has rightly secured for the victim the overwhelming sympathy of
the public, and where the accused is a friendless
member of a weaker race this irritation has sometimes passed into uncontrollable exasperation. As a
matter of fact, however, such procrastination is more
frequent to the popular imagination than to the observer of real events. In the presence of the crime
to which reference is made, American courts do not
impose delays. "The delay of the courts" is in
large measure a popular superstition. Where it
occurs, it occurs not in cases where the accused is
a helpless and ignorant member of society, but where
the defence can command those resources of legal
talent and of technical procedure which are possible
only to the rich. In the cases of heinous crime, the
American court, North or South, is usually conscious
of its obligation to the community. Surely, if the

end be justice rather than senseless and futile
slaughter, the court is not inferior to the mob., as
the instrument of an intelligent social verdict.   The
crude theory that "the people" may resume their
delegated powers has no place in a democratic order.
The mob is not "the people"; it is a temporary,
feverish minority, possessing only an incidental co-
herence, without a fixed identity, without continuity
or responsibility — assuming the most august prerogatives of society.   Every mob is, in truth, an
attack upon "the people," for it acts in repudiation
of those institutional forms which the majority have
established.   By its very existence it announces its
violation of the social compact and its rejection of
the freely established forms of popular administration; by its deliberate anonymity and its immediate
dissolution it confesses its irresponsibility and declares that its deeds were usurpations.   The only
real instruments of "the people" for the administration of social penalties are the constabulary and the
courts, and these instruments the people have established in order that one man alone, and he the
humblest, may not be without protection — if innocent — from even the collective power of the majority
itself.   For the constabulary and for the courts,
promptness and decision are important.   But the
paramount and essential end of every true judicial
process is not promptness but justice, is not "vengeance" — individual or social — but the solemn and
decisive determination of innocence or guilt.   It is
the business of the court to free the innocent, it is
its business to set apart the guilty for the penalties of
an outraged law.   All reasonable haste, all possible

diligence must be employed, but — as has been well suggested — in our effort to prevent the mob from turning itself into a court, let us not end by turning the court into a mob.

The methods of the mob are also defended upon the ground that they serve to protect the victim of crime from the ordeal of publicly testifying in the case. Many have regarded this as the strongest argument in the mob's behalf. Yet when we have eliminated the cases — by far the greater number — in which the prisoner of the mob was not even charged with any crime against women, but with arson or robbery or attempted murder; and when we have eliminated, among the cases of assault against women, the number in which death has resulted and the victim is thus prevented from all testimony, legal or extra-legal, the number of cases which come within the traditional excuse is extremely small. And even here, what is the high chivalry of the mob which some would substitute for the care and protection of an American court? Does the mob permit the woman to escape the ordeal of testimony? Does it accomplish the very protection which it proposes? Not at all. The judge has authority to clear the room of all but the direct parties to the case, has the power to spare the victim — under cross-examination — from any but the simpler and less offensive questions, has the right and would surely have the will — in the North or South — to arrange the place for the sitting of his court so as to provide effectively and considerately for the conditions of privacy. But under the régime of the mob, who is to protect the victim, in the hour of

wretchedness, from the morbid and miscellaneous
crowd about the rural home? Posses of men are
scouring the surrounding territory. Absent with
them are probably her father, or her husband, or her
brothers. As each suspected negro is caught, he
must be brought back for identification, and the
woman in her season of agony and humiliation is
called upon, again and again, to face a different
prisoner and to pass upon the question of his identity. In the dim light of her little room she knows,
and all know, that error is possible. But she is
forced to endure this thing — and not in such privacy as the court affords, but often in the gaze of
men — guards of the prisoner — whom she has never
before seen. And this is all supposed to be chivalry.
But men who have seen its crude devices do not call
it so; they regard it as a stupid, ignorant, pitiful
travesty of reserve. The crime of which the prisoner
is accused is perhaps the most unutterably infamous
of human wrongs, and in a vague way men have felt
it to be too personal, too domestic, to permit of formal rectification. Beneath this deep feeling there
is a certain touch of truth. Nor is the court a perfect instrument for the punishment of such a crime;
the crime is wholly outside our normal thinking and
feeling; it is, whether committed by black or white
men, from the barbaric or the degenerate elements
in our life; it is out of the very pit. There can be
no perfect instrument for its punishment, but the
court is the best instrument that we have — best for
the interests of privacy as well as for the interests
of justice — and in the defence of our courts the
very validity of our civilization is involved. The

mob, as we have seen, violates the very canons of
the chivalry which it presumes to guard; it thrusts
upon the victim of the crime an added martyrdom of
publicity; it increases by the power of criminal suggestion the crimes it has undertaken to prevent;
it substitutes the chance humor of an irresponsible
minority for the deliberately established processes of
the majority, and so becomes a peril both to justice
and to freedom.

IV

I think it may be fairly said, however, that the
relative number of lynchings is decreasing from year
to year.   In the South, especially, there is an evident
disposition upon the part of the more influential press
to accord to the negro the measure of exact justice
before the law.[1]   That this ideal will be attained

---

[1] The expressions of such journals as the *Constitution*, of Atlanta,
Ga., and the *Advertiser*, of Montgomery, Ala., are noteworthy, and
yet quite characteristic of the Southern press.

Said the *Constitution* under date of June 27, 1903: —

" The time when the lynching of a certain breed of brutes could be winked
at because of satisfaction that punishment came to him quickly and to the
uttermost, has given way to a time when the greater peril to society is the
mob itself that does the work of vengeance. Against the growth of that evil
the best sense of the nation needs to combine and enforce an adequate
protection."

Said the *Advertiser* under dates of September 16 and October 6,
1903: —

" The white race has a duty which is imperative. It is a duty which is
demanded by justice, by humanity, and by self-interest. Ours is and will
ever be the governing race. It will elect the lawmakers, make the laws, and
enforce them. That being so, that principle of eternal justice which bids the
strong protect the weak, makes it our duty to protect the negro in all his
legal, industrial, and social rights. We should see that he has equal and
exact justice in the courts, that the laws bear alike on the black and the
white, that he be paid for his labor just as the white man is paid, and that
no advantage be taken of his ignorance and credulity. . . .

" And the task is a simple and easy one. The courts and juries should immediately no one can predict. So long as any element of the population is, as a class, in a position of marked economic dependence upon stronger factions or classes, it will certainly suffer — however unfortunately or unjustly — from the pressure of civil and political prejudice. The intelligent negro may well ask of our public opinion a larger measure of discrimination; and yet he may well lay the greater stress upon his gains rather than upon his losses. Certainly his gains will be of small avail if the contemplation of his wrongs shall supersede in his life the positive acceptance and the definite using of his rights. The consciousness of grievances is not an inspiring social asset for a class or for a race. There need be no surrender of essential principles, and yet stress may well be laid, confidently and hopefully, upon the privileges that are actually available for the negro in American life. Here, in the using of the positive liberties and advantages of education and of industry, of religious and political freedom, the negro, through the acceptance of a programme of positive progress, may enter into a larger heritage than is open to any like number of his race in any quarter of the world. Important are some of the advantages he has not; but more important are the many advantages which he has.

Nor can it be said that these advantages are Northern

know no difference between whites and blacks when a question of right and justice is up for settlement. The man who employs a negro to work for him should deal as fairly with him as he would deal by a white man. The life of a negro who has done no wrong should be as sacred as the life of a white man. He is in our power, politically and otherwise, and justice, humanity, and good policy unite in demanding for him equal and exact justice. Keep the negroes among us, give them the full protection of the laws, and let them have justice in all things. That is the solution of the race question."

rather than Southern.   There are to-day almost nine
millions of negroes in the United States.   After thirty
years of freedom, nearly eight millions of them remain
within the borders of the South.   Why have they
remained ?   The broad and living decisions of great
masses of men possess a dumb but interesting significance.   They are never wholly irrational or sentimental.   The negro remains at the South because,
among the primary and the secondary rewards of
honest life, he gets more of the primary rewards at
the South than at the North.   There is no idle flattery of the South in this declaration of the Principal
of Tuskegee : —

"It is in the South that the black man finds an
open sesame in labor, industry, and business that is
not surpassed anywhere.   It is here that that form of
slavery which prevents a man from selling his labor
to whom he pleases on account of his color, is almost
unknown.   We have had slavery in the South, now
dead, that forced an individual to labor without a
salary, but none that compelled a man to live in idleness while his family starved."

The words are not too strong.[1]   The negro knows
that in the essential struggle for existence the spirit
of the South has been the spirit of kindliness and
helpfulness.   Nor is it true that the negro may there
perform only the deeds of drudgery, or those petty

[1] Referring to the statistics of the United States Census for 1900
(Vol. II, p. ccvii), Booker T. Washington says: "Here is the unique
fact, that from a penniless population just out of slavery, 372,414
owners of homes have emerged, and of these 255,156 are known to
own their homes absolutely free of encumbrance.   In these heads of
negro families lies the pledge of my race to American civilization." —
See the *Tradesman*, Chattanooga, Tenn., January 1, 1904, p. 99.

offices that are the badges of a menial dependence. The negro at the South is preacher, teacher, physician, and lawyer; he is in the dry goods business, the grocery business, the livery business, the real estate business, the wood and coal business; as well as in the business of running errands and blacking boots. He is shoemaker and carpenter and blacksmith. He is everywhere where there is anything to do, and if he can do it well, he is usually treated fairly and paid for it honestly. Except in professional capacities, he is employed by all, he does business with all. There is just one line drawn, however, and it is perhaps significant. In a Southern city, with the life of which I am familiar, there is a successful, respected negro man, with many industrial and commercial functions toward the community in which he lives. He is a keeper of carriages, a dealer in wood and coal, a butcher, and vendor of vegetables, — and an undertaker. There is one department of his varied establishment which has never had the monetary support of the white population, and which is sustained entirely by the people of his own race. The white people of the city will buy their supplies of him, will purchase his wood and his coal, will leave their horses in his stables, and will ride in his carriages; — but he may not bury their dead. There is in this simple incident a monograph upon the subject of the negro in the South.

But the South gives to the negro something more merciful than sentiment and something more necessary than the unnegotiable abstractions of social right. The South gives to him the best gift of a civilization to an individual — the opportunity to live industriously and honestly. As the representative of the negro race whom I have already quoted has also said, " If the negro would spend a dollar at the opera, he will find the fairest opportunity at the North ; if he would earn the dollar, his fairest opportunity is at the South. The opportunity to earn the dollar fairly is of much more importance to the negro just now than the opportunity to spend it at the opera." [1] The large and imperious development of trades-unionism at the North (the writer would not speak in criticism of organized labor in itself) is already eliminating the negro as an industrial factor. Du Bois's book on the negro in Philadelphia, to which I have already referred, is but a rescript of the story of his life in every community at the East. Nothing could be more searchingly relentless than the slow, silent, pitiless operation of the social and economic forces that are destroying the negro, body and soul, in the Northern city. None knows it so well as the negro himself. The race-prejudice, which Professor Shaler of Harvard has recently told us is as intense at the North as it is anywhere in the world, first forbids to the negro the membership of the labor union, and then forbids to the employer the services of non-union labor. If

[1] It is of some significance that in 1900 there were 732,362 farms operated by negroes in the South. We find that 150,000 Southern negroes now own their own farms, and 28,000 more are recorded as part owners. (Twelfth Census of the U.S., Vol. V, pp. xciii, 4, 172.) The value of the property in all the farms operated by negroes at the South was $469,506,555. In more than half the counties of Virginia over 70 per cent of the negro farmers are owners or managers, and in 33 counties of the State the proportion is over 80 per cent. — See the interesting papers in the *Southern Workman*, Hampton, Va., for October, 1902; and January, 1903. — See also the valuable monograph by Carl Kelsey, " The Negro Farmer "; Chicago, Ill., Jennings and Pye, 1903.

the employer turn wholly to the non-union men, he
finds that rather than work beside the negro, these
usually throw down their tools and walk out of the door
of factory or shop. And so the dreary tale proceeds.
The negro at the North can be a waiter in hotel and
restaurant (in some); he can be a butler or footman
in club or household (in some); or the haircutter or
bootblack in the barber shop (in some); and I say
"in some" because even the more menial offices of
industry are being slowly but gradually denied to
him. And what is the opportunity of such an environment to the development of self-dependence, what
is the value to his labor of so inadequate and restricted
a market for the complex capacities and the legitimate
ambitions of an awakening manhood? And what
lies at the background of the man? What of the
family, the wife, the mother, the children? What
are the possibilities, there, of self-respect, of decency,
of hope? what are the possibilities of bread?

The economic problem lies at the very heart of the
social welfare of any race. The possibility of honest
bread is the noblest possibility of a civilization; and
it is the indispensable condition of thrift, probity, and
truth. No people can do what is right or love what
is good if they cannot earn what they need. The
South has sins for which she must give account; but
it may be fairly said that as yet the South has no
problem so great, so intimately serious as this. The
South has sometimes abridged the negro's right to
vote, but the South has not yet abridged his right, in
any direction of human interest or of honest effort, to
earn his bread. To the negro, just now, the opportunity, by honest labor, to earn his bread is very much

more important than the opportunity to cast his vote. The one opportunity is secondary, the other is primary; the one is incidental, — the greater number of enlightened peoples have lived happily for centuries without it, — the other is elemental, structural, indispensable; it lies at the very basis of life and integrity — whether individual or social.

V

It is not possible or desirable, however, to ignore the political issues created by the presence of the negro in our national life. If the negro were the only factor to be considered, the questions affecting his political status might be temporarily postponed. But the negro is, in some respects, the least of the factors involved. The political and administrative organization of our country is democratic. Its institutional assumptions are the assumptions of a free democracy. Before all questions which touch the political status of any race or class of men there arises the primary question as to the effect upon our country and its constitution, upon its civic customs and its habits of thought, of the creation of a serf-class, a fixed non-voting population. Such a class can be ustablished and continued only through habitual disregard to all the moral presumptions of our organic law; and such disregard, in its reactive influence upon those who continue it, must result in a lowering of political standards and a vitiation of civic fibre, far more disastrous to the strong than to the weak. Such practices may begin with class discriminations, but these discriminations soon forget their class distinctions; white

men end by using against white men the devices
which they began by confining to black men; the
whole suffrage becomes corrupt; a corrupt suffrage
eliminates from political leadership the men who are
too free or too pure to use it; it becomes the basis of
control for an ever degenerating political leadership;
and what began as a denial of political privilege to
a despised faction at the bottom results in the control at the top of those very elements of an irresponsible ignorance which discrimination was intended
to eliminate. The retrogressive forces which were
dreaded in a faction become enthroned over all; and
the real mind and conscience of the State, in attempting to secure their freedom by protecting themselves
against the ignorant, are despoiled of their freedom
through the very processes of their self-protection;
are put, by their own methods, in bondage to the
cruder forces of society.

The difficulties of the situation have been supremely
serious, and complex beyond description. It is obviously true — as has just been stated — that a democracy cannot consent to the establishment of a
dependent class. And yet it is equally obvious that
within a number of our Southern States that is precisely what the negro is. He is so not primarily as
the result of political proscription, but simply because
he *is* so. A race which, while numbering from 30 to
50 per cent of the population, contributes but 4 or
5 per cent of the direct taxes of the State, is as yet
in an economic status which does not square with
those industrial assumptions which are as important
as the political assumptions of a genuinely democratic
order. The elementary contradiction of our situation

lies, therefore, just here — in the very presence within our life of the vast numbers of a backward and essentially unassimilable people.

In the years following the Civil War the North asserted, sometimes with a ruthless impatience and often through unworthy instruments, but with the sincere conviction of the masses of her people, that the actual political administration of the Southern States must be squared with the democratic assumptions of the Constitution. And the North was right. The South contended, upon the other hand, that where the choice must be made between civilization and democracy, between public order and a particular form of public order, between government and a specific conception of government, — civilization, order, government are primary, and that any forms or conceptions of them — however sacred — must await the stable and efficient reorganization of social life. And the South was right. It was opportune for the North to declare that the freedman could not protect himself unless given the ballot in the mass; it was equally opportune for the South — with whole States where the negroes were a majority, with many counties where the number of black men was treble the number of white men — to declare that the supreme question was not the protection of the negro but the protection of society itself; that white supremacy, at that stage in the development of the South, was necessary to the supremacy of intelligence, administrative capacity and public order, and involved even the existence of those economic and civic conditions upon which the progress of the negro was itself dependent. And here, also, the South was right.

The South was right and the North was right.
The North was strong and the South was weak.
The North imposed the forms of democracy. The
South clung to the substance of government.

Yet, because the very forms of government were
democratic and because these forms of government
were ruthlessly imposed by an irresistible and unsympathetic party power, the South in clinging to the
very substance of civilization was compelled to maintain a lie. Up to this point the historian will not
accord to her the larger measure of blame for the
moral tragedy which followed. The effort, however,
to avert fraud and ignorance at one door admitted
them at another. The effort to prevent the demoralization of government resulted — as has been suggested — in the compromise of all the safeguards of
the suffrage. The growing youth of the South became habitually familiar with ever lowering political
standards, as the subterfuges which were first employed against the black man came to be employed
between white men in the struggle of faction against
faction within the party. The better heart of the
South now rose in protest. An unlimited suffrage
was impossible, but the limitation of the suffrage
must be established not by fraud or force but under
legal conditions, and must be determined by a fixed
and equitable administration.

Thus the deeper moral significance of the recent
constitutional amendments of the Southern States
does not lie in the exclusion of the negro. The
exclusion of the negro had long since been accomplished. It lies in the emancipation of the white
man, an emancipation due to the awakening desire

to abandon the established habits of fraud, and to place the elimination of the undesirable elements of the suffrage squarely and finally under the terms of law. The negro has, in the ultimate result, everything to gain from such a course. Temporarily he must suffer the consequences of an undemocratic adjustment to democratic conditions, an adjustment due primarily to no wilfulness of the white man at the South and to no apathy of the white man at the North, but to the contradiction presented by his presence in the Nation. There are always disadvantages in securing for any adjustment a legal status through illegal means, and the direct elimination of all the undesirable elements of voting age might have seemed a comparatively simple undertaking. Had the negro masses presented the only illiterate elements, that method might have been pursued. But there were two defective classes — the unqualified negroes of voting age and the unqualified white men. Both could not be dropped at once. A working constitution is not an *a priori* theoretic creation; it must pass the people. The unqualified white men of voting age might be eliminated by gradual process, but they must first be included in the partnership of reorganization. Such a decision was a political necessity. They had been fused — by their participation in the military struggle of the Confederacy and by their growing participation in the industrial and political power of the South — into the conscious and dominant life of the State. Many of them possessed large political experience and political faculties of an unusual order. Moreover — and we touch here upon a far-reaching consideration — no amended Constitu-

tion, no suffrage reform, no legal status for a saner
and purer political administration, was possible without their votes.   They held the key to the political
situation — with all its moral and social issues — and
they demanded terms.

Terms were given them.[1]   Under skilfully drawn
provisions the mass of illiterate negro voters were
deprived of suffrage and the then voting white population — with certain variously defined exceptions —
was permitted to retain the ballot.   Care was taken,
however, that all the rising generation and all future
generations of white voters should be constrained to
accept the suffrage test, a test applicable, therefore,
after a brief fixed period, to white and black alike.
Such is the law.[2]

Lest, however, its technical and more strictly political provisions should be declared unconstitutional, its
practical administration is placed in the charge of
boards of registrars, having a large discretionary
power in the application of the law, and thus — by the

[1] In Alabama the Democratic State Convention went so far as to
pledge that no white man would be disfranchised " except for infamous crime."   In criticism of this pledge the writer pointed out that
its fulfilment would leave the ballot in the hands of all the white
vagrancy, perjury, and bribery of the State — as these offences were not
then " infamous " under the code ; and would be contrary to the permanent interests of both races.   The Constitutional Convention, largely
at the suggestion of the Press Association of Alabama, practically ignored
any literal interpretation of the unfortunate pledge, and the completed
instrument did, in effect, result in the disfranchisement of a large number of white voters.

[2] No attempt is here made to distinguish between the suffrage provisions of the different States.   A statement of these provisions in
detail, together with a discussion of some of the current proposals of
federal policy must be reserved for a later volume.

acceptance or rejection of candidates for registration — actually choosing and creating the permanent electorate of the State. A system of appeals has been provided, and in a number of test cases white juries have shown themselves willing to reverse the adverse decision of the registrars, and to return a verdict in the interest of negro applicants; but the system — as a system — is manifestly subject to grave abuses. If it be used as a responsible instrument for the fair and equitable administration of the law, it may prove an honorable and effective way out of an intolerable situation.

The essential principles involved, apart from all the exasperations of the discussion that has gathered about the National Amendments are, however, but the elementary principles of experience itself. In an open letter to the Constitutional Convention of Alabama, they were thus expressed : —

" Southern sentiment will not approve the disfranchisement of the illiterate Confederate soldier. In any civilization, there is a deep and rightful regard for the man who has fought in the armies of the State. But, with that exception, the State must eventually protect itself, and protect the interests of both races, by the just application of the suffrage test to the white and black alike. The South must, of course, secure the supremacy of intelligence and property. This we shall not secure, however, if we begin with the bald declaration that the negro is to be refused the suffrage although he have both intelligence and property, and that the illiterate white man is to be accorded the suffrage although he have neither. Such a policy would, upon its face, sustain the charge that we are not really interested in the supremacy of intelligence and property, but solely in the selfish and oppressive supremacy of a particular race.

"Such a course, through its depressing influence upon the educational and industrial ambitions of the negro, would but increase his idleness and lawlessness, and work injustice to the negro and to the State. Take out of his life all incentive to the franchise, and you will partly destroy his interest in the acquisition of knowledge and of property, because no people will, in the long run, accept as a working principle of life the theory of taxation without representation. I do not think the negro will riot or rebel, but I do think he will be discouraged in the task of acquiring something for the State to tax. It is not merely a question of justice to the negro. It is a question of enlightened self-interest. No State can live and thrive under the incubus of an unambitious, uneducated, unindustrious, and non-property-holding population. Put the privilege of suffrage among the prizes of legitimate ambition, and you have blessed both the negro and the State.

"If, on the other hand, we accept the administration of an educational and property test which is to enfranchise the negro on his acceptance of its provisions, and is to enfranchise the white man whether he accepts them or not, we shall have adopted a measure which will be an injustice to the white citizenship of the South. It will be an injustice to the white man for the reason that it places for the negro a premium upon knowledge and property — makes for him a broader incentive to the acquisition of an education and a home, leaves the white boy without such incentive, makes the ballot as cheap in his hands as ignorance

and idleness, and through indifference to the God-
given relation between fitness and reward, tempts the
race which is supreme to base its supremacy more
and more upon force rather than upon merit.

" No one shall justly accuse me of wanting to put
the negro over the white man. If anything, however,
could bring about that impossible result, it would be
the imposition of a suffrage test for the negro without
the application of the same test to the white man.
Such action will increase for the negro the incentives
to an education, to industry, and to good behavior ;
and leave the white man without the spur of those
incentives. Whatever such a course may be, in relation to the humbler classes of our white people, it is
not statesmanship. I do not assume that the average
illiterate negro has the political capacity of the average illiterate white man. The illiterate white man at
the South has attained — through the genius of race
and the training of generations — more political capacity than many a literate negro. Nor is illiteracy
a crime ; but literacy is a duty. Old conditions are
passing away. The white man of the future who
would claim the political capacity to vote must exercise enough political capacity to qualify. The obligation to qualify is an obligation of helpfulness. No
one is a true friend to our white people who increases
for the negro the encouragements and attractions of
progress and refuses those incentives and encouragements to the children of the white man. I am quite
sure that any suffrage test which establishes for the
negro an incentive to education and property, and
which makes the ballot in the hands of our white
population as free as ignorance and thriftlessness,

will serve, permanently, to injure the stronger race
rather than the weaker.

" To the white boy such a provision is an insult as
well as an injustice, for the reason that it assumes his
need of an adventitious advantage over the negro.
For us to ask the negro boy to submit to a test which
we are unwilling to apply to our own sons, would be,
in my judgment, a reflection upon the capacity of our
white population; and our people, wherever it may
be attempted by the politician of the hour, will come
so to regard it. The absolute supremacy of intelligence and property, secured through a suffrage test
that shall be evenly and equally applicable in theory
and in fact to white and black — this will be the ultimate solution of the South for the whole vexed question of political privilege." [1]

That this faith was not wholly justified by the issue
of the Alabama Convention need not obscure the
fact that the final proposals of the Convention were
far more conservative, far more truly democratic,
than at first seemed probable or possible. The
"temporary plan" with its intended inequalities has
already passed away. The permanent plan with its
just and equal provisions is still, however, under the
administration — as in Mississippi — of a system of
election boards.

If these boards of registrars — the essential and
distinctive provision in the suffrage system of the
South — be administered arbitrarily and unfairly, if
they perpetuate the moral confusion and the debas-
ing traditions which they were intended to supplant,

[1] From An Open Letter to the Constitutional Convention of Alabama, by Edgar Gardner Murphy, Montgomery, Ala., April, 1901.

then the South will stand condemned both to the world and to herself. She will have defeated the purpose of her own deepest political and moral forces. But let no one assume that such a result is now in evidence. There have been many instances of needless and intentional injustice. There are, upon the other hand, many evidences which indicate that while the old habits have widely affected the immediate action of the registrars, there is a growing disposition toward just administration, a disposition to exclude the unqualified white man and to admit the qualified negro to the ballot.[1]

A dogmatic impatience will avail nothing. The Nation owes to the South an adequate opportunity for the trial of the difficult experiment which she has undertaken. Adequate results, a full determination of success or failure, cannot be attained in five years or in ten. All criticism of the actual political readjustment of the South should, moreover, be positive as well as negative, and adverse discussion should deal sympathetically and constructively with the question, " If not this, what ? " What is the alternative ? One must recur again and again to the thought

[1] According to the Secretary of State for Mississippi more than 15,000 negroes are already registered there as voters ; in Virginia the number registered is approximately 23,000; in South Carolina, 22,000; in Louisiana, 6400; in North Carolina, 6250. In the latter State, as well as in Alabama, many negroes have been discouraged from offering to register by reason of the fact that the State organization of the party with which they have been associated recently refused to admit even their most respected representatives to its Conventions. Large numbers have also refrained from registration because of their unwillingness to meet the poll-tax requirement. The interest of the masses of the negroes in things political has, for quite different reasons, been much exaggerated by the representatives of both parties.

that the fundamental embarrassments lie in the elementary conditions that precede all the evils and all the remedies. Partially anomalous remedies will always arise out of essentially anomalous conditions.

The task is so complex, the difficulties are so inscrutably formidable, the issues — involving all the deepest and most fateful passions of races and parties — are so far-reaching, that one may well pause before attempting prematurely to substitute for a pending policy of extrication a policy — even though logically complete — which may be based upon more consistent but perhaps more academic conceptions of public right. As one who vigorously opposed the imposition of unequal or uneven tests the author feels that he may fitly say that there would be nothing gained and much lost by any return to older conditions, and that the whole Southern readjustment, whatever its theoretic inconsistencies, should be accorded a reasonable trial.

The situation presents issues for which men upon either side have often been willing to die. But for strong men it is sometimes easier to die than to wait. The need of the present is not martyrdom, with all its touching and tragic splendor, but just a little patience. Human nature is everywhere essentially the same. No movement of our human life can long support its own momentum, or conserve its own integrity, if it assume an irrational or unrighteous form. Political inequalities will not endure. With time, with reason, with patience, the moral forces of the South can accomplish something which all the enactments and threatening of the Nation can delay but cannot produce, — an equitable public temper, — with

which imperfect laws are just, and without which
Utopia itself would be but an institutional futility.
God has left no corner of the world without certain
of the resident forces of self-correction.   The South
feels, and feels justly, that in the view of history she
has dealt as scrupulously as the North with the literal
obligations of the Constitution, and that in the travail
of her extrication from an intolerable situation, her
policy is now entitled to considerate and adequate
trial.   She has given her own welfare as hostage, in
pledge for her sincerity.   With patience, and with
the rapidly increasing educational and industrial
quickening of the South, there is arising within her
popular life, a clearer outlook, a saner Americanism,
a freer and juster civic sense — and these are, at
last, the only ultimate security of our constitutional
assumptions.

The practical situation presents, not a problem of
theoretic politics, sociology, or ethics.   It is a problem
of flesh and blood, the elements of which are men
and women and little children ; the issues of which
lie not in the cheap and passing advantage of factions
and parties but in the happiness or the wretchedness
of millions of our human kind.   It is in many of its
aspects the greatest, the most difficult, problem in
American life — a problem all the greater because,
North as well as South, the forces of race prejudice
and of commercial and political self-absorption are
constantly and impatiently putting it out of sight.   But
it is here.   It is the problem of taking those institutions
and those principles which are the flowering of the
political consciousness of the most politically efficient
of all the races of mankind — institutions and prin-

ciples to which even the Anglo-Saxon is unequal save
in theory — and securing the just coördination under
them of this stronger race which has hardly tried
them with a race which had never dreamed them — a
race which, with all its virtues, is socially and politically almost the least efficient of the families of men;
— two races separated socially by antipathies of
blood, separated politically by the supposed division
of political interests; the weaker distrusting the
stronger, the stronger distrusting the weaker; each
knowing the other at its worst rather than at its
best, and each passionately resolved to be judged by
its best rather than by its worst; a situation of actual,
grotesque, far-reaching inequalities projected under
the conditions of a democratic order and continued
under the industrial and political assumption of the
parity of classes. A great problem! A problem
demanding many things — the temper of justice,
unselfishness, truth — but demanding most of all a
patient wisdom, a wise, conserving, and healing
patience — the patience of thought and of work; not
the patience of the opportunist but the deeper patience
of the patriot. Indeed, if one may speak of it with
anything of hopefulness, it is only because this
problem has now come for its adjustment into a day
when a deeper sense of nationality has merged within
its broader sympathies and its juster perspective the
divisive standpoints of the past, bringing into the
Nation's single and inclusive fate a new North as well
as a new South, a South with its boundaries at the
Lakes and the St. Lawrence, a North with its boundaries through the fields and the pines of a reunited
country at the waters of the Southern Gulf.

A NARRATIVE OF COÖPERATION

CHAPTER VII

I

A NARRATIVE of the general movement represented by the Southern Education Board and the General Education Board must be corrective before it can be descriptive. In phrases of loose and somewhat inaccurate reference, the reader of our current press has come to recognize it under such terms as "the Southern Conference Movement," "the Southern Educational Movement," "the Ogden Movement," and "the Conference for Education in the South." Of these terms only the last-named — "the Conference for Education in the South" need here enter into the essential structure of the story. While the Southern and General Education Boards are distinct from each other, and are distinct from the Conference for Education in the South, there can be no history of the Boards without a preceding and accompanying history of the Conference.

It was in the year 1897 that the Rev. Edward Abbott, D.D., of Cambridge, Massachusetts, made to Captain W. H. Sale of the Capon Springs Hotel, West Virginia, an informal suggestion of such a gathering. Dr. Abbott urged the advisability of holding at some point within the South a personal conference of men and women, Northern and Southern, who might be interested in the problems of Southern education.   Captain Sale assented to the proposal and extended to those who might attend the hospitality of an attractive and historic inn.   It was thought that such a meeting, comprising representatives both from the North and from the South, would be of service to the earnest educational forces of both sections — bringing to the South a clearer and juster perception of the motives and policies of the North, and bringing to the North a broader and more sympathetic appreciation of the needs and difficulties of the South.   Much was expected from the opportunity for personal association.   Accordingly, "the first Capon Springs Conference for Christian Education in the South assembled in the chapel on the grounds of the Capon Springs Hotel, on Wednesday, June 29, 1898, at 8.30 P.M.;"[1] and its membership formed a small but interested company.

The president of the first conference was the Rt. Rev. T. U. Dudley, LL.D., Bishop of Kentucky, an alumnus of the University of Virginia, late Chancellor of the University of the South at Sewanee, Tennessee.   Its vice-president was the Hon. J. L. M. Curry, agent of the Peabody and Slater Boards; its secretary and treasurer was the Rev. A. B. Hunter of St. Augustine's School, Raleigh, North Carolina.   Upon its executive committee were Dr. J. A. Quarles of Washington and Lee University, Lexington, Virginia, and the Hon. John Eaton, formerly United States Commissioner of Education.

The Conference, though small in attendance, touched

[1] Proceedings of the First Capon Springs Conference, p. 3.

a note of reality which gave its work significance and made its existence permanent. Its continuous life was made possible largely through the broad sympathies and the executive effort of Dr. Hollis Burke Frissell, of Hampton, Virginia. The second Capon Springs Conference met on the 20th of June, 1899; and the third met — also at Capon Springs — on the 27th of June, 1900. Of the second conference Dr. J. L. M. Curry was the president; of the third, Mr. Robert C. Ogden of New York was president. Mr. Ogden, by the unanimous request of both the Southern and the Northern members, has from that time continued in service as the presiding officer.[1]

---

[1] Among the men closely associated with the work of the Conference during the period of its sessions at Capon Springs, we find a number of representative names, in addition to those already mentioned. Among the members from the North were Dr. James McAlister, president of the Drexel Institute, Philadelphia; William H. Baldwin, Jr., William J. Shieffelin, George Foster Peabody, George McAneny, R. Fulton Cutting, the Rev. David H. Greer, Charles E. Bigelow, Albert Shaw, and Everett P. Wheeler, of New York; the Rev. A. D. Mayo, D.D., and General Guy V. Henry, of Washington; the Rev. S. D. McConnell, of Brooklyn; George S. Dickerman, of New Haven; and Herbert Welsh of Philadelphia.

Among the members from the South were Dr. Ormand Stone, Dr. A. H. Tuttle, and Dr. Charles W. Kent, professors in the University of Virginia; Dr. A. K. Nelson and Dr. H. St. G. Tucker, professors in Washington and Lee University; Dr. Julius D. Dreher, president of Roanoke College; Dr. J. E. Gilbert of Washington, D.C.; Dr. Charles E. Meserve, president of Shaw University; the Rt. Rev. C. K. Nelson, D.D., Bishop of Georgia; the Rt. Rev. Howard E. Rondthaler of North Carolina; Dr. F. G. Woodworth, of Tougaloo University, Mississippi; Captain C. E. Vawter of Virginia; Lyman Ward of Camp Hill, Alabama; and — by no means least — the Hon. William L. Wilson, then president of Washington and Lee University. For a year as a member of its executive committee, and always as an interested and active participant, Mr. Wilson continued

Many of the papers and addresses of these early
meetings are of permanent value. Dealing frankly
and explicitly with almost every phase of the general
subject of education — for both races — there is a
definiteness of attack, a practicality of purpose, a
generosity of temper, which made possible — and
helpful — the expression of personal and sectional
differences. These differences served but to illustrate two truths — the truth that upon the larger
number of cardinal issues there is, between North
and South, more of agreement than of disagreement;
and the truth that the frank and courteous expression of such differences as may remain serves only
to create an atmosphere of mutual understanding
which soon establishes the possibility of intelligent
coöperation. If a literal and unvarying agreement
were the sole condition of coöperation, coöperation —
among the living forces in any department of activity
— would be impossible. There can be little coöperation between those, upon either side, who know only
their own opinions and can test that knowledge only
in the light of their own experience; there can be
little coöperation between those who withhold or dis-
guise what they really think. But between those who
are ready to learn as well as to teach, and who sincerely attempt to throw into clear and ample light
the landmarks of their respective positions, there is
possible a common outlook and a common work.

his association with the Conference until failing health forced him to
retire from active public service. No man carried greater weight
among his associates in these early and formative occasions. If
Dr. Curry was the presiding genius, men like President Wilson, from
the South, and Dr. Shaw and Mr. Ogden, from the North, were high
among the counsellors.

Where, upon the other hand, there is mutual ignorance, there is likely to be mutual suspicion.
Where there is mutual knowledge, there may be
something of disagreement, but there is sure to be
more of confidence; and confidence rather than agreement is the essential basis of intelligent coöperation.

Among the formal resolutions of the first Conference were the following : —

"Thoroughness in elementary instruction is of the
first importance, and in facilitating the advance along
higher lines the utmost care should be taken to allow
no faster or further progress than is consistent with
solid and durable foundations."

"Longer school terms, and a longer school life,
better qualified teachers and more thorough work, are
greatly to be desired in the public schools.   Industrial education is to be encouraged in all schools, and
at least the elements of it in the public schools.
While deprecating the unnecessary multiplication of
rival institutions with high-sounding titles, we heartily
believe that in a few institutions well equipped for it,
provision should be made for the liberal or higher
education of those called to leadership as preachers,
teachers, editors, etc."

"The principles now widely applied, tending to
prevent the bestowal of gifts upon unworthy persons, have a proper field for exercise in the support
of institutions of learning . . . and while fully realizing the difficulties in the way of any such application
of those principles, we are of the opinion that the
gifts of the North in aid of the educational work of
the South should proceed upon the lines of intelligent,
equitable, and discriminate selection. . . ."

"Upon the principle that if one member of the Union of States suffers, all the members suffer with it, the duty of the whole country to foster education in every part of it is manifest, and the question of a larger and more energetic national aid in behalf of efforts for the education of illiterate masses, deserves the most serious consideration of all patriotic citizens, and never more so than at the present time."

It will be noted that this resolution is not, in a technical and explicit sense, an acceptance of the proposal of national aid as a formal element in the policy of the Conference; but that suggestion is given a cordial measure of approval. In the third Conference a more explicit declaration in favor of national aid was first accepted and then withdrawn. The proposal from that day forward has gained increasing consideration, and yet there has been much unwillingness to make the suggestion an explicit part of a formal programme. It has seemed right as well as wise that those who accept it and those who reject it should remain — without the introduction of a divisive issue — as colaborers in the immediate practical advancement of the general programme of educational revival.

With the second Conference the word "Christian" was dropped from the titular description of the gathering. This change was probably the result, not of a desire to ignore any aspect of religious education, but in order that the supposedly "secular" department of "public" education might have appropriate and increasing recognition. The sessions of the Conference are still opened with prayer, and the coöperation of the leading representatives of denominational education has always been requested and accorded.

Among the resolutions of the second and third Conferences at Capon Springs, were expressions commending the idea of "the travelling library as especially applicable to conditions in the South," commending the administration of the Peabody and Slater Boards, suggesting a wiser discrimination in the use of money contributed at the North for negro education, advising the establishment of industrial reformatories for youthful incorrigibles, encouraging the development of secondary schools, and emphasizing the importance of industrial education as a basis of coöperation between the sections (and presumably between the races). The resolutions, as well as the papers and addresses, of the first three Conferences deal fully and freely with many of the interesting and appealing phases of negro education. All the more impressive, therefore, are the opening clauses of the first resolution of the second Conference: " Resolved, that the education of the white race in the South is the pressing and imperative need, and the noble achievements of the Southern Commonwealths in the creation of common school systems for both races deserve not merely the sympathetic recognition of the country and of the world at large, but also give the old and high-spirited colleges and universities of the South a strong claim upon a generous share of that stream of private wealth in the United States that is enriching and vitalizing the higher education of the North and West." [1]

Such a resolution is an explicit recognition not only of the importance of white education, its importance

[1] Proceedings of the Second Capon Springs Conference, p. 8.

to the Nation, to the welfare of the negro, and to the white population of the South, but also a recognition of the nature of the claims for endowment which have often been made in behalf of certain of the institutions of higher learning in the Southern States. The "wealth" to which reference is made is not the wealth of the North, peculiarly, but the wealth "of the United States," South as well as North. The appeal to that wealth is not based upon a sense of unworthy poverty but upon the consciousness that the Southern institution — like the Western or the Eastern — has the power to serve, — to serve the whole Nation. Its service is all the more real if it stand and work where true work is hard, and if it minister, with inadequate equipment and under difficult conditions, to the reality of our culture and to the breadth and fulness of our national experience.[1]

When Harvard or Yale or Princeton University asks or receives a gift from a Southern man, the in-

[1] " Within the past five years the benefactions to the institutions of higher learning in the United States have amounted to a little more than $61,000,000. Out of a total of $157,000,000 of productive funds held by American colleges the South has but $15,000,000. Out of the 8,500,000 books in college libraries the South holds but 1,250,000. The value of scientific apparatus in the South is a little over $1,000,000 against a total valuation of $17,000,000 in the whole country. The valuation of buildings and grounds of Southern colleges is $8,500,000 in a total of $146,000,000. The total annual income available for higher education in Virginia, North Carolina, South Carolina, Georgia, Alabama, Mississippi, Louisiana, Tennessee, and Kentucky is $19,000 less than the yearly income of Harvard University.

" Out of forty institutions in the United States with productive funds amounting to $1,000,000 or over, but five are in the South ; of twenty-one with productive funds of between $500,000 and $1,000,000 but one is in the South." From " Educational Endowments of the South," by Elizabeth M. Howe ; *The Popular Science Monthly*, October, 1903.

stitution is not said to have asked or received, in any
political or sectional sense, "money from the South."
Nor does a Southern institution, in asking or receiving a gift from a Northern man, ask or receive, in
any political or sectional sense, "money from the
North." The South, like the West, is contributing
to the prosperity of the country as a whole; the
South, like the West, may not improperly share in
that prosperity. The man, however, North or South,
who desires to add to the educational equipment with
which the Nation is meeting anywhere the issues
which involve the clearness of its thinking, the freedom of its decisions, the wisdom and righteousness
of its life, adds to that equipment, not as to a local or
irrelevant memorial, but as to an expanding asset —
to the informing and liberalizing equipment of his
country and his age.

It was at Winston-Salem, North Carolina, that the
Fourth Conference for Education in the South opened
its sessions on the 18th day of April, 1901. The
death of the kindly and courteous proprietor of the
Capon Springs Hotel had suggested the advisability
of holding the annual gatherings at other points
within the Southern States. The striking development of educational interest in North Carolina gave
especial appropriateness to the invitations from the
city of Winston-Salem, and this session of the Conference marked the beginning of permanent and far-
reaching changes in its policy and method.[1] The

[1] Addresses of peculiar interest and value were made by the Hon.
Charles B. Aycock, Governor of North Carolina ; Dr. G. S. Dickerman of Connecticut ; Dr. Charles W. Dabney, president of the University of Tennessee ; Dr. James E. Russell, dean of the Teachers

needs for specific work were set forth with such clearness and fulness, the interest of the representatives of the South and the North was so deeply serious, the method of coöperation, after the past years of experiment, seemed to possess such genuine validity, the truly national significance of the whole subject seemed so increasingly evident, that there arose within the Conference a spontaneous demand for more effective organization. The cause seemed to be too great to be wholly left to the inspirational force of an annual meeting. There seemed to be a clear need for an executive body, a body which might give continuous and more general influence to the purposes and policies which the Conference had come to represent. The following resolutions, accompanied by their preamble, were unanimously adopted : —

"The Conference for Education in the South, on the occasion of its fourth annual meeting, reaffirms its conviction that the overshadowing and supreme public need of our time, as we pass the threshold of a new century, is the education of the children of all the people.

"We declare such education to be the foremost task of our statesmanship, and the most worthy object of philanthropy. With the expansion of our population and the growth of industry and economic resources, we recognize in a fitting and universal educa-

College of New York ; Hon. G. R. Glenn, state superintendent of education for Georgia ; Dr. Truman J. Backus of Brooklyn, New York ; Dr. Charles D. McIver, president of the State Normal College of North Carolina ; Dr. Francis G. Peabody and Dr. John Graham Brooks of Cambridge, Massachusetts ; Dr. Lyman Abbott of New York ; Mr. Carleton B. Gibson of Georgia ; and Dr. George T. Winston, president of the Agricultural and Mechanical College of North Carolina.

tion and training for the home, for the farm and the workshop, and for the exercise of the duties of citizenship, the only salvation for our American standards of family and social life and the only hope for the perpetuity of our institutions, founded by our forefathers on the four corner-stones of intelligence, virtue, economic efficiency, and capacity for political self-control.

"We recognize the value of efforts hitherto made to solve our educational problems, both as respects the methods to be used, and also as regards the sheer quantity of work to be done. But we also find in the facts as presented at the sessions of this Conference the imperative need of renewed efforts on a larger scale; and we find in the improved financial outlook of the country and in the advancing state of public opinion better hopes than ever before of a larger response to this greater need.

"As the first great need of our people is adequate elementary instruction, and as this instruction must come to children so largely through mothers and women-teachers in their homes and primary schools, we desire to emphasize our belief in the wisdom of making the most liberal investments possible in the education of girls and women.

"Whereas, therefore, the conditions existing in the Southern States seem now fully ripe for the large development as well as further improvement of the schools; and,

"Whereas, This Conference desires to associate itself actively with the work of organizing better school systems and extending their advantages to all the people:—

"Resolved, that this Conference proceed to organize by the appointment of an Executive Board of seven, who shall be fully authorized and empowered to conduct : —

"1. A campaign of education for free schools for all the people, by supplying literature to the newspaper and periodical press, by participation in educational meetings and by general correspondence; and,

"2. To conduct a Bureau of Information and Advice on Legislation and School Organization.

"For these purposes this Board is authorized to raise funds and disburse them, to employ a secretary or agent, and to do whatever may be necessary to carry out effectively these measures and others that may from time to time be found feasible and desirable." [1]

The appointment of this executive body was assigned as a duty to Mr. Robert C. Ogden, of New York, the presiding officer of the Conference, and — by special resolution — the president was made the eighth member of the Board. Mr. Ogden's broad appreciation of Southern educational conditions, his executive power, and his well-tried capacity for disinterested and patriotic service, made his personal relation to the Board an indispensable condition of its success.

The president took no immediate action. It was only after several months of extended correspondence and of careful deliberation that he called together the following gentlemen: the Hon. J. L. M. Curry, agent of the Peabody and Slater Boards, Washington, D.C.; Dr. Edwin A. Alderman, formerly presi-

[1] Proceedings of the Fourth Conference for Education in the South, p. 11.

dent of the University of North Carolina and now president of Tulane University, New Orleans, Louisiana; Dr. Wallace Buttrick of Albany, New York; Dr. Charles W. Dabney, president of the University of Tennessee, Knoxville, Tennessee; Dr. Hollis Burke Frissell, principal of Hampton Institute, Hampton, Virginia; Mr. George Foster Peabody, a native of Georgia, now a citizen of Brooklyn, New York; and Dr. Charles D. McIver, president of the State Normal College of North Carolina. These gentlemen, five from the South and three from the North, met for organization in the city of New York on November 3, 1901. They added to their number Mr. William H. Baldwin, Jr., president of the Long Island R.R.; Dr. Albert Shaw, editor of the *Review of Reviews;* Dr. Walter H. Page, editor of *The World's Work;* and the Hon. H. H. Hanna of Indianapolis, Indiana. Mr. Edgar Gardner Murphy of Montgomery, Alabama, was appointed as the executive secretary, associated with the president, and was later added to the membership of the Board as its active executive officer. Although not members of the Board, Dr. G. S. Dickerman of New Haven, Connecticut, and Dr. Booker T. Washington of Tuskegee, Alabama, were associated — as field agents — with its working force. Dr. Washington has been a wise counsellor in reference to the educational problems affecting the colored people of the South, and Dr. Dickerman had served for two years with great acceptability as the special agent of the Conference.

The Southern Education Board was organized with Robert C. Ogden as president, Charles D. McIver as recording secretary, George Foster Peabody as

treasurer, and J. L. M. Curry as supervising direc-
tor.   The active work at the South was committed to
a campaign committee altogether consisting of Southern members and acting under the general direction
of Dr. Curry.   The Board had no funds to disburse.
Its operating expenses for an experimental period of
two years had been underwritten by one of its
members.   These expenses involved the inaugura-
tion of a Bureau of Investigation and Publicity, at
Knoxville, under the direction of Dr. Dabney, and
the conduct of a general " campaign " in certain sections of the South, where coöperation might be requested for the bettering of the public school facilities
and for the enlargement of school appropriations.

Shortly after the organization of the Southern
Education Board, and largely as an additional result
of the forces which had been called into existence by
the Conference, there was also organized " the General Education Board."   Its chairman was Mr.
William H. Baldwin, Jr., and among its members
were Messrs. Curry, Ogden, Peabody, Buttrick, Shaw,
and Page, of the Southern Board.   In addition to
these gentlemen, there were elected Mr. Frederick T.
Gates, Mr. John D. Rockefeller, Jr., and Mr. Morris
K. Jesup, of New York, and Dr. Daniel C. Gilman,
president of the Carnegie Institution.   Dr. Wallace
Buttrick became the secretary and executive officer,
the Board was incorporated by special act of Congress, and permanent offices were opened at 54
William St., New York City.

The Southern Education Board, as has been explained, makes no direct gifts to educational institu-

tions. It exists to aid in the development and in the
wise direction of educational sentiment. Though
working at the South to secure larger policies of local
support for popular education, and though working,
North and South, to encourage larger policies of philanthropy in relation to the educational needs of rural
localities, it does not hold nor distribute funds for
educational purposes.

This is the work of the General Education Board,
a body with three distinctive functions which may be
thus defined : —

(a) The careful investigation and the accurate collection and presentation of the facts as to the educational situation at the South. I say the South, and
yet the South is in no final or exclusive sense the
one field of its interest. Wherever public education,
as the chief constructive policy in American life, needs
the support of exact inquiry and of intelligent and sympathetic interest, the General Education Board may find
its work. The educational situation at the South, from
causes both preceding and following the Civil War,
claims at present the especial interest not merely of
the Nation but of the world. To secure not only the
statistics, but the facts back of the statistics, to appre-
hend and truly to record the life which lies behind
the formal phenomena of schoolhouses and school
administration, to perceive just what the South has,
in order rightly to understand just what the South
needs — this is the work with which the General
Education Board has thus far been primarily concerned. So fully has it had the intelligent and appre-
ciative coöperation of the educational authorities of
the South that its data from the State of Mississippi

(for example) form a more comprehensive collection than any body of reports to be found in Mississippi. What is true of this State is true of others. Such results have necessarily been dependent, in large degree, upon the aid of the officials and teachers of the South. The Board may be of service to them only because it has been served by them.

(*b*) In addition to the work of investigation, the Board is also committed — subject to the discretion of its authorities and the limit of its resources — to a policy of assistance. This policy represents in its purpose no mere effort of the wealth of one section to meet the needs of another section. The Board was organized under Act of the National Congress in order that the sources of its support might become as broadly national as its interests, might be found in the wealth of the South as well as in the wealth of the North and East and West. Nor have the gifts of the General Education Board represented a substitute for local effort. They have represented an answer to it. They have not forestalled initiative. They have asked it. Their gifts have been so tendered as to awaken and stimulate those forces of self-help which form the amplest security of public investments. The resources of the Board have been too limited, moreover, for any policy of general aid. They have permitted, however, certain small conditional appropriations to well-accredited institutions of both races within the South. Especially in Georgia, Alabama, North Carolina, and Tennessee, these gifts have served as an indication of the spirit, and as an earnest of the sympathetic and inclusive purpose of the organization. With increasing means, this work may be done with broader power and more far-reaching benefit.

(*c*) No limitation of means has served, however, to arrest the work which many have regarded as of more preliminary importance than the gifts of aid. This has been the conduct of certain phases of coöperative experiment, in order to determine just how the influences represented by the Board and the influences represented in the South may most wisely join their forces. At one point, a rural county having a short school term has been enabled to lengthen its school period at one end of the year upon condition that the county from its own resources would add a month at the other end. At another point a model country school has been established, with its "teacherage" and its school farm; at a number of the State Universities of the South, such as the University of Tennessee, the University of Georgia, the University of North Carolina, the University of Mississippi, and the University of Virginia, assistance has been given in the conduct of "Summer Schools" for teachers. There is an indication of the moral earnestness of the teaching force of the South in the mere recital of the fact that in the summer of 1903 more than ten thousand of these young men and women thus gave their vacation period to the work of securing a broader and fuller equipment for their profession. For two summers in succession more than two thousand have gathered at one university alone — the University of Tennessee.

Perhaps, however, the most striking of the coöperative experiments of the General Education Board is to be found in the series of personal conferences

between the representatives of the Board and the
county superintendents of education. In ten of the
Southern States these conferences have thus far been
held; and the States which have not yet been visited
have taken the initiative in requesting them. Coming
to an accessible common point within the State, the
superintendents of education from the several counties
have met with the representatives of the Board in
frank and cordial interchange of information and
ideas. Elaborate bulletins of data from each county
have been filled out, signed, and filed. The vivid
interests and forces which can never be crowded into
"reports" have come naturally and rightly to the
surface; misunderstandings have been adjusted,
misinformation has been corrected, and in the common and supreme concern for the life and training of
the child, the representatives of every phase of feeling
and opinion have found the deep and serious basis of
coöperation. Thus in contact with men coming
directly from the people, the authorities of the Board
have sought that fulness and freedom of information
which might place its policies and its activities in
close and helpful touch with the actual South. The
Board, in every Southern State, has been accorded the
interest and aid of the State Department of Education.

Thus, through the gathering and classifying of
information, through the extension of aid under the
form of conditional appropriations to certain selected
educational institutions, and through the effort to
bring its policies into intelligent and practical relation
with the real working forces of the South, the
General Education Board has attempted, and has
made, what may be called a demonstration of method.

It has established a working basis not only for its own
activities but for the activities of others. The
resources of philanthropy, however large or however
varied, whether representing the wealth of the North
or of the South, may find in its large experience and
its ample records a helpful if not an authoritative
measure of information and suggestion. Its files are
not for any self-interested or private use. Its facilities and its reports are at the service of the public.

The Southern Education Board, as already stated,
has found its distinctive service in the deepening and
quickening of educational sentiment within the South.
Its work has not been that of employing the resources
of philanthropy. It has been the task of directly
appealing to the resources of taxation, to those local
forces of self-interest and self-development by which
the State expends a little money for a larger life and
through which the community builds the schoolhouse
as the temple of its own consecration to the joy, the
usefulness, and the liberties·of its children.

No work for the future of the South can be conducted in forgetfulness of what the South has done.
The nature of her progress, when considered in relation to her difficulties, must bring a sense of gratitude
to the true citizen of the Nation, whether he be
Southerner or Northerner. And yet no true work
for the future can find the goal of its attainment in
the memory of the past or in the mere consideration
of the present. There remains how much to do!
The task of the South must still bring for many a
year a searching test to her patience, her generosity,
her wisdom. To help directly with this task ; to

increase in the treasury of her local heart the South's best capital of enterprise, — her fund of interest, of sane and well-measured self-command, of civic hope, of true yet unstrident confidence in herself, her children, her resources, and her future ; to stand for a patriotism which is not merely retrospective but constructive, — this, as many have conceived it, is the broader service of the Southern Education Board.

It is a work to which thousands of men and women have long given themselves. For this Board does not assume that it has created the educational revival at the South. Its work is but a part of that revival — has advanced it and has been advanced by it. Within an enlarging confederacy of local interests and local forces, it has served to commend and to reënforce the responsibility of the people for the education of all the people, thus taking its vigorous part in the creation of an educational sentiment which may answer the gifts of philanthropy with the larger gifts of taxation, and which — with or without philanthropy — may provide for the children of the State a longer school term and a better school equipment.

Its bureau of publication has circulated the literature of the subject. Through circulars and special bulletins the press of the South has been freely informed as to educational needs and helpful educational methods. Under the auspices of the Board, or in coöperation with the local authorities, hundreds of public meetings have been organized, and eager audiences, sometimes in the towns, sometimes in the country, have been addressed by trusted and effective speakers. Its Southern representatives have entered vigorously and untiringly into the definite campaign

to secure a larger measure of local taxation for the
public schools; and, in the State of North Carolina,
where, under Dr. McIver and his associates, this work
has been most successfully conducted, there are now in
one county more " local-tax districts" (school districts
in which the additional tax for schools has been voted
by the people) than existed in the whole State prior to
the activity of the Board.   In 1902, North Carolina
had 56 local tax communities; in January of 1904 there
were 186, with an anticipated additional increase of
nearly 100 within the next half year.   In other Southern States similar work has been accomplished.   It
cannot be said that the results attained are wholly due
to this Board alone.   Its part in this work, however,
has been conspicuous, and, at many points, decisive.

For their popular interpretation, both the General
Education Board and the Southern Education Board
are still much indebted to the Conference for Education in the South.   The existence of the Boards has
not made the Conference obsolete.   Its annual sessions have grown both in numbers and in popular
authority.   It still brings together the interested and
representative forces of all sections.   It still makes
from its platform a palpable and inspiring demonstration of coöperative statesmanship, speakers from the
North and from the South dealing in candor and fraternity, with those industrial, social, or political conditions which retard or advance the popular development of the educated life.   The fifth Conference, by
special invitation of the legislature of the State,
gathered at Athens, the home of the University of
Georgia, April 24, 1902.   The sixth Conference, by

invitation of the Governor, the legislature, the University of Virginia, and the educational forces of the State, met at Richmond, Virginia, on April 22, 1903.

Of the deep enthusiasm of the crowded audiences at both these Conferences one may not write at length. Nor is it possible to dwell upon any of the interesting details of what were, in fact, memorable occasions.[1]

II

Through these annual Conferences as well as through the printed issues and the public declarations of the members of the Southern and General Education Boards, the educational situation at the South has been brought more clearly and more

[1] Among those in attendance at one or the other of these later meetings, many of the speakers being present at both, were the Governor of Virginia, the Governor of North Carolina, the State superintendents of education from Virginia, North Carolina, South Carolina, Georgia, Florida, Alabama, Tennessee, Mississippi, Louisiana, and Texas ; John W. Abercrombie, president of the University of Alabama ; J. H. Kirkland, president of Vanderbilt University ; F. P. Venable, president of the University of North Carolina ; B. C. Caldwell, president of the State Normal College of Louisiana ; B. L. Wiggins, chancellor of the University of the South, Sewanee, Tennessee ; Clark Howell, editor of the *Atlanta Constitution ;* John B. Knox and Sydney J. Bowie of Alabama ; Hoke Smith of Georgia ; Hamilton W. Mabie, associate editor of the *Outlook*, New York ; Richard Watson Gilder, editor of the *Century*, New York ; L. H. Bailey, professor in Cornell University, Ithaca, New York ; Dr. Felix Adler, New York ; Dr. Richard S. Jesse, president of the University of Missouri ; R. Fulton Cutting of New York ; Josephus Daniels of North Carolina ; Walter B. Hill, chancellor of the University of Georgia ; W. W. Stetson, state superintendent of public instruction for Maine; R. Heath Dabney, Paul B. Barringer, and Charles W. Kent, professors in the University of Virginia, Dr. W. T. Harris, U. S. Commissioner of Education, and others who have been named in reference to their connection with the earlier Conferences.

fully into the national consciousness. The intelligent forces of American opinion have been won to a fairer appreciation of Southern difficulties. The revelation of Southern needs has brought into only more evident relief the abundant heroism of those human forces with which the South is responding to her task. In proportion to her *means* the South is perhaps expending as much for public education, per capita of her children of school age, as States like Michigan in the West or New York in the East.[1] Yet those whose burdens are abnormal need the expenditure of more than normal power, and those whose educational progress has been so long and so unhappily retarded — and yet whose populations are constantly in competition with the more generally educated masses of other sections — can equalize the conditions of competition only by increasing the volume of expenditure. The man who is toward the rear in the march of progress will never get to the front simply by moving as fast as the others move. If he is to get to the front, he must expend sufficient energy

---

[1] The amount raised for public education per capita of the school population, is $22.37 in Massachusetts and $20.88 in New York, as contrasted with $2.87 in Tennessee and $2.28 in North Carolina ; but, according to Dr. Charles W. Dabney, back of each child in Tennessee there is only $509 of taxable property, and in North Carolina only $337, as contrasted with $1996 in Michigan and $2661 in New York. (See Report of the Sixth Conference for Education in the South, p. 40.) We may note also that in the Northern and Western States the proportion of adult males to the children of school age is from 50 to 100 per cent greater than at the South. (See the Appendix to this volume, p. 304, Table VII, columns 8 and 13.) The male producer at the South may thus be called upon to bear a larger economic burden, under the system of public education, than a like producer at the North. This burden is still further distributed at the North by the much larger number of women engaged in the higher productive employments.

to move as fast as the others move, *plus* the energy
which must be expended to bring him from the rear
to the front. The South is finding her duty, therefore, not merely in the measure of her resources but
in the appalling measure of her needs.

Let us turn again, therefore, to a brief statement
of her educational situation. I quote from Dr. Charles
W. Dabney, president of the University of Tennessee. "Our Southern problem," says Dr. Dabney,
"is the education of all the people of the South.
First, who are these people? In 1900 the States
south of the Potomac and east of the Mississippi contained, in round numbers, 16,400,000 people, 10,400,000
of them white and 6,000,000 black. In these States
there are 3,981,000 white and 2,420,000 colored children of school age (five to twenty years), a total of
6,401,000. They are distributed among the States as
follows : —

	White	Colored	Total
Virginia	436,000	269,000	705,000
West Virginia	342,000	15,000	357,000
North Carolina	491,000	263,000	754,000
South Carolina	218,000	342,000	560,000
Georgia	458,000	428,000	886,000
Florida	110,000	87,000	197,000
Alabama	390,000	340,000	730,000
Mississippi	253,000	380,000	633,000
Tennessee	590,000	191,000	781,000
Kentucky	693,000	105,000	798,000
Totals [1]	3,981,000	2,420,000	6,401,000

[1] To these totals might well be added the children of school age in
Arkansas, Louisiana, and Texas. Arkansas has 380,815 white, 148,534
colored ; Louisiana 276,563 white, 261,453 colored ; Texas 955,906
white, 259,491 colored.

"What an army of young people to be educated! How they are marching on! Many of them are already beyond our help; all will be in less than ten years; and still they come marching up from the cradles into American citizenship.

"The important question is, What are we in the South doing for these children? Let us see. Only 60 per cent of them were enrolled in the schools in 1900. The average daily attendance was only 70 per cent of those enrolled. *Only 42 per cent are actually at school.* One-half of the negroes get no schooling whatever. One white child in five is left wholly illiterate. Careful analysis of the reports of State superintendents showing the attendance by grades, indicates that the average child, whites and blacks together, who attends school at all stops with the third grade.

"In North Carolina the average citizen gets only 2.6 years, in South Carolina, 2.5 years, in Alabama, 2.4 years of schooling, both private and public. In the whole South the average citizen gets only three years of schooling of all kinds in his entire life; and what schooling it is! This is the way we are educating these citizens of the Republic, the voters who will have to determine the destinies not only of this people but of millions of others beyond the seas.

"But why is it that the children get so little education? Have we no schools in the country? Yes, but what kind of schools? The average value of a school property in North Carolina is $180, in South Carolina, $178, in Georgia, $523, and in Alabama, $512. The average monthly salary of a teacher in North Carolina is $23.36, in South Carolina, $23.20,

in Georgia, $27, and in Alabama, $27.50. The schools
have been open in North Carolina an average of only
70.8 days in the whole year, in South Carolina, 88.4,
in Georgia, 112, and in Alabama, 78.3. The average
expenditure per pupil in average attendance has been,
in North Carolina $4.34, in South Carolina $4.44, in
Georgia $6.64, and in Alabama about $4.00 per annum. [I am glad to say that these *per capita* ex-
penditures are now a little larger and the school
terms a little longer than when this statement was
made.] In other words, in these States, in schoolhouses costing an average of $276 each, under teach-
ers receiving an average salary of $25 a month, we
have been giving the children in actual attendance
five cents' worth of education a day for 87 days only
in the year. This is the way we have been schooling
the children." [1]

The reading of Dr. Dabney's figures is not a cheer-
ing diversion. And yet it were folly to assume that
we can aid the South by the exercise of a blind affection which would blink or conceal the facts. These
facts are not taken from the tale of an enemy; they
are taken from the reports of our own superintendents of public instruction, they form a part of our
local as well as our national records. The first duty
of the physician who would apply a remedy lies in a
sympathetic, but fearless diagnosis. The first duty
of a wise educational statesmanship is a clear and
unflinching perception of the situation. There is no
disgrace in our illiteracy. It is due to historic and
formidable forces. There would be every disgrace,

[1] See also Report of the Proceedings of the Sixth Conference for
Education in the South, 1903, p. 37.

however, in a policy which would now perpetuate it by concealment, and which would feed its indifference upon the husks of a flattering and senseless optimism.

It has been said that we must educate. When we say "we," it is evident that we must count all of our people within the fellowship of responsibility. Within the partnership of obligation, the great masses of our white people should hold the first place of initiative, dignity, and service. No man can go to them with "alms." To rouse them to see their duty, their duty to their children, to themselves, and to their country, and then to help them see how bravely and how well they themselves can perform this duty — we have here the fundamental and distinctive element in the policy of the Southern Board.

But the principle of initiative may well be supplemented by the principle of coöperation. It is an established principle in every form of commercial, religious, or educational effort. No man, North or South, shares any privilege of this life for which he has paid all the cost. How many of us who go to church have paid our full share of the cost of what we get? How many men in business refuse to be benefited by policies and facilities of the community which, in their value, are out of all proportion to what these men have paid? Who goes to a college North or South and really pays there, in full, for all he gets? He may pay what is asked or charged, but what is asked or charged is a small element of the cost of what he gets. The man who goes to Yale or Harvard University, the young woman who goes to Vassar, is directly the beneficiary of buildings and endowments which philanthropy has

given and which express the enduring truth that
the education of our children, whether the children
of the rich or of the poor, represents a great task
of collective consecration, the task of society and of
humanity.

Who shall presume, therefore, to assert that the
principle of coöperation may be accepted by the
sons of wealth, but that it may not be accepted by
the children of the poor? Surely, if any children in
our land may lay rightful and honorable claim upon
the generous interest of all our countrymen, these
are the children of our rural South. The children of
a people isolated from the busy life of trade, often
thinly settled upon undeveloped lands, they yet represent an uncorrupted stock, full of native vigor and
native wit. It is a noble wealth which awaits us in
their capacities and faculties. The South's intense
preoccupation with the problem of the negro has
largely shut these people out from the care and the
provisions of the State. For this preoccupation and
for all its unfortunate results, our whole country has
been responsible.

The Federal Government freed the slaves, but the
Federal Government spent little indeed in fitting
them to use their freedom well. Hundreds of thousands of ignorant negro men were introduced to the
suffrage without any introduction into the capacity
for its exercise, and the South, — defeated, impoverished, desolate, — was forced to assume the task of
providing for the education of two populations out
of the poverty of one.

The very hypothesis of intervention on behalf of
the negro, as has also been previously suggested,

was that the condition of the black man was the
care and responsibility, not of a section, but of the
whole country.   The very essence of the theory
of emancipation was that the status of the black
man was the charge of the Nation.   Yet the issue
of emancipation left the negro, in his helplessness,
at the threshold of the South.   The South, with
peculiar heroism, has risen to that responsibility.   For
one dollar contributed for his education by philanthropy from the North, four dollars have been contributed through taxation from the South.   The negro
has shared this burden, but his vast numbers, his
great needs, and his low productive capacity have
necessarily reduced the amount which the South
could expend upon her white children.

The utter impossibility, to the impoverished South,
of speedily securing the negro's educational development, made the thought of his political power an all-
absorbing anxiety.   From this preoccupation of our
public interest (largely caused, as I have said, by the
neglect of the freedmen by the Federal Government)
the chief sufferers were the white children of the
masses of our rural population.   That they have so
suffered may be called the fault of the South; yet it
is also the fault of that negligence of all our countrymen through which the South with inadequate
resources has been largely left to bear alone a
national burden and to discharge a national responsibility.   When, therefore, the wealth of our common
country, North or South, generously invests its revenues in the education of the children of these Southern
States, I do not call it the extension of "charity";
I venture to call it the acceptance of obligation.

This is the obligation which was so nobly assumed by the founder of the Peabody Fund, — a fund left by a Northern man for the educational needs of white and black, a fund which has for these thirty years — through the South's glad and faithful use of it — put forever beyond question not only the acceptability of educational philanthropy at the South, but the practical wisdom of the comprehensive policy for which it stands.

There are many who see, therefore, in this educational situation at the South a challenge to the wisest and deepest forces of a national patriotism. This, however, is no mere question of the duty of the North to the South. A similar situation in New England or the West should arouse a like response from South as well as North. It is a question of the duty of the Nation to the children of the Nation. Our conditions, as I have said, are those of a rural population thinly settled upon undeveloped lands. May I again recall some of the peculiar phenomena of its distribution?

"Let us turn to the figures of the last census. The one State of Massachusetts, as we have seen, has 20 cities of over 25,000 inhabitants. The 10 States south of Virginia, Kentucky, and Missouri, with an area 85 times as great have only 19, and the aggregate population of the Massachusetts cities exceeds that of the latter by 417,000.

"Again, Massachusetts has 110 communities of over 4000 inhabitants, with an aggregate population of 2,437,994. Her entire population is 2,805,346, so that the number in smaller places is but 366,352.

"These 10 Southern States have altogether only

146 communities of this rank, with an aggregate population of 2,148,262. But the total population of these 10 States is 17,121,481, so that the number dwelling in places smaller than towns of 4000 inhabitants is 14,972,738, as contrasted with 366,352.

"By comparison with the census of 1890 we may see the trend of population. During the ten years from 1890 to 1900 the population of Massachusetts increased 566,399, and the increase in her 110 large places was 551,555. In the 10 Southern States, the total increase was 3,071,276, of which only 505,781 was in their 146 cities.

"Outside of the larger places Massachusetts increased only 14,844; these 10 States of the South increased their population outside of their cities of this size, by 2,565,495. Massachusetts people live in cities and the growth is there. Southern people live in the country and are to do so in the future. Only a small part live in communities of even 1000 inhabitants. The 608 places of this size or larger contain but 3,029,000, while 14,090,000 remain for the strictly rural population. This is for the 10 most southern States. If we add Maryland, Virginia, and Kentucky, the number will rise to over 17,000,000. How many people has Massachusetts or Rhode Island in communities of less than 1000 inhabitants? So few as to be hardly appreciable as an influence in their educational policy.

"Now it is a serious question in the North, how to provide good schools for the country. Even in Massachusetts there are many little places where educational opportunities are by no means of a high order. Else why has Berkshire County 415 native

white illiterate men of over twenty-one years of age?
One county in northern Maine has over 15 per cent of
its native white voters who cannot read and write.
New England has not yet answered in her own
domain the question of education for her rural people. But in the South this is the main question.
Southern cities, like Northern cities, have institutions
which are their pride; but the cities are few in the
South and play a subordinate part. The multitudes
of people are widely scattered. The neglected few
in Massachusetts or Maine multiply into millions.
To make the situation harder, the South has the two
races to complicate everything, two peoples so unlike
yet bound together in so many of their interests.

"The Nation has yet to open its eyes to the possibilities lying dormant in these great Southern States
— 17,000,000 people in these stretches of territory,
none of whom live in a village of 1000 inhabitants!
Ten million whites of our native American stock,
with few exceptions, and having 3,500,000 children
of school age usually unprovided with good schools!
Seven million negroes, with 2,500,000 children, and
these vitally identified in their rise or deterioration
with the whites about them! Who grasps the scope
of these figures, and comprehends the task of the
men who have to wrestle with these problems? Do
they deserve no recognition from the Nation? Can
the Nation in a prudent regard for its own permanence and future growth afford to go on heedless
of what is done or not done in this great section of
our territorial domain?

"There is no end of the bounty bestowed on institutions for the common people in Northern cities.

Why, as an American, should I be more interested in the children of Boston or of New Haven than in those of the Carolinas and Georgia? Who are the children of Boston? Sixty-seven per cent of them are of parentage from beyond the sea. Eighty per cent of the children of New York are of such parentage, and the story is the same for other great cities — Cleveland, Chicago, San Francisco. More than three-quarters of their people are of foreign antecedents: Irish, Germans, French, Italians, Hungarians, Poles, Russians, Armenians, Chinese.

" Not that I would disparage the beneficent ministries of education for any of these. It is all an occasion of joy. I only speak of what we are doing for them to emphasize what we ought to do for those of our own blood. It was the apostle to the Gentiles, engaged with all his might in efforts for the people of other races, who wrote: 'If any provideth not for his own, and especially his own household, he hath denied the faith and is worse than an infidel.' And so, to-day, our interest in other people should deepen our sense of responsibility for those who are our nearest of kin.

" Who are these 10,000,000 whites of the South? They are the children of the colonial pioneers, of the soldiers who made the continental army, of the fathers who established the Republic. They are many of them descendants from a New England ancestry as well as from settlers of Virginia and the Carolinas. A cursory study of the subject leads me to believe that in some counties of Georgia a larger proportion of the people can trace back through some line to a New England sire than in the city of Boston. The cracker is of the same blood with the merchant prince. This is to be seen in their very names. The people, North and South, are one, in features and in native force, cherishing common religious beliefs and conserving the immemorial traditions of freedom and independence.

" What is due from the prosperity of the great cities of New England, New York, and Pennsylvania to their kinsfolk in the rural South ? This is only a new direction to a very old question. For a full hundred years these cities have generously recognized their obligations to their own children as they went to Ohio, Michigan, and all the region beyond to the Pacific Coast. What academy or college was planted anywhere in these states during their pioneer days that was not helped from the older and wealthier communities of the East ? We see the results to-day in the whole life of the Northwest." [1]

Our Southern States must look with larger and more active confidence to the resources of local taxation, and yet the conditions which have been here outlined possess indeed a national significance and should challenge a national response. The child in Alabama is not the child of Alabama alone. Our children — let me again suggest — are the Nation's children. In their potential citizenship lie the social and political forces which are to have a part in the making of their country's government, in the shaping of their country's destiny. Yet there is reason for

---

[1] Quoted from George S. Dickerman, New Haven, Connecticut, — one of the wisest and most conservative of the Northern students of Southern conditions. Further statistics as to the density and the distribution of population will be found in Table VII of the Appendix, p. 304, columns 2 and 3.

reflection in a startling contrast to which the records of our government will point us. The child of Alaska is the subject of the Nation's considerate provision. He is not in any immediate sense a potential voter. Yet in Alaska the expenditure upon the children of the Nation — though 60 per cent of them are the children of the Eskimo — is annually $17.78 per capita of the enrolment. The children of Alabama are not the subject of a national provision, and the expenditure in Alabama per capita of the pupils in average attendance is now annually $4.41. For the child of the Nation in Alaska an annual investment of $17.78, actually paid in part, though indirectly, by the people of Alabama; — for the child of the Nation in Alabama an annual investment of $4.41 — though the child of Alabama represents in his growing and eager life the potential electorate of the richest and noblest land in history.

We may well be grateful for every dollar that is being expended upon the children of our territories. I also know the explanations with which some would attempt to modify the appalling contrast which I have cited. But when we see what our great government can spend and what this government can compass when it tries, how insistently and successfully it can find needs to meet and tasks to accomplish from the Eskimo to the Filipino, and from Porto Rico to Guam, has not the time fully come to look straight and clear before us to the home acre of our own undeveloped citizenship? It is well to aid and to bless the governed. We shall not fail to do so if we have something of a care for those who are going to do the governing. No rule will ever be wiser than the rulers, and no republic can be freer than its own people. To enlarge the lot and to increase the inspirations of the children of these United States, North and South and East and West, is, therefore, not a gratuitous charity : it is not merely the obligation of one section to another ; it is the responsibility of the Nation to its world-influence as well as to its citizenship ; it is the supreme duty of our national capacities and of our national self-interest.

There have been objections to any policy of "federal aid." Unquestionably such a policy might take objectionable forms. With, however, the safeguarding of the principle of self-help and with a broad and satisfactory recognition of the principle of local administration, such a policy would seem to be as commendable as it would be effective. Nor should such a policy rest upon the merely local or sectional necessities of the South ; it should be national in its whole conception. Representing a constructive policy of the State, it should be available throughout our country wherever the illiteracy of the individual county rises beyond a fixed percentage ; — wherever, in other words, the standard of American citizenship is threatened by the unusual massing of ignorant or untutored life.

And yet it should not be a policy of constraint. Federal assistance should not be forced upon the unwilling, for under such conditions the county would certainly be averse to the acceptance of the necessary terms of aid, and the appropriation — when given — would not receive sympathetic or effective administration. But where the county, through its own people or its own authorities, makes request, and where the county meets the conditions of self-help, the general government should be free to extend its practical coöperation. The labor of the schools is labor for a citizenship which is national as well as local. Ignorance in America cannot be fenced off into negligible provinces of life and interest. Though the Nation neglect its ignorance, ignorance will not neglect the Nation. It thinks, it hates, it drags down — by crude and wasteful work — the standard of intelligent and effective labor ; ignorance helps to make others ignorant, its poverty helps to make others poor ; it votes ; and, because it votes, it creates the perennial opportunity of the demagogue and an ever attendant peril of the State. There are in the United States to-day more than 6,000,000 of people who cannot read and write, among them nearly 2,300,000 of illiterate men of voting age, and, sadder still, more than 2,600,000 of illiterate adult women — possible mothers of our citizenship.

Shall a Nation which waged a tragic war over the issues involved in the formal emancipation of its slaves, pause before the problem of that real emancipation which finds its argument and its appeal in the presence of every ignorant and ineffective life? The freedom to possess one's self is, for white men or for black men, by no means all the battle. The freedom to possess one's self holds little of security or joy till it is followed by at least some measure of the freedom of knowledge and some share in the freedom of training. Life without fitness for life is hardly happiness, and work without fitness for work is almost slavery. Even if there should first be necessary an amendment to the national Constitution, what more

sacred dogma could stand in the organic law of a
modern democracy than a provision according at
least the opportunities of elementary knowledge and
elementary training to every child of the land?

As for the South, there are those who tell us that
she would object to "outside aid." The apprehension is theoretic. That the South would object — as
other sections and localities would object — to a policy
of enforced relief, is true. That the South — whatever the course of her political representatives in the
past — would now oppose such a policy as I have
attempted to suggest is altogether incredible. In
substance, she has accepted it. The revenues of the
Peabody Fund, a fund given in 1867 by a citizen of
Massachusetts, have been accepted, freely, gladly,
gratefully, and for more than thirty years, by the public school authorities of every Southern State. The
educational funds represented by the Slater Board
and the General Education Board have also been
accepted, and — like those of the Peabody Board —
have been wholly inadequate to meet the cogent and
overwhelming appeals from practically every quarter.
The agricultural and mechanical colleges of the States
are directly the creation of federal appropriations,
appropriations based upon the values of public lands,
and now everywhere cordially accepted and utilized
in the educational policy of the South.

Is it urged that these revenues belong in part to
the States themselves? — that they hardly represent
the acceptance of "outside aid"? It is true. It is
also true that, in the strict analysis of the expression,
there is no such thing within the whole domain of our
national administration as "outside aid" — nor can

there be. If the South asks for a federal public
building, it asks no "charity"; if any section of the
South asks for a special mail-train, it asks no " outside aid." For the South is not one land and the
Nation another. The South is within the Nation —
may make its legitimate requisitions upon the national
expenditure because toward that expenditure it makes
its ample contributions. No section of the Nation
receives, proportionately, so little of the national revenues. The South is predominantly agricultural. In
the vast sums collected in the form of a protective
tariff, but contributed indirectly by American con-
sumption — Northern and Southern — to the upbuilding of our country's manufacturing interests, the South
has had little share. She has contributed her portion
toward the $140,000,000 which the country annually
distributes through the national pensions.[1] Yet these
revenues are received and expended, for the most
part, within the States of the North and West. I do
not call in question the principle of pension relief. It
is of some economic significance, however, that the
fiscal policies and the relief provisions of the government should operate chiefly to the advantage of the
sections outside the South. This is not in itself a
reason why pensions should be discontinued or why
the tariff should be readjusted. And yet it is a reason why there need be no sensitiveness on the part
of the South if the South should be included in a
policy of federal aid in relation to public education.

---

[1] Since 1893 the cost of the pension system per capita of the whole
population has gradually fallen, but in that year this cost was $2.44.
The expenditure for public education, per capita of the whole population, was in the same year $2.48.

But even if it were otherwise, no section or State could well hesitate to receive and use — under a wise and equitable system — national revenues appropriated for national ends. For these revenues are themselves a contribution from the people of the States. The South may well receive some portion of what the South has given. The Nation's resources, I may repeat, are not the vague revenues of a mysterious paternalism outside the Northern or Southern States. "Outside aid" is an impossible misnomer. In the United States of America there *is* no "outside" : nor can there be. The land is one land ; and a democracy which is everywhere opening to its people an equality of political obligation must, in the interest of government itself, provide for a fairer distribution of educational opportunity.

One of our greatest Presidents has said that it is "the duty of the people to support the government, not of the government to support the people." Like many an epigram, its truth is wholly dependent upon its context and its application. That the expression should sometimes have been quoted in criticism of the policy of federal appropriations for public education brings us an explicit perversion of its intended sense. And yet even here I would not hesitate to hold the maxim sound. For as thus applied, the saying may but enforce the truth that when government educates it supports itself. What the State appropriates for the education of its people, it appropriates not to their support but to the support of those stabilities of mind and temper, those habits and efficiencies of the popular life, which make of democracy a rational and consistent order, an institution combining flexibility with permanence and force with freedom. When the people, through their government, educate themselves, they educate themselves for government.

III

The movement represented by the Southern and General Education Boards — as already stated — is in no sense formally identified with the proposal for national aid. And yet this movement, however unconsciously, has perhaps contributed to that proposal. It has brought into the national mind, it has brought into the national heart, and has laid upon the national conscience, the needs of the rural child, — the child not only of the rural South but of the North and West as well. And, for one, I am glad that it has done so. It is apparent that while philanthropy may appropriately serve to make at certain points its demonstrations of method, may touch here and there with inspiring force a locality, an institution, or an individual, and so may turn failure into success, yet the task is too appalling in its complexity and its magnitude for the resources or the administrations of private bodies. These organizations must continue — they have worked out all the essential policies of a wise and constructive programme — and their field will remain even after the coöperation of the national government is secured. But it is to our national and collective interest, as found and expressed through our national legislature, that we may look henceforth for a clearer and juster perception of the needs of our rural life. How long we may have to wait, no man can say; but in this day, not of socialism, but of vivid social obligations, the stars in their courses seem to fight for those who believe that the function of government is not merely the function of a national police, is not merely negative, corrective, regulative, but positive and affirmative.

In the meanwhile we may rejoice that there are those who, under the pure impulses of a generous patriotism, are trying to aid in doing personally what the Nation has not done officially. While it is true that the Nation has a duty to its citizenship, these are also proving that a true citizenship has a duty to the Nation. Every true gift of a genuine philanthropy represents the thought of what is due not only to the child but to our country. Such a gift is the acceptance of the holiest and deepest obligation of the citizen to the State. It is his effort to add to the forces by which it rebuilds and reconstitutes its life.

And yet, let us suppose that such a gift were made solely for the child's sake, were indeed that real thing which the world calls charity, — not the charity of condescension, but the charity of a reverent and tender love, the motive of that fine, ennobling, human grace which puts a man's strength at the service of his friend, which puts God's power at the service of those who pray, which always places and always will place the whole world's wisdom and goodness and greatness at the service of a little child, — who then will care to stand, as a forbidding and darkening barrier, between charity and the children?

May I close this chapter, therefore, with a story; not an " historic illustration," but a true story out of life? It illustrates, as in a simple, human parable, that truth of a coöperative and coöperating patriotism

upon which we have dwelt so long. It is a story of
one of the children of Alabama. As its meaning
comes home to us, we may well leave the mood of
argument and abstraction for that mood of tender
and personal affection which makes the deeper nerve
of every civic cause, of every social faith.

Some twenty years ago, in one of the smaller
cities of Alabama, there was born to an honored Confederate soldier and his noble wife, a little daughter.

For a few brief months she dwelt among them as
a little presence of bodily happiness and responsive
charm. Clear eyes, lighted with the strange wisdom
of innocent babyhood; soft prattle, making audible
her rapturous content with the wonder of this great,
kindly, befriending, human world; and then, within
the bitter fate of a few swift hours, there came the
desolating change.

It was not death; it was that tragic compromise by
which life comes back from death, leaving its laurels
in death's hands, — life without the seals and symbols of our living world, — life without sight or hearing or utterance. Through the tender body of the
child there had swept a fever, like a scourge of flame,
that left her forevermore a child of darkness and of
silence.

The fever did not take her from her father, her
mother, her friends, her loved and happy world; but
from her it took — all. For seven long years, — deaf,
speechless, blind, she knew no converse with any
human or living thing.

You may teach the deaf through the ministry of
vision; you may instruct the blind by hearing and by
speech, but when the blind one cannot hear, and

when the deaf cannot see, how may love find a way? Dwelling thus in a silence without light, in a night that gave back to her no earthly or heavenly voice, the child lived on, her prison darkening as her young heart grew older in its warfare.

And then on a wonderful and ever memorable day, there came another change. To this little girl in her Southern home there was brought one who found a clew, one whose patient and unwearied labor, whose brooding insight, found at last a symbol, a common term, between her own mind and Helen Keller's imprisoned life. Following that clew, and by adding symbol to symbol and term to term, the devoted teacher built up for the struggling and eager child, upon the single sense of touch, a language; and that language has unlocked for her the whole vast, radiant world of books and art and hope and truth and love. Helen Keller, now a successful student of Radcliffe College in Harvard University, familiar with five of the great literatures of our civilization, shares a life which, though still deaf and still sightless, is rich in human interests and friendships. Out of the dark and silent prison-house there was but one door into the glad provinces of culture, fellowship, and light, — but one door, and her teacher found for her its hidden threshold, opened it, led her forth, and keeps her hand in hers to-day; — the hand no longer of a sad, baffled, despairing child, but of a useful and happy woman.

Was it worth doing? Was it worth permitting? That teacher's hand was the hand of a wise, patient, tender, devoted woman of the North. The means that have made possible this strange and beautiful emancipation have come largely through the considerate aid of Northern friends, — friends who forgot North and South and East and West in the presence of a great, saddening, appealing calamity of our human life, remembering only that a little child in need is the rightful heir of all that this world holds.

A little child in need, — the child in its helplessness, with its back toward the darkness and the silence, with its face toward a day dawning over the battle-ground of ideas, of institutions, of nations, of men, of great, naked, furious, relentless destinies, — clashing, contending, devouring, till the doom of God; the child facing the battle; the child in a democracy, with an outlook from the chariot of the King; the child, — and all humanity within him. There lies the constraining motive, the fundamental and inclusive motive, of all the educational policies of Church or State, of legislation or philanthropy, — the child, in whose presence sectionalisms become meaningless and humanity becomes supreme.

The policy of education may be, indeed, a policy of national or local self-interest. But the self of which we think is the self-hood of our future — the locality, the State, the Nation, of our children. Their hands rule us while we work. Toward the threshold of their enfranchisement they move to-day, through all our country, out of the valleys of silence and of darkness — hearts breathing toward the hills, faces lifted toward the light. Their souls inherit from us all things but the strange and fatuous passions that divide man from man. Their uplifted hands bear no blood-stains of war. Their waiting and eager lives know nothing of factions and sections and nations.

They are here, they are ready, and the world is theirs.

The glory, the largess, of all humanity belongs to every one of them. Just as no man can prevent the poetry of our Lanier from speaking to the child of the North, just as no man can prevent the music of Longfellow from blessing the child of the Sout'a, so the wealth and good and truth of all belong forever to us all.

Education, all education, is but philanthropy; and philanthropy is but humanity believing in itself and in its God, — humanity, with its hand in the child's hand, before that door that opens ever Eastward, out of the world of the helpless and silent night into the world of the far, free day — the world of voices and fellowship, of serious, grave, implacable liberties, of a little happiness, of much duty and struggle and patience, and — if God will — an honest work inspiring, sustaining, contenting.

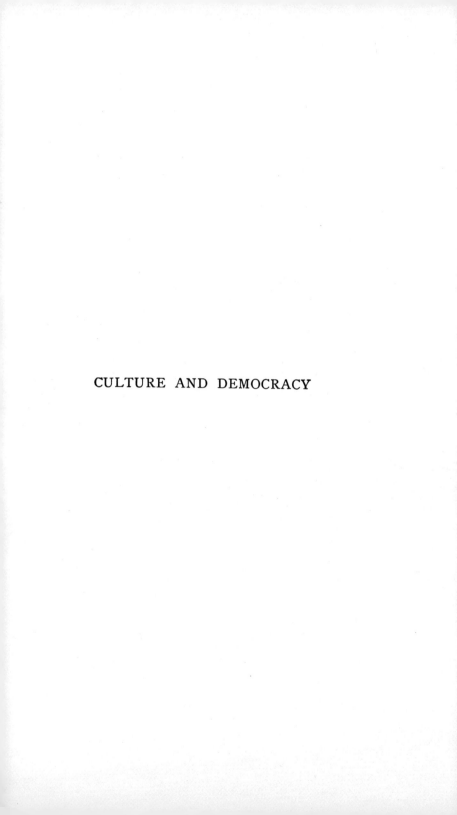

CULTURE AND DEMOCRACY

CHAPTER VIII

CULTURE AND DEMOCRACY

I

CULTURE, in a democracy, is the aspiration of the many; and a democracy is to culture but the challenge of practical occasions. In the world with which we have now to do culture is everybody's creed; and democracy is everybody's chance to put the creed to work.

Manifestly, therefore, culture is more than knowledge, just as democracy means more than a form of government. We need not pause for fixed and ultimate definitions. We have no sooner fixed them than they cease to be ultimate. Our danger lies not in the descriptions we should accept so much as in the possible truth of those we might omit; for all are true. Culture — in a broad and liberal sense — is but the estate of the human mind when touched by the joy of achievement, just as democracy is the rule of human numbers come to their conscious power. We may find aspects of culture in the savage, phases of democracy in the Russias. Wherever the achievements of the mind are pleasurably and consciously possessed, we have the beginnings of those aristocracies of sentiment and of those distinctions of feeling which have builded the kingdom of ideas. Out of small beginnings has come

the reign of truth and the authority of loveliness.
And wherever human multitudes have tasted the
consciousness of power, of power in their own right,
we have the vague foreshadowings of a government
of the people.   Government, however, is the least of
the forms through which the people rule, just as
scholastic knowledge is the least of the offerings of
culture.   The power of ideas and the power of numbers — through all the range of our human life —
act and react upon each other.   Out of this action
and reaction, out of these reciprocities of influence,
what may we say as to the obligation of culture to
democracy, and as to the obligation of democracy to
culture?

It were perhaps a simple matter to discuss such
questions merely as the abstract and unrelated questions of social criticism.   But such inquiries, for an
age dominated by a certain imperious sense of actu-
ality, possess an inevitable context.   They fit into
given scenes and touch upon living issues.   It would
be interesting to discuss them in relation to the
intellectual habits and the social institutions of
China.   But the American must discuss them in
America.   It would be interesting to point out their
significance at the North, to trace there the obligations
of the educated life toward the deep human issues
that arise in the struggle between labor and capital;
to indicate the perils there of a crude emotionalism
upon the one hand, and of an occasional self-
sufficiency upon the other, to show, upon both sides,
the survivals of tyranny and the failure of the fruits
of freedom, the negation of culture by the cultivated
and the rejection of democracy among the multitude;

but the citizen of the South, writing from within the conditions of Southern thought, must discuss these questions in their application to the South.

What, then, is the obligation of democracy to culture? First of all, the right to live. The obligation to accord to the educated life the opportunities of knowledge, and then in the interest of democracy itself to permit the founding and extending of the prerogatives of intellectual freedom. Such liberties are far more familiar to the South than the world has understood. Recent tests of the principle of academic freedom, at the University of Texas, in Tennessee, in Virginia, in North Carolina, have indicated that the South has not altogether failed to keep pace with the broader university traditions. There have been some Southern lapses, and there have been a few, at least, in the North and at the West. But the freedom of the intellectual life is never fully measured by the standard or the precedents of the university, nor by the traditions of journalistic or political expression; nor even by the truer tests of literature. Social life is a thing of vast complexity, and yet a thing of local and individual character. A civilization has many ways of talking out its mind. Its way may be wholly different from the way which is accepted by other civilizations and other worlds; but the fact that its method of expression is different does not argue that it is without expression. The South is not a land of book-making; it is so essentially and predominantly rural that it is not a land of great newspapers; it has been so long the land of a fixed political minority that it knows little of the clash of great and sincere debate;

but it is peculiarly a land of conversation. The North may think it knows something of conversation, but the North, as compared with the South, may be said never to have enjoyed a conversation. About the village courthouse, within the hospitable doors of some central store, in the office of the local daily or weekly paper, or — above all — in the leisurely and genial intercourse around the fireside in winter or on the inviting porch in summer, of friend with friends, there will be heard a conversation which in wit, in the charm and force of its illustrations, and in the directness and freedom of its criticism is not surpassed in American life to-day.

It is the product of leisure, of a world without haste, without ruthless preoccupations, without those resources of expression and of interest which belong to the crowded and overweighted existence of the commercial city. It is, moreover, part of the tradition of the Cavalier. It is part of the genius of climate, and soil, and social habit. The Southern speaker who addresses a Northern audience is often asked where he gets his "stories." They are stories, usually, not only with humor but with meaning. He hardly knows. They are vivid, inherited possessions. They have come down to him from a land in which conversation is an art, and in which it is not mere art alone but the supreme vehicle of social criticism.

That this vehicle — despite its individuality and efficiency — is increasingly inadequate must be evident enough. The complexity and the activities of industrial transformation are making an end of the old leisure and of the old possibilities which it involved, and are thus making a larger demand for a more explicit and more active leadership in politics, in the press, the pulpit, the university. This leadership is fast appearing. In politics it will probably be longest delayed — through causes as operative in the North as in the South — and yet there are men in the political life of the South who, though holding no longer the centre of the national stage, are truly the heirs of whatever is noblest and freest in the public service of their country.

The press, as with the press of the world at large, is sometimes chargeable with a hysteria and a perversity which are the despair of a rational hopefulness, and yet upon the really vital issues in the life of the South the press has been a free and patriotic force. What newspapers of our country have stood more persistently and effectively for law and order than the *Atlanta Constitution*, the *Montgomery Advertiser*, the *New Orleans Times-Democrat*, the *Raleigh News and Observer*, the *Charleston News and Courier* — not to mention a score of others whose course has been as honorable? The writer has examined nearly two thousand editorials of the American press on the subject of child labor. No editorials have been comparable to those of the South in fulness of knowledge, intensity of interest, or vigor and directness of expression. The files of the daily *State* of Columbia, South Carolina, represent for a course of two years the ablest handling of a human industrial issue that our country has known since the period of emancipation. As for the pulpit of the South, a popular writer has charged it with a cowardly silence in relation to our industrial problems, and has intimated, with grotesque inaptness, that the child-labor abuses of the South were due to the complicity of the Christian clergy. At the very time when this criticism was written, the reform committees in charge of the propaganda for protective legislation in the several Southern States were, almost without exception, headed by a clergyman of the Christian Church. The South is the subject of a general national interest, but it is not the subject, unfortunately, of a general national information. There have been clergymen who from motives good or bad have not aided sympathetically in the pressing of industrial reforms. But, upon the whole, the clergy of the South rang nobly true upon that especial issue, and they spoke from individual pulpits and through the action of church assemblies with a freedom and a vigor which the clergy of the North — upon like issues — have not surpassed.

The universities of the South have shared in the common national struggle for the freedom of the teacher, and while much remains to be accomplished, the conflict — as has been suggested — has not been without its signal triumphs. Another, and yet a cognate, struggle for the raising of academic standards has been quite as inspiring; and the leadership of men like Kirkland of Vanderbilt, Wiggins of Sewanee, Denny of Washington and Lee, and Alderman of Tulane, is achieving definite and permanent results. More important still are those forces of popular leadership which — through the whole domain of our Southern States — have issued from our universities for the upbuilding of the common schools. To the support of popular education, to the enlargement of the life, the training, the freedom, of the masses of the people these men have unselfishly dedicated capacity and energy and labor, and in an educational revival which has become one of the most significant movements of our century they are helping to make of our democracy not merely a theory of politics but a civic creed.

And yet with explicit appreciation of the vigor and the freedom of the leadership which now exists — in politics, the press, the pulpit, the university — it is obvious that the conditions which have made its existence difficult have reduced its volume and will continually threaten its efficiency. The South possesses a peculiar " problem " — bequeathed to it under tragic conditions and continued under every circumstance which might increase its perplexities and its burdens. The political solution which was attempted by the North was apparently involved — by those who undertook it — with a number of unwise and unsympathetic methods in negro education and with what was popularly regarded as an experiment in " social equality." The three proposals — political, educational, social — thus became identified, however mistakenly, in the popular imagination of the South, and each phase of Northern activity became so intimately associated with the other — especially in the thought of the ignorant — that the task of clarification has seemed almost impossible. To the baffling confusion of the situation was added the fact that the responsible interest of the South was largely ignored and — upon the assumption that the South's opposition to the freedman's social and political assimilation involved the South's opposition to his every right — the problem was assumed to be wholly a problem of the North. Beneath the North's serious and rightful sense of obligation the South saw only an intolerant "interference." Beneath the South's natural suspicion and solicitude the North saw only an undiscriminating enmity to herself and to the negro. Both interpretations were unfounded. The South, however, passed from a mood of comparative indifference to a mood of active and unyielding criticism, a criticism which expressed — in one form or another — the central contention that the problem had never been the North's and must always remain the South's; that having attempted its solution upon the basis of universal suffrage, and, in 1876, having confessed its failure by the withdrawal of its military support of the reconstruction governments, the North was bound to remand the problem to the Southern States. In the stricter sense, the problem is not the South's or the North's, but the Nation's; and yet, as has been suggested, its local home does lie within the South, and the ultimate forces of its solution must therefore be predominantly Southern in their genius and environment. In any event, it is evident to-day that the popular forces of American life are only too ready to leave the question — in its deepest issues — with the people of the Southern States; and therefore, to-day, as never before, the negro problem is, in fact, the South's.

In an older period, when the question was within the physical as well as the moral control of alien and unsympathetic forces, it was natural that the attitude of Southern thought should have been an attitude of protest, and that its criticism should have been chiefly negative and corrective. That period made men naturally resentful of " advice," naturally suspicious and contemptuous of " theories." It was the period of reconstruction, — a period of much administrative sordidness, but also of memorable heroism among numbers of the men and women who undertook the freedmen's initiation into the experience of the citizen. Its successes, however, were hidden, deep, not easily observable; its blunders were observable and conspicuous. It was to have been expected, therefore, that in the presence of palpable mistakes which it was powerless to rectify, the mind of the South should have become reticent or indifferent or occasionally cynical, and that its tendency to deal with the whole question negatively rather than positively should have become an established intellectual habit.

But that period has passed, and with the passing of that period there arises a larger and clearer need for the contribution to this question, as to every question of the South, of a positive and constructive leadership, — a leadership no longer reactionary or obstructive, but, while awed by responsibility, equipped with learning, vital with suggestion, altogether untrammelled in utterance, and therefore consciously and confidently free.

It is in the interest of the South herself that such a leadership — not in one profession or one class but in all — should be more largely developed and sustained. Dark indeed must be the fate of any land if compelled to approach the solution of any significant problem of its life with its lips sealed and its reason bound. In the interest of her own solution of her own problems, the South will, of necessity, assume that her policies are not to be determined from the standpoint of the ignorant or from the standpoint of the crude devices of party tactics, but from the standpoint of her best life — desiring the total good. For the very reason that her problems are so difficult and so acute, the South is entitled to the largest knowledge, and to the freest, clearest thinking of which her sons are capable. For the reason that the problem is so largely committed to the South, the life and thought of the South are under every obligation to deal with it affirmatively and constructively. In the leadership which would respond to this obligation there will be errors, — some of them really serious, some of them serious only to those who fail to realize that all progressive movement anywhere must necessarily involve a little of that trait of the injudicious which is the fine infirmity of disinterested courage. When great issues are at stake the counsels of caution become sometimes an intolerable and impossible fetich. Mistakes will, of course, be made, but the South will also make a demonstration of capacity and courage which will accomplish real results. Anything is better than a situation in which — North and South — we too often find the ignorant assertive and the educated silent, the ignorant aggressive and the educated acquiescent, the ignorant recording with a pathetic but sinister intolerance the decrees of academic or political policy, and the educated exhausting their powers only in the familiar exercises of private lamentation. It is true, upon the other hand, that in a democracy the influence of the best experience is often limited or defeated by the alliance of the traditional forces of leadership with the very ignorance which needs correction. The political platform, the pulpit, the university, the journalism of the hour, are expected to prey — for their existence — upon the errors which demand redress. The multitudes of a democracy should insist, however, that in their own interest the forces of leadership shall really lead. The people must come to expect service rather than flattery — a service which may involve, in the interest of its usefulness, the examination and criticism of popular misconceptions.

For the errors of a democracy are attended with peculiar and disastrous cost. In a monarchy or oligarchy, general administrative wrongs are willed from above downward upon the masses of social life. The people may endure them or approve them, but the people have never willed them, have never spiritually accepted them. When, however, a democracy goes wrong, the people have done more than go wrong; they have willed to go wrong. Wrong has entered, by a certain process of collective participation, into the national life and the national spirit. Its effect is not registered in the life of the majority alone. The consequences of elective action pass back from the action itself into the will; and multitudes who, before, were faintly right or at least not convinced of error, grow in a subtle way to feel that what the majority has ordered is to be henceforth accepted not only as an authoritative policy, but as a moral finality. Unless, therefore, a democracy is to give a spiritual authority to occasional majorities which they ought hardly to possess, and unless there is to be no effective appeal from the tyranny of popular moods, the conditions of a genuine moral and intellectual leadership must be consistently sustained. The essential obligation of democracy to culture is thus no mere obligation to the æsthetic arts or to academic science —sacred as these must be—but an obligation to accord trust and reverence everywhere to the policies of freedom, an obligation consistent with the rights of the majority, but consistent also with that larger perspective of history in which it has not infrequently appeared that those who have served democracy most truly are those who have saved the people from themselves.

II

Turning thus more directly to the thought of the obligation of culture toward a democratic order, it must be obvious that its first duty is in large measure to itself. Its own light—in the Church, in the university, in the home of the citizen—must be kept pure and clear. No enthusiasm for the education of "the masses" should be suffered to obscure the dignity and the necessity of the scholar's life. But the law of self-preservation is, after all, but an aspect of the law of service. And the law of service is but an aspect of the law of self-preservation. A culture which holds itself in detachment from the vital issues of experience, which has things to say in reference to the economic heresies of Germany or Russia, but nothing to say in reference to the economic perils of its own land, which deals at the North only with the "problems of the backward South" or at the South only with the problems of the "materialistic North," a culture which ignores its own context, will not long be taken seriously even by itself. If it be not interested in life, it will soon cease to be interested in anything; and, consuming itself upon itself, it will pass at length into the dry-rot of a nerveless and unfruitful cynicism.

The quickening of the nerve of culture within the life of the South has been largely due to the response which its educated men, and especially its educated women, are giving to social needs. For example, the teaching force in the schools and universities of the South is, in its personnel, as noble a social force as a democracy has known. It is not surpassed even by the inspiring standards of early New England. And yet culture, as a force of citizenship, may not busy itself exclusively with the traditional interests of technical education. A rising generation is educated not only by its schools but by the forces of established custom, by the pressure of traditional truth or traditional error, by the habits of opinion, the assumptions of popular feeling, the dogmas of collective sentiment, within which it looks outward and upward into life. These bear with intimate and often with decisive pressure upon those who are just beginning to accept for their own land and time the larger heritage of womanhood and manhood. Culture has, therefore, a duty toward the scholastic training of our democratic life; but it has also a duty toward that vast body of traditional prepossessions which form the broader educative forces of society. It is an obligation of sympathetic, intelligent, but unflinching criticism.

If we turn for illustrations to the South, it is not because I could not find them at the North, but because the North — for the purposes of this volume — is "another story." And the thought of the

South must, for the sake of the South, concern itself supremely with certain confusions of sentiment within the Southern States. Indeed, a few of these illustrations are chosen for us; chosen both by the obtrusive and persistent form of the errors themselves and by the gratifying and increasing evidence of Southern protest. There was a time when one of the most potent of these prepossessions had reality and authority, when the cry of "negro domination" rang through the heart of the South with an intelligible although an indescribable terror. Yet for now more than twenty years, a negro officialism or the preponderance of an ignorant negro vote has been impossible. The negro vote may hold the balance of power at this or that point where the white vote is evenly divided. That is true of New York City with its 18,651 negro votes; or of the city of Philadelphia with its 20,000. The negro, however, votes nowhere as a unit except at the South, and the solidity of his vote is largely due to the force of that external pressure which thus creates the very " peril " it has attempted to defeat. If the negro votes were not driven together in a mass, there could be no decisive power in the minority which they represent. And even where they represent a majority, — where do they rule? or where have they ruled for these twenty years? The South, with all its millions of negroes, has to-day not a negro congressman, not a negro governor or senator. A few obscure justices of the peace, a few negro mayors in small villages of negro people, and — if we omit the few federal appointees — we have written the total of all the negro officials of our Southern States. Every possibility of negro domination vanishes to a more shadowy and more distant point with every year, with every dollar invested in Southern properties, with every white man come into the South to live, with every mile of railways, telegraphs, and telephones, with every penny expended for public education. The peril of the supremacy of the colored population is the merest "bogie." It was never possible, except through the support of military force. That force has been, for nearly thirty years, withdrawn. It will never enter the South again. The whole country has so willed it; and if it could come again, our intelligent and conservative negroes would be the first to suspect its motive and to repudiate its odious compulsion. Among all the absurdities of conjecture, and among all the ridiculous imaginations of theoretic horror, there is just now no phantom so spectral in its substance or so pitifully trivial in its proportions as this "peril" of negro domination. And yet in certain sections of our Southern States it is still an "issue," is still the first theme of political oratory and the last excuse of civic negligence. In counties where there are hardly enough negroes to form a docile and amused "example," and where probably less than a hundred negro votes have been cast within a decade, gaping crowds are yet thrilled by stentorian assertion of "the white man's unalterable vow—in the face of all the legions of brutal and insidious conspiracy — to maintain inviolate the proud dominion of the Caucasian,"—and so forth. The real interests of party are forgotten; the educative power of sincere political debate, the progressive and wholesome influence of the division of men and factions upon contemporary issues and in reference to legitimate political ideas,

are all but abandoned, and the political education of
large and potentially efficient masses of American
voters is dominated by a crude frenzy of the hustings
which seldom has either sincerity or validity except
as a party lash.   And this, even, is a failing function.
Sober and responsible men throughout the South are
growing very, very tired of it.   The red-shirt brigades
of one Southern State were called into existence not
so much to awe the negroes as to "arouse" the white
vote.   In another of our Southern States the vote for
the constitutional convention, distinctly solicited on
the old issue of "white supremacy," received the
suffrages of less than a third of the Democratic voters.
Not that anybody was opposed to "white supremacy."
That was precisely the reason why two-thirds of the
voters stayed at home.   They knew perfectly well that
no one was opposed to it, and that the cry which called
them to preserve it and to perpetuate it was a strident
but familiar fiction.   Those who voted for the convention voted for it not because they thought white
supremacy was in danger but because they wished to
put the supremacy of the intelligence and property
of the State under the securities of law.

"Negro domination" as a force of party control,
as a weapon of political constraint, is fast losing its
authority.   Great masses of the people are beginning
to "know better."   Its passing, as a party cry, will
help both the Democracy and the South.   The sooner
the Democratic party comes to understand that, if it
would hold the allegiance of the intelligent masses
of our Southern States, it must represent, not a futile
programme of negation, animosity, and alarm, but a
policy of simple ideals and of constructive suggestion

— a course which has given the party its historic
position in our life — the better it will be both for the
party and for the South. The South can then divide,
and can make its divisions turn upon thought, fact,
conviction. Every party and every section demands,
in the interest of its broadest welfare, that there shall
work within its regions, its traditions, and its ideas,
the searching, sifting, divisive, regenerative forces of
truth upon its merits. If this is not to be the privilege of the South, and if the masses of our people —
through the wanton provocation of the North, or
through the failure of our own party leadership —
are to be still possessed by the old benumbing and
baffling terror, then we shall have, as we have had in
part already, a form of negro domination which we
have least suspected. The soldier of old who bound
his captive to his wrist bound more than the wretched
captive. If his slave was bound to him, he was
hardly the less in bondage to his slave. If the supreme apprehension of the South is to be the apprehension of negro domination, if our intensest effort,
our characteristic and prevailing policies, our deepest
social faiths, are to look no further than the negro,
are to be ever busied with the crude fictions of negro
power, and ever clouded by the outworn demand for
the negro's bondage, then, at either end of this
clanking chain, there is a life bound. If we are
so morbidly afraid of the spectral possibilities of
the negro's freedom that we must keep him ever
in a prison, then let us remember that on both
sides of the prison door there is a man in duress;
for he who keeps a jail is hardly freer than his prisoner. This is the domination that we have really

to fear, the domination wrought upon the mind of
a strong and sensitive people by the presence of a
weaker race; a domination so possessing the imagination, with an alarm half uncontrollable and half
contemptuous; so inducing perplexity to thought,
and so constraining into fixed and peculiar forms
the course of its whole experience, that the weaker
race acts upon the social nerve of the stronger race
as the occasion of habitual hysteria, touching even
its saner moments as the all-absorbing preoccupation
of its culture and its life. This indeed would be
negro domination. Its existence upon any wide or
inclusive scale would make impossible the simplest
assumptions of a truly democratic order. To protest
against it, to define its possibility, and yet to destroy
its possibility by the demonstration of its needless-
ness — this, of definite tasks, is among the first of the
obligations of our culture to our democracy.

III

The educated life of the South, capable of clear
thinking and of just discriminations, will also deal
with some of the misconceptions which have gathered
about the topic of "social equality" between the
races. But while dealing with misconception it will
be compelled, in order to prevent blunders greater
than those it would correct, to conceive and restate,
in positive forms, the implicit racial passion which
underlies the cruder phases of racial antipathy.
Here, as always, the recognition of truth may well
precede the correction of error. And this truth is
quite as vital to the interest of the negro as to the

interest of the white man. The total abandonment
of the dogma of racial integrity at the South would
mean a land — not white, nor part white and part
black — but a land all black; with perhaps many of
those reversions of the standards of political and
social life which have been exhibited in Hayti and
San Domingo. The possibility of racial fusion is
not now repugnant to the instinct of the average
negro, repugnant as it is to the instinct of the average white man, and this fact — the fact that the instinct of the black man is usually ready to abandon
the individuality of his race — puts the white population upon its guard and leads it to perceive a sinister
significance in some of the most harmless occasions
of racial contact. A number of the wisest leaders of
the negro race are seeking to develop a deeper sense
of racial pride. Until negro feeling and opinion are
generally organized, however, into more tenacious
and more articulate support of negro race integrity,
we may expect that the instinct of racial integrity
among the masses of our white people will lead
always to apprehension, sometimes to suspicion,
and occasionally to unreasonable and uncontrollable
assertion.

For, whatever the supreme interest of the negro
race, it is obvious that the supreme interest of the
white race is the interest of racial purity, a purity
necessarily inconsistent with the slightest compromise
in the direction of racial fusion. That the individuality of the white race has been sometimes betrayed by
its own representatives — betrayed in response to the
lowest passions — is conspicuously evident. That public opinion should have dealt too leniently with such

offences is due to two causes — to the fact that those
who are guilty of them are for the most part too
ignoble to be amenable to any opinion whatever; and
to the fact that all social life, Northern or Southern,
European or American, deals inconsistently and in-
sincerely with social evils.   Explanations, however,
are not excuses; and with the existence of so much
natural antipathy toward the negro who would trans-
gress the barriers of race, there must arise a clearer
perception of the truth that the racial integrity of
the Caucasian is threatened, most seriously and in-
sidiously, not by the negro but by the degraded
white man.

The formative assumptions, the ultimate dogmas
of a civilization are to be determined, however, not
from the failures of the few but from the conceptions, the laws, the habits, of the many.   The present
evidences of racial admixture are due not primarily
to the period of slavery (for the old negroes are the
black negroes), nor chiefly to the period of the present, but rather to the period immediately following
the Civil War, when the presence at the South of
vast numbers of the military forces of both sections
— the lower classes of the Northern army demoralized
by idleness, the lower classes of the Southern army
demoralized by defeat — were thrown into contact
with the negro masses at the moment of their greatest
helplessness.   Here and there in specific groups
within selected negro communities racial admixture
may now seem to be increasing, but this increase
is apparent rather than real.   It is only the perpetuation of an admixture that, once existent, will naturally
continue in its own line.   Among the great masses

of the race, especially through the illimitable stretches
of the rural South, the black people are still black.
Every tendency of the present seems to be making
not toward their disintegration but toward that social
and domestic segregation demanded by their own interest as well as by the interest of the stronger race
about them.

And yet it is inconceivable that this segregation of
the race should involve its degradation.   That would
be a conclusion as unworthy of logic as it would be
unworthy of life; a conclusion disastrous to every
interest of the South.   The perils involved in the
progress of the negro are as nothing compared to the
perils invited by his failure.   And yet if any race is
to live it must have something to live for.   It will
hardly cling with pride to its race integrity if its race
world is a world wholly synonymous with deprivation,
and if the world of the white man is the only generous
and honorable world of which it knows.   It will hardly
hold with tenacity to its racial standpoint, it will
hardly give any deep spiritual or conscious allegiance
to its racial future if its race life is to be forever burdened with contempt, and denied the larger possibilities of thought and effort.   The true hope, therefore,
of race integrity for the negro lies in establishing for
him, within his own racial life, the possibilities of
social differentiation.

A race which must ever be tempted to go outside
of itself for any share in the largeness and the freedom of experience will never be securely anchored in
its racial self-respect, can never achieve any legitimate
racial standpoint, and must be perpetually tempted —
as its members rise — to desert its own distinctive

life and its own distinctive service to the world.
There is no hope for a race which begins by de-
spising itself. The winning of generic confidence,
of a legitimate racial pride, will come with the
larger creation — for the capable — of opportunity
within the race. The clew to racial integrity for
the negro is thus to be found, as stated in an
earlier chapter, not in race suppression but in race
sufficiency. For the very reason that the race, in the
apartness of its social life, is to work out its destiny
as the separate member of a larger group, it must
be accorded its own leaders and thinkers, its own
scholars, artists, prophets; and while the development of the higher life may come slowly, even blun-
deringly, it is distinctly to be welcomed. As the
race comes to have within itself, within its own social
resources, a world that is worth living for, it will gain
that individual foothold among the families of men
which will check the despairing passion of its self-
obliteration; and instead of the temptation to abandon
its place among the races of the world it will begin
to claim its own name and its own life. That is the
only real, the only permanent security of race integrity for the negro. Its assumption is not degradation,
but opportunity.

Thus understood, I think the educated opinion of
the South has no war with the progress of the negro.
It has feared the consequences of that progress only
when they have seemed to encroach upon the life of
the stronger race.[1] It is willing that the negro, within

[1] " There is a certain amount of race hatred, of course, and there are
reasons for this, but the best Southern people not only do not hate the
negro, but come nearer to having affection for him than any other peo-

his own social world, shall become as great, as true, as really free, as nobly gifted as he has capacity to be. It has fixed its barriers — in no enmity of temper but in the interest of itself and its civilization, and not without regard to the ultimate welfare of the negro. It cannot base its social distinctions on an assertion of universal "inferiority" — for in that case every gifted or truly educated negro might shake the structure of social usage. It bases its distinctions partly upon the far-reaching consideration that the racial stock of the two families of men is so unlike that nothing is to be gained and much is to be lost from the interblending of such divergent types; partly upon the broad consideration of practical expediency, in that the attempt to unite them actually brings unhappiness; partly upon the inevitable persistence of the odium of slavery; partly upon a complex,

ple. They are too wise not to realize that posterity will judge them according to the wisdom they use in this great concern. They are too just not to know that there is but one thing to do with a human being, and that thing is to give him a chance, and that it is a solemn duty of the white man to see that the negro gets his chance in everything save 'social equality' and political control.

"The Southern people believe with their usual intensity that it is the duty of civilization always to protect the higher groups against the deteriorating influence of the lower groups. This does not mean that the lower should be prevented from rising, but that it should not be permitted to break down the higher.

"The improvement and progress of the backward nations and races should all come by improving the conditions of their own group, but should never be permitted to come at the expense of the higher or more advanced group, nation, or race. Social equality or political control would mean deterioration of the advanced group, and the South is serving the Nation when it says it shall not be so." — EDWIN A. ALDERMAN, LL.D., President of Tulane University, New Orleans, Louisiana, before the American Economic Association, December 29, 1903.

indefinable, but assertive social instinct.[1] This instinct
operates almost as remorselessly at the North as at
the South.[2] The North is sometimes inclined to
think that it exercises a loftier discrimination because
it accords a genial social recognition to this or that
gifted negro visitor from the South. Such an act
involves little more than a transient courtesy. It is
no test of the real attitude of the North toward the
question of "social equality." That test is found in
the attitude of the social forces of the Northern city
toward the negroes of their community, toward their
own fellow townsmen and townswomen, toward the
whole permanent and complex problem of social reciprocities between families as well as between individuals. What is the social status of the negro family
whose home is in Boston, or Philadelphia, or New
York? Is it essentially different from its status at
the South? Are not the few courtesies extended only
the more bitter because through them it feels the
emphasis upon those which are withheld? Is not the

[1] See a selected passage from the *Romanes Lecture*, by James Bryce,
on page 330, of the Appendix of this volume.

[2] In the city of Boston, Massachusetts, for example, in a population
of a half million inhabitants, including twelve thousand negroes, there
is practically no intermarriage of the races. The instances that occur
are usually confined to the lower elements of both races and possess no
serious social significance. "Such couples are usually absorbed by the
negro race, although if they belong to the more educated class they
enter into natural relations with neither race." . . . "Barred out from
the society he most admires, his mimicry only excites mirth, and when
he touches the white race on grounds of social equality, it is the meeting of outcast with outcast." — See "Americans in Process," a settlement study of the North and West Ends, Boston, by residents and
associates of the South End House; edited by Robert A. Woods, pp.
60, 148; Boston; Houghton, Mifflin & Co., 1902.

custom of the South, save when pressed to morbid and unusual conclusions, happier as a *modus vivendi* than the custom of the North?

But be that as it may, the South in establishing the dogma of race integrity has done so, not in order to enforce a policy of degradation, but simply to express her own faith in a policy of separation. Her desire is not to condemn the negro forever to a lower place but to accord to him another place. She believes that where two great racial masses, so widely divergent in history and character, are involved in so much of local and industrial contact, a clear demarcation of racial life is in the interest of intelligent coöperation, and — in spite of occasional hardships — is upon the whole conservative of the happiness of both. During the opening of the great Southwest to private settlers there was an extended period of a *quasi*-collective ownership upon the unrestricted prairies. Men grazed their herds at will. There soon arose, however, the confusion of boundaries and a consequent multiplicity of feuds. Then a number of the settlers, in order to define their limits, began to put up fences. Those who first did so were regarded as the intolerant enemies of peace. Soon, however, men began to see that peace is sometimes the result of intelligent divisions, that the attempt to maintain a collective policy through the confusion of individual rights had broken down; that clear lines, recognized and well-defined, made mightily for good will; that the best friends were the men who had the best fences. And so there arose the saying, " Good fences make good neighbors."

Certainly, however, the educated life of the South

must do its utmost to see that racial divisions are in
fact intelligently made and that the dogma of race
integrity is not subjected to morbid and irrational
applications. In the direct interest of its existence
and its usefulness, it must not be made ridiculous.
To assume that every incident at the North — however unwise — of rumored or actual departure from
Southern customs is an "insult" to the South or an
"attack" upon its life is to assume that the South
may dictate not only for itself but for all the Nation,
and it is to imply that the North must be denied
the very liberty which the South is so rightfully
jealous to assert. The two sections are so largely
different in social feeling and domestic custom
that it will long be difficult, however, for one to
understand the other. In the South, the table,
simple though its fare may be, possesses the sanctity
of an intimate social institution. To break bread
together involves, or may involve, everything. In
the North, especially in its larger cities, the table
of the social dinner or of the general banquet is
often but a useful device for getting together those
who perhaps could not possibly be induced to get
together under any other conceivable conditions.
The social occasion usually involves nothing beyond
itself. In this respect, and in others equally important, Northern conditions and Southern conditions
are unlike. That this unlikeness in conditions is
becoming more generally understood by the discriminating public, North and South, is evident. But that
this clearer and broader understanding will obtain in
either section, among every element of the population, is not immediately probable. Here and there

at the North the journalism of moral petulancy,
abandoning the standpoint of the broader representatives of the Northern press, will still insist upon reading "pro-slavery" designs into the elementary and
most imperative policies of the South, and will find
"hatred of the negro" in customs which have pro-
tected him from hatred and have made possible his
existence and his happiness. In recent years nothing
has been more marked, however, than the growing
appreciation of the perplexities and difficulties of the
South upon the part of the press of the North. As
it approaches a truly national standpoint, it will contribute to truly national ends.

And at the South we may also expect to find, here
and there, those who will too readily contribute to
sectional misunderstandings, who will misinterpret
the feeling of the North, who will continue to seize
upon every pretext which may be twisted into a
sinister significance, and will discover in incidents
to which the North is wholly indifferent a studied
and malignant plot against the life and peace of
the Southern States. Here, too, is the golden opportunity of the politician of the lower type. Dread-
ing lest the masses of the people should begin to
think beyond his leading and to divide upon the
varied legitimate issues of principle or policy, he
seizes upon almost any excuse to raise and to
vitalize the fading terror of "negro domination,"
thus to perpetuate still further — in order that he
may still profit by — the political solidarity which
was created by it. Not only at the North but within
many sections of the South itself, the slightest contact with the negro upon the part of white men who

may be interested in his welfare is often watched with a sensitive anxiety, and the fear lest there may be some possible or shadowy indiscretion is often the basis of unjust and unreasonable rumor, or the occasion, if there be enmity toward the helper or the helped, for fertile and mischievous detraction.

It should be the duty of educated opinion, as expressed through the pulpit, the press, the university, to insist calmly but resolutely upon the function of discrimination. Such an exercise of discrimination is in no sense inconsistent with the opinion that this or that incident of racial contact, North or South, is injudicious or unfortunate. Blunders, vicious or ingenuous, will necessarily be thought about and talked about. To exaggerate, however, this or that trivial incident into a vast and ominous peril, to receive the evidence of an exhibition of questionable discretion, here or there, in North or South, as though it involved a legitimate occasion for the frenzy of multitudes, as though it seriously threatened the fate of peoples and the very stability of a civilization, is to take issue with common sense, is to suggest that if the dogma of race integrity is so easily disturbed, it cannot be deeply rooted, and is likely to remove that dogma — in the opinion of the world — from the category of legitimate social hypotheses — where it belongs — to the category of malignant and fanciful prepossessions, to be opposed in the strong and to be humored only in the weak.

A little discrimination, a little poise, a little of that equable capacity which can note the distinction between incidents great and small, a little clear-headed appreciation of the perspective of events, a due sense of proportion, will aid — as nothing else can aid — in the secure establishment of the doctrine of race individuality and integrity. No doctrine or dogma can be so injuriously compromised as by its wanton and unintelligent exaggerations. A doctrine is always held most strongly when it is held sanely.

IV

The culture of the South will find, however, the occasions of its supreme and immediate interest, not in the issues presented by the negro, but in the problems presented by the undeveloped forces of the stronger race. These must largely constitute the determining factor, even in the problem presented by the negro; for the negro question is not primarily a question of the negro among negroes, but a question of the negro surrounded by another and a stronger people. The negro is in a white environment; the white man is largely the market for his labor and the opportunity for his progress, as well as the social and political model of his imitative spirit. Where we find the negro in relation to the trained and educated representatives of the stronger race, we find few of the evidences of racial friction.

But the white race, in the interest of the efficiency and the happiness of the masses of its own life, must bring its culture still more closely into relation with social needs. That the presence of child labor has called out strong and wholesome protest, that all the more helpless factors of our industrial system have commanded a deep and effective public interest, has been recorded. And yet in certain sections and among certain forces of the South there has been encountered much indifference or positive opposition to the bettering of industrial conditions. The causes for opposition are many, and have been stated in an earlier chapter. Among these causes, however, the most serious is one which is not peculiar to the South, but which is finding, throughout our country, an increasing power in the shaping of our social decisions. It is the exaggeration of the importance of the money element as contrasted with the human element in the world's work. For many years the South struggled against almost inconceivable odds in order to regain her place in the commercial experience of our country. She had men, women, children, resources, but little else. The process of rehabilitation is now rising to completion. Business is growing. Wealth, slowly but surely, is coming into her life. How much is it worth? There are those who seem to think that it is worth the exploitation of the ignorant and the helpless, who regard all "reforms" as the phases of a Pecksniffian hypocrisy, who not infrequently have stock in the enterprises affected by the suggestions of amendment, but who are "good" people and who give largely to charitable and semi-charitable institutions. There are others, however, who, while sensible of the good which men may accomplish with their money, are sensible also of the fact that, with money gotten under false conditions, any blessing which its giving brings can never equal the curse which its getting leaves, — leaves in that region out of sight where the ignorant and the poor go with a bitter silence to their fate, and the young, in their tender strength, give life itself when they are only paid for labor. To those who have seen these things, all that money can add to a trade, an industry, a civilization, does not equal what it takes away ; and the zest of action, the joy of success, the consciousness of increasing power, the gains of external privilege and comfort, are not matters of such weight as the sob of the child in the humid clatter of the mill. The mind of a true culture, a presence of fine and actual power throughout the South, will help her people everywhere to understand that culture of the deepest and broadest type, despite all sophistries, is never builded in violation of elementary human interests; that a prosperity which means the prosperity of the strong at the expense of the weak, carries at its heart the curse of blunted perceptions, intellectual and moral; that if the material elements of progress are to outweigh the spiritual, and if the crude masses of democratic feeling are to be commercialized before they are moralized, the South will lose that distinctive sensitiveness of temper, that quality of charm, that generous imagination, that capacity for reverence, that alert and responsive heart, which have constituted her peculiar birthright.

Yet the social interests of the educated life will not be negative alone. They cannot rest within the circle of corrective policies. They must press on into the reënforcement of those positive and affirmative proposals to which the methods of remedy and prevention are but contributory. What the child may do is of more importance than what it should not do. The movement against child labor, the movement for the relief of degrading penal conditions for adults and for children, are but an impera-

tive part of the constructive movement— through the
kindergartens, the schools, the churches — for freer,
more wholesome possibilities.   Through all the agencies of a positive social progress the South is rousing
herself as never before in order that her children
may be born into a land — not merely of greater
wealth — but of more immediate, more abundant
opportunity.   Upon the many evidences of this
arousal I have dwelt in previous chapters.   That
it will be sustained is clear.   Yet there is no proba-
bility that — with all its moral resources — it will too
soon overtake its task.   The vast stretches of rural
territory (more than seventeen millions of human
beings living in places of less than a thousand inhabitants), the prevailing isolation, the few railways,
the poor roads, the absence of strong centres of social
organization, the remaining poverty, the comparative
lack of diversity in industrial life, the schools, — inadequate and not effectively distributed, — and last, but
not least, the two races dividing the lands, dividing
the churches, dividing the schools — races to whom
coexistence seems imperative, but between whom
coalescence would be intolerable; here indeed is a
task for stout hearts, a task in the presence of which
men — if they are ever to accomplish anything —
must learn to know, to think clearly, to be patient,
and to love.

Where difficulties are so great, none but the great
and elemental human forces will prevail.   It is therefore of deep and hopeful significance that the power
and influence of religious institutions is so general.
As these come to deal more definitely and explicitly
with the phases of social need, there will enter into

social enthusiasms a high and serious confidence, a touch of authority and yet a touch of tenderness, which will draw the world to the Church while it draws the Church to the quickening and freeing of the world. Among civic forces the various organizations of the women of the South are yielding an inspiring measure of disinterested service. An increasing commercial activity is at length touching almost every section of our life, inaugurating more varied interests and opening new possibilities to thought, energy, ambition. The home — the individual American home — here, as everywhere, is the most intimate and most conservative of social forces. But it is to the school — the school in its every form, from the rural "primary" to the university — that our democracy must look, and may look, for the more satisfactory adjustment of the problems which accompany and affect its progress. The university touches life less intimately and less deeply than the home, but more broadly and more explicitly. The university may not be so popular in its appeal as the civic club or so concrete in its influence as the business career, but it is more informing than the one and more varied, more emancipating, than the other. It cannot touch the soul as does the Church, it cannot usurp the spiritual functions or wield the directive and healing influence of the Christian ministry, but it can touch the temporal conditions of the soul more broadly than the Church has touched them, can invest and teach the whole body of knowledge with a fulness which the Church does not assume, and can give to the specific issues of our civil and industrial life a clearer, more definite, more explicit criticism than has seemed practically possible to a divided Christian fellowship. Under the actual conditions of Southern society, it may be said that the university may become — if it would meet the measure of its ideal — not only the best gift of a democracy to culture, but the best gift of culture to our democracy.

That it will teach knowledge — knowledge in its fulness and its freedom — goes without saying. But it may also bring, through the truth and value of the scholar's standpoint, the influence of perspective into the consideration of our Southern tasks — a perspective in which men may see more clearly the world-position of the problems of Southern life, may understand that we are laboring with difficulties common, in large measure, to every civilization; that the South has everywhere something to teach and something to learn, whether from the industrial history of Lancashire or from those points — at Ceylon, or Bagdad, at Johannesburg, or Algiers — where white men and brown and black are struggling with the age-long divisive fate of racial cleavage.

The university may not only establish among us a clearer sense of perspective; it may help to make the method of political and social criticism a method of ideas. It may contribute to the dethronement of a method of popular adjudication which in many quarters of the South has long made conventions and conventional traditions unhappily supreme. Of these, many have been necessary, many have been beautiful and satisfying, many — just because of tender and compelling associations — must long remain; and yet there is need that the supreme method of judgment, the supreme process of social and political definition,

shall be more truly a method of ideas; that fulness
and exactness of knowledge, clearness and veracity of
thought, truth and accuracy of statement, shall —
along with breadth of sympathy and fertility of suggestion — take a larger place in the shaping of popular opinion. When a great section gives itself over
to a prolonged and exclusive emphasis upon one or
two ideas, however true, there is danger that it may
at length cease to have ideas.

And yet the collective progress, the social momentum, of a huge body of democratic life is not easily
secured except in relation to a few clear, elementary
conceptions. These become, therefore, of such con-
trolling and significant importance that it is all the
more needful that they should be intelligently and
fruitfully possessed. The developments which they
suggest or necessitate, their broader meaning, their
varied applications, should be discussed and interpreted in an atmosphere of reverence, of sympathy,
and yet of consistent freedom. In its contribution to
the creation of such an atmosphere the university
may render its most signal service. It may contribute
to our social development not merely a sense of perspective and a more vital method of social criticism,
but it may henceforth become in our democracy an
effective organ of its self-correction.

If it is to be so, however, it will first become intimately, supremely human, like, at least in some
degree, that teaching force which entered into our
civilization nearly twenty centuries ago, as the pro-
foundest social possession of the Western world.
And believing, with Him, in the fertility of every
unreclaimed or isolated province of social need, it

will find at length its benediction in the face of One who taught men democracy by His culture — who, in the richness and serenity of His spirit and out of that fulness of His interests which has been rightly called the fulness of His love, taught the dignity and the freedom of the individual heart; who taught men culture by His democracy — opening the fulness of truth through the simplicity of His faith in life, opening the wonder and promise of our earth from the standpoint of a soul giving to all knowledge the perspective and the dignity of imperishable use. His supreme gift was personal, but it has revealed an institutional ideal. The largest service of the university as an institution of culture, only arises as it comes to touch the enfolding and educative forces of the familiar world and assumes, in simplicity and sympathy, its more human function as supremely an institution of democracy.

APPENDICES

APPENDIX A

STATISTICS OF POPULATION, ILLITERACY, ETC.[1]

THE Twelfth Census shows that in June, 1900, there were in the United States 2,288,470 men of voting age (twenty-one years and over) who were unable to read and write. This was nearly 11 per cent of the total number — 21,134,299.

At the last presidential election the total vote was 13,961,-566; and the plurality of the successful candidate was 849,790. In the nearly 2,300,000 illiterate voters, there is thus no small opportunity for those who would appeal to the class feeling of the ignorant. If the greater number of this mass of ignorant voters could be thrown to one side in a closely contested election, involving the national credit or the national honor, there would be a more vivid appreciation of the possibilities which they involve.

Who are these illiterates and where are they? Many are of the negro race, 976,610; but more are white, 1,249,897. In 1870 the greater number were negroes, 862,243 to 748,970 white, an excess of more than 100,000. But within the intervening thirty years this has been changed, and now the white illiterates outnumber the negro by over 273,000.

Of the white illiterates a large number are foreign-born, 562,000; but the number of the native-born is 687,000, or 125,000 more than the foreign-born illiterates. It appears

---

[1] The matter of this Appendix (A) is largely taken from the Report of the United States Commissioner of Education for 1902. The tables of statistics, I, II, III, VIII, were compiled for Chapter XVIII of Vol. I of that publication by Dr. George S. Dickerman of New Haven, Conn. Table VII is from p. lxviii of Vol. I, and Tables IV, V, VI, IX, are from Vol. II.

also that the percentage of illiterates among the native-born sons of native parents is nearly three times as great as among the native-born sons of foreign parents. With the former it is 5.9 per cent, with the latter 2 per cent, indicating that our schools have been reaching the children of the foreigner more effectively than they have reached the children of the native-born. Not confining ourselves to the figures for adult males, but taking into view the whole native white population ten years of age and over, we find the persistence of the same tendency. Even in States like New York, Pennsylvania, and New Jersey the percentage of illiteracy among the native white population of native parentage is greater than among the native white population of foreign parentage.[1]

This is due to a number of causes, — chiefly, perhaps, to the fact that the children of the foreign-born are being reared largely within the cities, where schools are accessible and compulsory education laws enforceable, whereas the illiteracy among the children of the native-born is due to the inadequacy of school privileges among the rural population. And yet, the presence in our national life of 2,288,000 illiterate men of voting age — 618,000 of whom are native-born representatives of our native white population — may well be an occasion for serious reflection.

In the tables which follow, Table I presents the statistics as to the white males of voting age, with percentage unable to read and write, classified as native of native parents, native of foreign parents, and foreign-born.

Table II presents the statistics as to the negro males of voting age, with percentage unable to read and write, in 1870 and in 1900.

Table III affords a striking illustration of the fact that the problem of illiteracy, North as well as South, is largely rural. It presents the statistics as to the white males (twenty-one years of age and upward) with proportion unable to read

[1] See Twelfth Census of the United States, Vol. II, Table LX, p. cvi.

and write, classified by parentage and by their distribution within or without the centres of population.

Table IV illustrates the distribution of the three elements of our national population in the year 1900.

Tables V and VI indicate the progress of the several States in the reduction of the illiteracy of the native white population and of the colored population in the twenty years from 1880 to 1900.

Table VII presents in close juxtaposition certain facts as to the distribution of population, the per capita value of manufactures, the relation between the adult male and the school population, etc. Attention is called especially to columns 3, 8, 12, 13.

Table VIII presents the statistics as to the counties in the several States in which the proportion of white males of voting age, native and foreign, who cannot read and write is 20 per cent and upward.

Table IX indicates the rank of each State according to the percentage of the illiteracy of the native white population.

In reprinting the following illustrative material upon the subject of illiteracy, the author has had no desire to exaggerate its significance. But, inasmuch as the statistics have not been easily available in popular form, it has seemed well to include the data in this volume. Among the many preoccupations of our national interest, the significance of our illiteracy is perhaps more likely to be ignored than to be exaggerated.

TABLE I

WHITE MALES OF VOTING AGE (21 YEARS AND UPWARD), WITH PERCENTAGE UNABLE TO READ AND WRITE, CLASSIFIED AS (1) NATIVE OF NATIVE PARENTS, (2) NATIVE OF FOREIGN PARENTS, AND (3) FOREIGN-BORN, BY STATES AND TERRITORIES, ARRANGED GEOGRAPHICALLY, 1900

STATE OR TERRITORY	1. NATIVE WHITE OF NATIVE PARENTS			2. NATIVE WHITE OF FOREIGN PARENTS			3. FOREIGN-BORN WHITE		
	Total	Illiterate	Per cent	Total	Illiterate	Per cent	Total	Illiterate	Per cent
The United States	10,569,743	618,606	5.9	3,444,684	68,975	2.0	4,904,270	562,316	11.5
NORTH ATLANTIC DIVISION	2,760,103	57,767	2.1	1,257,195	24,085	1.9	2,108,698	320,189	15.2
Maine	157,377	3,420	2.2	20,964	2,089	10.0	38,515	8,223	21.4
New Hampshire	82,383	1,189	1.4	13,496	706	5.2	34,759	8,333	24.0
Vermont	68,857	1,759	2.6	18,324	1,858	10.1	20,846	4,862	23.3
Massachusetts	320,943	1,927	.6	165,584	2,422	1.5	343,522	47,436	13.8
Rhode Island	44,893	550	1.2	25,340	841	3.3	53,768	9,795	18.2
Connecticut	113,768	1,040	.9	54,955	663	1.2	105,403	16,562	15.6
New York	782,487	15,201	1.9	533,090	8,240	1.5	829,474	100,776	12.1
New Jersey	224,644	6,370	2.8	111,508	1,285	1.2	196,598	26,300	13.4
Pennsylvania	964,751	26,311	2.7	313,928	5,981	1.9	484,803	97,902	20.2
SOUTH ATLANTIC DIVISION	1,466,826	178,564	12.2	105,484	2,555	2.4	104,183	11,768	11.3
Delaware	33,270	2,666	8.0	5,575	93	1.7	6,747	1,186	17.6
Maryland	172,003	10,191	5.9	46,965	1,006	2.1	42,011	4,481	10.7
District of Columbia	39,557	391	1.0	11,161	75	.7	9,600	478	5.0
Virginia	280,881	35,057	12.5	9,413	270	2.9	11,085	1,166	10.5
West Virginia	205,216	23,024	11.2	15,035	553	3.7	12,878	2,895	22.5
North Carolina	284,601	54,208	19.0	2,211	126	5.7	2,451	140	5.7
South Carolina	124,097	15,643	12.6	3,299	68	2.1	2,979	154	5.2
Georgia	263,929	31,914	12.1	6,860	168	2.4	6,707	376	5.6
Florida	63,272	5,470	8.6	4,965	196	3.9	9,725	892	9.2

SOUTH CENTRAL DIVISION	2,055,858	237,239	11.5	176,686	9,946	5.6	178,376	33,566	18.8
Kentucky	402,244	62,182	15.5	41,823	1,166	2.8	25,139	2,169	8.6
Tennessee	353,621	51,244	14.5	11,916	444	3.7	9,509	730	7.7
Alabama	216,050	30,680	14.2	8,162	286	3.5	8,082	648	8.0
Mississippi	140,065	11,613	8.3	5,750	233	4.1	4,715	447	9.5
Louisiana	121,356	24,681	20.3	31,182	1,120	3.6	25,340	6,238	24.6
Texas	458,863	24,180	5.3	55,325	5,837	10.6	85,773	21,773	25.4
Indian Territory	71,736	7,792	10.9	3,186	192	6.0	2,943	493	16.8
Oklahoma	82,956	2,321	2.8	9,990	219	2.2	8,597	540	6.3
Arkansas	208,967	22,546	10.8	9,352	449	4.8	8,278	528	6.4
NORTH CENTRAL DIVISION	3,656,293	127,480	3.5	1,640,913	28,675	1.8	2,074,626	163,161	7.9
Ohio	697,956	25,476	3.7	256,955	4,688	1.8	225,688	21,605	9.6
Indiana	517,446	24,937	4.8	111,228	2,944	2.6	73,087	7,022	9.6
Illinois	586,773	20,952	3.6	316,313	4,139	1.3	407,123	36,608	7.8
Michigan	288,293	6,406	2.2	162,537	4,413	2.7	261,415	26,693	10.2
Wisconsin	116,943	1,744	1.5	192,966	4,022	2.1	257,304	23,893	9.3
Minnesota	104,577	737	.7	137,054	1,766	1.3	260,753	16,720	6.4
Iowa	321,513	5,944	1.8	151,246	1,791	1.2	157,906	8,246	5.2
Missouri	551,438	34,773	6.3	145,876	3,021	2.1	112,483	7,666	6.3
North Dakota	19,777	153	.8	17,902	220	1.2	55,558	3,597	6.3
South Dakota	35,381	219	.6	26,526	259	1.0	45,446	2,215	3.4
Nebraska	147,508	1,629	1.1	59,384	535	.9	90,925	4,677	5.1
Kansas	268,688	4,660	1.7	62,926	877	1.4	66,938	4,309	6.4
WESTERN DIVISION	630,663	17,556	2.8	264,406	3,714	1.4	438,387	33,632	7.7
Montana	35,130	237	.7	19,760	186	.9	39,983	2,675	6.7
Wyoming	18,012	166	.9	7,639	46	.6	10,011	828	7.8
Colorado	99,563	2,834	2.8	30,691	361	1.2	51,162	3,052	7.1
New Mexico	39,171	9,589	24.5	4,382	671	15.3	7,251	2,244	30.9
Arizona	16,183	526	3.3	6,507	491	7.5	12,161	3,759	30.9
Utah	18,321	290	1.6	22,478	200	.9	24,406	1,129	4.6
Nevada	5,431	44	.8	3,424	25	.7	5,797	406	7.0
Idaho	25,786	289	1.1	11,051	106	1.0	13,491	770	5.7
Washington	92,262	460	.5	29,992	169	.6	61,745	2,413	3.9
Oregon	79,220	881	1.1	20,555	198	1.0	31,486	1,681	3.4
California	201,584	2,240	1.1	107,667	1,261	1.2	180,294	14,675	8.1

TABLE II

NEGRO MALES OF VOTING AGE, WITH PERCENTAGE UNABLE TO READ
AND WRITE, IN 1870 AND IN 1900, BY STATES AND TERRITORIES

	NEGRO MALES OF VOTING AGE					
	1900			1870		
	Total	Illiterate	Per cent	Total	Illiterate	Per cent
The United States	2,060,302	976,610	47.4	1,032,475	862,243	83.5
NORTH ATLANTIC DIVISION	123,328	18,808	15.3	48,656	14,443	29.7
Maine	445	77	17.3	497	69	13.9
New Hampshire	230	34	14.8	176	38	21.6
Vermont	289	57	19.7	278	45	16.2
Massachusetts	10,456	1,100	10.5	4,073	822	20.1
Rhode Island	2,765	425	15.4	1,404	291	20.7
Connecticut	4,576	598	13.1	2,700	627	23 2
New York	31,425	3,541	11.3	14,586	3,912	26.8
New Jersey	21,474	3,925	18.3	7,870	2,881	36.6
Pennsylvania	51,668	9,051	17.5	17,072	5,758	33.7
SOUTH ATLANTIC DIVISION	817,224	417,400	51.1	456,448	396,437	86.9
Delaware	8,374	3,578	42.7	5,224	3,765	72.1
Maryland	60,406	24,462	40.5	39,120	27,123	69.3
District of Columbia	23,072	6,024	26.1	10,143	7,599	74.9
Virginia	146,122	76,764	52.5	107,691	97,908	90.9
West Virginia	14,786	5,584	37.8	3,972	3,186	80.2
North Carolina	127,114	67,489	53.1	78,019	68,669	88.0
South Carolina	152,860	83,618	54.7	85,475	70,830	82.9
Georgia	223,073	125,710	56.4	107,962	100,551	93.1
Florida	61,417	24,171	39.4	18,842	16,806	89.2
SOUTH CENTRAL DIVISION	951,724	500,093	52.5	461,478	413,182	89.5
Kentucky	74,728	36,990	49.5	44,321	37,889	85.5
Tennessee	112,236	53,396	47.6	64,131	55,938	87.2
Alabama	181,471	107,997	59.5	97,823	91,017	93.0
Mississippi	197,936	105,331	53.2	89,926	80,810	89.9
Louisiana	147,348	90,262	61.3	86,913	76,612	88.1
Texas	136,875	61,744	45.1	51,575	47,235	91.6
Indian Territory	9,146	3,776	41.3	—	—	—
Oklahoma	4,827	1,543	32.0	—	—	—
Arkansas	87,157	39,054	44.8	26,789	23,681	88.4
NORTH CENTRAL DIVISION	155,701	38,652	24.8	63,166	37,434	59.3
Ohio	31,235	6,813	21.8	15,614	7,531	48.2
Indiana	18,186	5,042	27.7	6,113	3,182	52.0
Illinois	29,762	5,551	18.7	7,694	3,969	51.6
Michigan	5,193	726	14.0	3,130	1,015	32.4
Wisconsin	1,006	128	12.7	642	185	28.8
Minnesota	2,168	150	6.9	246	44	17.9
Iowa	4,441	975	22.0	1,542	635	41.2
Missouri	46,418	14,829	31.9	23,882	18,002	75.4
North Dakota	115	19	16.5	} 28	} 6	21.4
South Dakota	184	30	16.3			
Nebraska	2,298	267	11.6	290	93	32.1
Kansas	14,695	4,122	28.1	3,985	2,772	69.6
WESTERN DIVISION	12,325	1,657	13.4	2,727	747	27.4
Montana	711	74	10.4	108	34	31.5
Wyoming	481	102	21.2	101	33	32.7
Colorado	3,215	448	13.9	197	63	32.0
New Mexico	775	126	16.3	85	58	68.2
Arizona	1,084	120	11.1	18	1	5.6
Utah	358	17	4.7	36	8	22.2
Nevada	70	16	22.9	203	15	7.4
Idaho	130	20	15.4	38	4	10.5
Washington	1,230	141	11.5	67	15	22.3
Oregon	560	53	9.5	143	48	33.6
California	3,711	540	14.6	1,731	468	27.0

TABLE III

WHITE MALES (21 YEARS OF AGE AND UPWARD), WITH PERCENTAGE UNABLE TO READ AND WRITE, CLASSIFIED AS (1) NATIVE OF NATIVE PARENTS, (2) NATIVE OF FOREIGN PARENTS, (3) FOREIGN-BORN FOR THE UNITED STATES, FOR THE NORTH AND WEST, AND FOR THE SOUTH, 1900

LOCATION	Number of cities	1. NATIVE OF NATIVE PARENTS.			2. NATIVE OF FOREIGN PARENTS			3. FOREIGN-BORN		
		Total	Illiterate	Per cent	Total	Illiterate	Per cent	Total	Illiterate	Per cent
In all quarters:										
The United States		10,569,743	618,606	5.9	3,444,684	68,975	2.0	4,904,270	562,316	11.5
The North and West		7,047,059	202,803	2.9	3,163,514	56,474	1.8	4,621,711	516,982	11.2
The South		3,522,684	415,803	11.8	281,170	12,501	4.4	282,559	45,334	16.0
In cities of 25,000 and over:										
The United States	160	1,863,367	14,520	.8	1,425,149	10,022	.7	2,274,889	222,938	9.8
The North and West	131	1,513,297	9,449	.6	1,298,337	8,350	.6	2,170,920	213,140	9.8
The South	29	350,070	5,091	1.5	126,812	1,672	1.3	103,969	9,798	9.5
In cities of 4,000 and over:										
The United States	1,158	2,683,248	20,909	.8	2,052,215	14,432	.7	3,275,840	321,031	9.8
The North and West	951	2,114,735	12,642	.6	1,846,273	11,717	.6	3,107,595	305,124	9.8
The South	207	568,513	8,267	1.5	295,942	2,715	1.3	168,245	15,907	9.5
Outside of cities of 25,000 and over:										
The United States		8,706,376	604,086	6.9	2,019,535	58,953	2.9	2,629,381	339,378	12.5
The North and West		5,533,762	193,374	3.5	1,865,177	48,124	2.5	2,450,791	303,842	12.4
The South		3,172,614	410,712	12.9	154,358	10,829	7.0	178,590	35,536	19.9
Outside of cities of 4,000 and over:										
The United States		7,886,495	597,697	7.6	1,392,469	54,543	3.9	1,628,430	241,285	14.8
The North and West		4,932,324	190,161	3.9	1,317,241	44,757	3.4	1,514,116	211,858	13.9
The South		2,954,171	407,536	13.9	75,228	9,786	13.0	114,314	29,427	25.7

TABLE IV

THE THREE ELEMENTS OF POPULATION IN 1900

STATE OR TERRITORY	Total population	Native White	Per cent	Foreign-born White	Per cent	Colored	Per cent
UNITED STATES	75,994,575	56,595,379	74.5	10,213,817	13.4	9,185,379 [1]	12.1
North Atlantic Division	21,046,695	15,898,900	75.6	4,738,988	22.5	408,807	1.9
South Atlantic Division	10,443,480	6,497,175	62.2	208,883	2.0	3,737,422	35.8
South Central Division	14,080,047	9,462,220	67.2	353,692	2.5	4,264,135	30.3
North Central Division	26,333,004	21,624,468	82.1	4,151,402	15.8	557,134	2.1
Western Division	4,091,349	3,112,016	76.1	766,852	18.6	217,881	5.3
NORTH ATLANTIC DIVISION:							
Maine	694,466	599,291	86.3	92,935	13.4	2,240	0.3
New Hampshire	411,588	322,830	78.4	87,961	21.4	797	0.2
Vermont	343,641	298,077	86.7	44,694	13.0	870	0.3
Massachusetts	2,805,346	1,929,650	68.8	840,114	29.9	35,582	1.3
Rhode Island	428,556	285,278	66.6	133,772	31.2	9,506	2.2
Connecticut	908,420	655,028	72.1	237,396	26.1	15,996	1.8
New York	7,268,894	5,267,358	72.5	1,889,523	26.0	112,013	1.5
New Jersey	1,883,669	1,382,267	73.4	430,050	22.8	71,352	3.8
Pennsylvania	6,302,115	5,159,121	81.9	982,543	15.6	160,451	2.5
SOUTH ATLANTIC DIVISION:							
Delaware	184,735	140,248	75.9	13,729	7.4	30,758	16.7
Maryland	1,188,044	859,280	72.3	93,144	7.9	235,620	19.8
District of Columbia	278,718	172,012	61.7	19,520	7.0	87,186	31.3
Virginia	1,854,184	1,173,787	63.3	19,068	1.0	661,329	35.7
West Virginia	958,800	892,854	93.1	22,379	2.3	43,567	4.6
North Carolina	1,893,810	1,259,209	66.5	4,394	0.2	630,207	33.3
South Carolina	1,340,316	552,436	41.2	5,371	0.4	782,509	58.4
Georgia	2,216,331	1,169,273	52.8	12,021	0.5	1,035,037	46.7
Florida	528,542	278,076	52.6	19,257	3.6	231,209	43.8

South Central Division:						
Kentucky	2,147,174	1,812,176	84.4	50,133	2.3	284,865	13.3
Tennessee	2,020,616	1,522,600	75.3	17,586	0.9	480,430	23.8
Alabama	1,828,697	986,814	54.0	14,338	0.8	827,545	45.2
Mississippi	1,551,270	633,575	40.8	7,625	0.5	910,070	58.7
Louisiana	1,381,625	677,759	49.1	51,853	3.7	652,013	47.2
Texas	3,048,710	2,249,088	73.8	177,581	5.8	622,041	20.4
Arkansas	1,311,564	930,394	70.9	14,186	1.1	366,984	28.0
Oklahoma	398,331	351,920	88.4	15,604	3.9	30,807	7.7
Indian Territory	392,060	297,894	76.0	4,786	1.2	89,380	22.8
North Central Division:						
Ohio	4,157,545	3,602,394	86.7	457,000	11.0	97,341	2.3
Indiana	2,516,462	2,316,641	92.1	141,861	5.6	57,960	2.3
Illinois	4,821,550	3,770,238	78.2	964,635	20.0	86,677	1.8
Michigan	2,420,982	1,858,367	76.8	540,196	22.3	22,419	0.9
Wisconsin	2,069,042	1,542,206	74.5	515,705	24.9	11,131	0.6
Minnesota	1,751,394	1,232,101	70.4	504,935	28.8	14,358	0.8
Iowa	2,231,853	1,912,885	85.7	305,782	13.7	13,186	0.6
Missouri	3,106,665	2,729,068	87.9	215,775	6.9	161,822	5.2
North Dakota	319,146	199,122	62.4	112,590	35.3	7,434	2.3
South Dakota	401,570	292,385	72.8	88,399	22.0	20,856	5.2
Nebraska	1,066,300	879,409	82.5	177,117	16.6	9,774	0.9
Kansas	1,470,495	1,259,742	87.7	126,577	8.6	54,176	3.7
Western Division:						
Montana	243,329	163,910	67.4	62,373	25.6	17,046	7.0
Wyoming	92,531	72,469	78.3	16,582	17.9	3,480	3.8
Colorado	539,700	438,571	81.2	90,475	16.8	10,654	2.0
New Mexico	195,310	166,946	85.5	13,261	6.8	15,103	7.7
Arizona	122,931	70,508	57.4	22,395	18.2	30,028	24.4
Utah	276,749	219,661	79.4	52,804	19.1	4,284	1.5
Nevada	42,335	26,824	63.3	8,581	20.3	6,930	16.4
Idaho	161,772	132,605	82.0	21,890	13.5	7,277	4.5
Washington	518,103	394,179	76.1	102,125	19.7	21,799	4.2
Oregon	413,536	340,721	82.4	53,861	13.0	18,954	4.6
California	1,485,053	1,086,222	73.2	316,505	21.3	82,326	5.5

¹ The term "colored" as here used by the U.S. Census includes 237,196 Indians and 114,189 Mongolians.

TABLE V

ILLITERATES IN THE NATIVE WHITE POPULATION 10 YEARS OF AGE AND OVER, 1880 AND 1900

STATE OR TERRITORY	1900				1880			
	Total native white population	Native white population 10 years of age and over	Illiterates Number	Illiterates Per cent	Total native white population	Native white population 10 years of age and over	Illiterates Number	Illiterates Per cent
UNITED STATES	56,595,379	41,236,662	1,913,611	4.6	36,843,291	25,785,789	2,255,460	8.7
North Atlantic Division	15,808,900	11,729,536	192,052	1.6	11,465,448	8,351,065	234,576	2.8
South Atlantic Division	6,497,175	4,748,622	541,530	11.4	4,481,144	3,144,714	630,062	20.0
South Central Division	9,462,220	6,723,766	754,057	11.2	5,630,217	3,806,063	836,489	22.0
North Central Division	21,624,468	15,730,473	363,672	2.3	14,049,225	9,646,617	482,103	5.0
Western Division	3,112,616	2,298,265	61,390	2.7	1,215,257	837,330	72,230	8.6
NORTH ATLANTIC DIVISION:								
Maine	599,291	474,821	11,394	2.4	588,193	463,158	8,775	1.9
New Hampshire	322,830	253,636	3,840	1.5	299,995	242,811	2,710	1.1
Vermont	298,077	235,117	6,934	2.9	290,281	224,361	5,354	2.4
Massachusetts	1,929,650	1,420,219	10,739	0.8	1,321,844	990,160	6,933	0.7
Rhode Island	285,278	207,953	3,714	1.8	196,108	144,596	4,261	2.9
Connecticut	655,028	485,367	3,678	0.8	481,060	361,733	3,728	1.0
New York	5,267,358	3,861,371	47,350	1.2	3,807,317	2,742,847	59,516	2.2
New Jersey	1,382,267	1,000,700	17,031	1.7	870,697	618,941	20,093	3.2
Pennsylvania	5,159,121	3,799,352	87,372	2.3	3,699,953	2,562,458	123,206	4.8
SOUTH ATLANTIC DIVISION:								
Delaware	140,248	108,389	6,072	5.6	110,720	82,318	6,630	8.1
Maryland	859,280	649,197	26,432	4.1	642,165	462,697	36,027	7.8
District of Columbia	172,012	140,114	1,138	0.8	101,026	75,025	1,950	2.6
Virginia	1,173,787	866,295	96,117	11.1	866,248	616,314	113,915	18.5
West Virginia	892,854	645,250	64,281	10.0	574,309	392,242	72,826	18.6
North Carolina	1,259,209	900,664	175,645	19.5	863,550	605,244	191,913	31.7
South Carolina	552,436	399,540	54,375	13.6	383,651	265,356	59,415	22.4
Georgia	1,160,273	841,200	100,431	11.9	806,573	553,769	128,362	23.2
Florida	278,076	197,973	17,039	8.6	134,902	91,749	19,024	20.7

SOUTH CENTRAL DIVISION:								
Kentucky	1,812,176	1,319,982	169,324	12.8	1,317,725	914,311	208,796	22.8
Tennessee	1,522,600	1,108,629	157,396	14.2	1,122,236	774,411	214,994	27.8
Alabama	986,814	700,823	103,570	14.8	652,664	443,327	111,040	25.0
Mississippi	633,575	459,952	36,038	8.0	470,403	319,385	52,910	16.6
Louisiana	677,759	474,621	82,227	17.3	402,177	268,600	53,261	19.8
Texas	2,249,088	1,554,994	95,006	6.1	1,083,656	701,969	97,498	13.9
Arkansas	930,394	656,438	76,036	11.6	581,356	384,060	97,990	25.5
Oklahoma	351,920	249,064	6,279	2.5				
Indian Territory	297,894	208,263	29,091	14.0				
NORTH CENTRAL DIVISION:								
Ohio	3,602,304	2,758,138	67,155	2.4	2,723,582	1,952,858	83,183	4.3
Indiana	2,316,641	1,780,458	63,800	3.6	1,794,764	1,297,159	87,786	6.8
Illinois	3,770,238	2,703,296	58,037	2.1	2,448,172	1,666,214	88,519	5.3
Michigan	1,858,367	1,348,352	22,277	1.7	1,228,127	854,925	19,981	2.3
Wisconsin	1,542,206	1,042,940	13,989	1.3	904,300	566,745	11,494	2.0
Minnesota	1,232,101	795,959	6,338	0.8	599,373	300,747	5,671	1.9
Iowa	1,912,885	1,397,581	16,522	1.2	1,353,046	918,723	23,660	2.6
Missouri	2,729,068	2,027,613	96,405	4.8	1,811,407	1,244,738	137,949	11.1
North Dakota	199,122	115,544	1,063	0.9	81,770	51,229	933	1.8
South Dakota	294,385	192,240	1,204	0.6				
Nebraska	879,409	616,473	4,717	0.8	352,413	224,899	5,102	2.3
Kansas	1,289,742	957,879	12,165	1.3	842,211	568,380	17,825	3.1
WESTERN DIVISION:								
Montana	163,910	116,475	752	0.6	25,898	19,628	272	1.4
Wyoming	72,469	52,816	348	0.7	14,509	10,458	177	1.7
Colorado	438,571	327,143	8,692	2.7	151,978	117,132	8,373	7.1
New Mexico	166,946	117,338	34,525	29.4	100,673	72,219	46,329	64.2
Arizona	70,508	50,122	3,096	6.2	20,609	15,200	1,225	8.1
Utah	219,661	141,036	1,108	0.8	98,958	53,944	3,183	5.9
Nevada	26,824	20,621	133	0.6	33,350	22,660	240	1.1
Idaho	132,605	92,008	862	0.9	22,414	15,011	443	3.0
Washington	394,179	289,007	1,374	0.5	54,896	37,278	895	2.4
Oregon	340,721	258,056	2,180	0.8	142,143	99,028	3,433	3.5
California	1,086,222	833,643	8,320	1.0	549,529	374,772	7,660	2.0

TABLE VI

ILLITERATES IN THE COLORED POPULATION 10 YEARS OF AGE AND OVER, 1880 AND 1900

STATE OR TERRITORY	1900				1880			
	Total colored population	Colored population 10 years of age and over	Illiterates Number	Illiterates Per cent	Total colored population	Colored population 10 years of age and over	Illiterates Number	Illiterates Per cent
UNITED STATES	9,185,379	6,698,906	2,979,323	44.5	6,752,813	4,601,207	3,220,878	70.0
North Atlantic Division	408,807	341,969	50,060	14.6	233,563	183,986	44,552	24.2
South Atlantic Division	3,737,422	2,662,338	1,253,379	47.1	2,943,085	1,973,725	1,482,745	75.1
South Central Division	4,264,135	3,057,507	1,455,273	48.6	3,018,056	2,007,453	1,525,245	76.0
North Central Division	557,134	452,272	110,674	24.6	402,688	294,276	121,216	41.2
Western Division	217,881	186,830	79,937	42.8	155,421	141,767	47,120	33.2
NORTH ATLANTIC DIVISION:								
Maine	2,240	1,823	471	25.8	2,084	1,658	412	24.8
New Hampshire	797	715	109	15.2	762	594	94	15.8
Vermont	870	721	108	15.0	1,068	807	156	19.3
Massachusetts	35,582	30,021	3,722	12.4	19,303	15,416	2,322	15.1
Rhode Island	9,506	7,970	1,133	14.2	6,592	5,303	1,249	23.6
Connecticut	15,996	13,270	1,572	11.8	11,931	9,523	1,661	17.4
New York	112,013	95,978	12,327	12.8	66,849	53,825	11,425	21.2
New Jersey	71,352	59,033	10,230	17.5	39,099	30,206	9,200	30.5
Pennsylvania	160,451	132,438	20,298	15.3	85,875	66,654	18,033	27.1
SOUTH ATLANTIC DIVISION:								
Delaware	30,758	23,587	8,983	38.1	26,448	19,245	11,068	57.5
Maryland	235,620	179,909	63,233	35.2	210,230	151,278	90,172	59.6
District of Columbia	87,186	72,414	17,548	24.2	59,618	45,035	21,790	48.4
Virginia	661,329	479,464	213,900	44.6	631,707	428,450	315,660	73.7
West Virginia	43,567	34,371	11,094	32.3	25,920	18,446	10,139	55.0
North Carolina	630,207	441,756	210,344	47.6	533,508	331,145	271,943	77.4
South Carolina	782,509	537,542	283,940	52.8	604,472	394,750	310,701	78.5
Georgia	1,035,037	724,305	379,156	52.3	725,274	479,863	391,482	81.6
Florida	231,209	168,980	65,101	38.5	126,888	85,513	60,420	70.7

SOUTH CENTRAL DIVISION:

Kentucky	284,865	219,843	88,186	40.1	271,511	190,223	133,895	70.4
Tennessee	480,430	354,980	147,844	41.6	493,528	271,386	194,495	71.7
Alabama	827,545	589,820	338,707	57.4	600,320	399,058	321,680	80.6
Mississippi	910,070	640,424	314,677	49.1	652,199	425,397	319,753	75.2
Louisiana	652,013	465,611	284,594	61.1	484,992	328,153	259,429	79.1
Texas	622,041	438,883	167,531	38.2	394,512	255,265	192,520	75.4
Arkansas	366,984	203,923	113,495	43.0	210,994	137,971	103,473	75.0
Oklahoma	30,807	22,651	8,227	36.3				
Indian Territory	89,380	61,372	22,072	36.0				

NORTH CENTRAL DIVISION:

Ohio	97,341	79,663	14,231	17.9	80,142	59,839	16,356	27.3
Indiana	57,960	47,355	10,680	22.6	39,503	29,140	10,363	35.6
Illinois	86,677	72,748	13,253	18.2	46,720	34,837	12,971	37.2
Michigan	22,419	18,182	3,806	20.9	22,377	16,780	4,791	28.6
Wisconsin	11,131	8,576	3,394	39.6	5,879	4,279	1,325	31.0
Minnesota	14,358	10,832	4,466	41.2	3,889	2,794	1,040	37.2
Iowa	13,186	10,982	4,219	20.2	10,015	7,578	2,272	30.0
Missouri	161,822	130,161	36,495	28.0	145,554	104,393	56,244	53.9
North Dakota	7,434	5,450	3,224	59.2	2,030	1,501	664	44.2
South Dakota	20,856	15,294	7,793	51.0	2,638	1,959	602	30.7
Nebraska	9,774	8,020	1,369	17.1				
Kansas	54,176	43,009	9,744	22.7	43,941	31,176	14,588	46.8

WESTERN DIVISION:

Montana	17,046	13,815	6,659	48.2	3,774	3,003	1,076	35.8
Wyoming	3,480	2,872	1,181	41.1	1,352	1,239	182	14.7
Colorado	10,654	9,123	1,823	20.0	3,201	2,764	568	20.5
New Mexico	15,103	11,324	8,049	71.1	10,454	8,199	7,559	92.2
Arizona	30,028	22,646	16,659	73.6	5,280	4,288	1,518	23.8
Utah	4,284	3,585	1,866	52.1	1,540	1,318	689	52.3
Nevada	6,930	5,794	3,871	66.8	8,710	8,071	2,154	26.7
Idaho	7,277	6,191	3,338	53.9	3,597	3,524	994	28.2
Washington	21,799	18,948	6,820	36.0	7,917	6,451	2,460	38.1
Oregon	18,954	17,434	6,299	36.1	11,693	11,083	3,080	27.8
California	82,326	75,098	23,372	31.1	97,513	91,827	27,340	29.8

TABLE VII

DENSITY OF POPULATION, URBAN POPULATION, NATIVITY AND RACE CLASSIFICATION, VALUE OF MANUFACTURES, ILLITERACY, AND RELATIONS OF THE ADULT MALE AND OF THE SCHOOL POPULATION

[NOTE.—The statistics in this table, except those in column 12, are from the United States Census of 1900.]

STATE OR TERRITORY	The total population					Value of manufactured products per capita of population[2]	The adult male population (21 years and over)				Number of children 5 to 18 years of age to every 100 persons of the total population	
	No. of persons to a sq. mile	Per cent in incorporated places of 8000 and over	Per cent of native and foreign white and of colored				No. to every 100 children 5 to 18 years of age	Per cent of illiterates (unable to write) among adult males			1870	1900
			Native white	Foreign white	Colored[1]			Native white	Foreign white	Negro		
1	2	3	4	5	6	7	8	9	10	11	12	13
UNITED STATES	25.6	32.6	74.4	13.4	12.2	$74.53	98.3	4.9	11.5	47.4	31.3	28.3
North Atlantic Division	129.8	57.0	75.6	22.5	1.9	140.22	121.8	2.0	15.2	15.3	28.3	24.4
South Atlantic Division	38.9	17.0	62.2	2.0	35.8	35.48	75.2	11.5	11.3	51.1	33.0	31.8
South Central Division	23.1	11.4	67.2	2.5	30.3	29.44	73.1	11.1	18.8	52.5	33.9	32.8
North Central Division	34.9	30.6	82.1	15.8	2.1	68.98	101.6	2.9	7.9	24.8	32.4	28.2
Western Division	3.5	31.2	76.1	18.6	5.3	63.96	141.1	2.4	7.7	13.4	25.6	25.1
NORTH ATLANTIC DIVISION:												
Maine	23.2	23.7	86.3	13.4	.3	84.23	135.3	3.1	21.4	17.3	28.0	23.2
New Hampshire	45.7	38.6	78.4	21.4	.2	127.22	147.5	2.0	24.0	14.8	24.8	21.6
Vermont	37.6	11.2	86.7	13.0	.3	86.80	134.9	4.1	23.3	19.7	27.2	23.4
Massachusetts	348.9	67.0	68.8	29.9	1.3	171.99	135.4	.9	13.8	10.5	25.5	22.2
Rhode Island	407.0	66.1	66.6	31.2	2.2	204.66	126.3	2.0	18.2	15.4	25.7	23.5
Connecticut	187.5	52.0	72.1	26.1	1.8	184.04	134.6	1.0	15.6	13.1	25.9	22.9
New York	152.6	68.5	72.5	26.0	1.5	141.97	125.7	1.8	12.1	11.3	28.1	23.9
New Jersey	250.3	61.2	73.4	22.8	3.8	133.15	118.0	2.3	13.4	18.3	29.0	25.0
Pennsylvania	140.1	45.5	81.9	15.6	2.5	125.73	108.7	2.5	20.2	17.5	30.6	26.5
SOUTH ATLANTIC DIVISION:												
Delaware	94.3	41.4	75.9	7.5	16.6	101.42	110.3	7.1	17.6	42.7	31.8	26.5
Maryland	120.5	46.9	72.3	7.9	19.8	82.62	97.0	5.1	10.7	40.5	31.3	27.9
District of Columbia	4,645.3	100.0	61.7	7.0	31.3	101.53	138.4	.9	5.0	26.1	27.0	21.7
Virginia	40.2	14.7	63.3	1.0	35.7	30.91	76.4	12.2	10.5	52.5	32.4	31.6

	1	2	3	4	5	6	7	8	9	10	11	12
West Virginia	38.9	7.7	93.8	2.4	4.5	33.20	83.9	10.7	22.5	37.8	34.1	30.8
North Carolina	39.0	5.1	66.5	.2	33.3	22.10	66.3	18.9	5.7	53.1	33.6	33.3
South Carolina	44.4	7.5	41.2	.4	58.4	18.44	61.1	12.3	5.2	54.7	33.2	34.6
Georgia	37.6	11.0	52.7	.6	46.7	21.85	67.7	11.8	5.6	56.4	34.4	33.4
Florida	9.7	15.0	52.6	3.7	43.7	40.06	85.4	8.3	9.2	39.4	34.0	30.9
SOUTH CENTRAL DIVISION:												
Kentucky	53.7	16.9	84.4	2.3	13.3	33.22	81.8	14.3	8.6	49.5	34.4	31.0
Tennessee	48.4	13.4	75.3	.8	23.8	21.92	75.4	14.1	7.7	47.6	34.1	32.0
Alabama	35.5	7.3	53.9	.5	45.3	20.04	67.8	13.8	8.0	59.5	34.1	33.4
Mississippi	33.5	2.6	40.8	3.7	58.7	12.08	66.2	8.1	9.5	53.2	33.7	34.0
Louisiana	30.4	22.8	49.1	5.8	47.2	28.14	72.5	16.9	24.6	61.3	31.1	32.6
Texas	11.6	11.3	73.8	1.1	20.4	17.16	72.3	5.8	25.4	45.1	34.8	33.5
Arkansas	24.7	5.4	70.9	3.9	28.0	16.19	70.8	10.5	6.4	44.8	34.2	33.8
Oklahoma	10.3	5.0	88.4	1.2	7.7	6.61	87.5	2.7	6.3	32.0		31.3
Indian Territory	12.6	0.0	76.0		22.8	4.25	72.8	10.7	16.8	41.3		34.1
NORTH CENTRAL DIVISION:												
Ohio	102.0	38.5	86.7	11.0	2.3	92.50	110.2	3.2	9.6	21.8	31.7	26.5
Indiana	70.1	24.2	92.1	5.6	5.6	64.84	103.5	4.4	9.6	27.7	33.8	27.7
Illinois	86.1	47.1	78.2	20.0	1.8	107.84	106.2	2.8	7.8	18.7	32.2	27.4
Michigan	42.2	30.9	74.6	22.3	.9	65.01	109.9	2.4	10.2	14.0	30.3	27.1
Wisconsin	38.0	30.7	74.6	24.9	.5	73.45	93.0	1.9	9.3	12.7	33.6	29.7
Minnesota	22.1	26.8	70.4	28.8	.8	50.95	98.5	1.6	6.4	6.9	32.5	29.4
Iowa	40.2	16.8	85.7	13.7	.6	28.43	99.9	1.6	6.8	2.0	33.1	28.5
Missouri	45.2	30.8	87.9	6.9	5.2	54.88	93.6	5.4	6.3	31.9	33.6	29.5
North Dakota	4.5	3.0	62.4	35.3	2.3	11.18	99.6	1.0	4.9	16.5	23.7	30.0
South Dakota	5.2	2.6	72.8	26.6	5.2	10.97	90.6	.8	5.1	16.3	28.1	31.0
Nebraska	13.9	15.8	82.5	16.6	.9	39.19	93.5	1.0	5.1	11.6	29.8	30.1
Kansas	18.0	14.0	87.7	8.6	3.7	29.00	94.8	1.7	6.4	28.1		29.7
WESTERN DIVISION:												
Montana	1.7	27.0	67.4	25.6	7.0	100.17	188.2	.8	6.7	10.4	10.2	22.3
Wyoming	.9	24.1	78.3	17.9	3.8	26.11	171.5	.8	7.8	21.2	9.4	23.9
Colorado	5.2	38.1	81.2	16.8	2.0	66.60	139.3	2.4	7.1	13.9	22.5	24.7
New Mexico	1.6	0.0	85.5	6.8	7.7	13.78	92.1	23.6	30.9	16.8	31.9	30.6
Arizona	1.1	0.0	57.4	18.2	24.4	104.54	138.7	4.5	30.9	11.1	16.8	25.9
Utah	3.4	25.2	79.4	19.1	16.4	30.00	74.5	1.2	4.6	4.7	35.1	32.6
Nevada	.4	0.0	63.3	20.3	4.5	19.31	196.5	.8	7.0	22.9	12.6	21.3
Idaho	1.9	0.0	82.0	13.5	4.2	12.15	116.4	1.1	5.7	11.5	11.3	28.6
Washington	7.7	31.9	76.1	19.7	4.6	72.76	149.3	.5	3.9	11.5	27.0	25.3
Oregon	4.4	23.9	82.4	13.0	5.5	48.10	132.7	1.1	3.4	9.5	32.3	26.3
California	9.5	43.7	73.2	21.3		77.27	160.5	1.1	8.1	14.6	24.5	22.8

1 Including Mongolians and Indians.   2 Less cost of raw material.

TABLE VIII

COUNTIES IN THE SEVERAL STATES IN WHICH THE PROPORTION OF WHITE MALES OF VOTING AGE, NATIVE AND FOREIGN, WHO CANNOT READ AND WRITE, IS 20 PER CENT AND UPWARD

	Total	Illiterate	Per cent		Total	Illiterate	Per cent
MAINE				**N. CAROLINA — con.**			
Aroostook	16,271	3,755	23.1	Nash	3,556	814	22.9
NEW YORK				Duplin	3,288	758	23.1
Clinton	13,602	3,345	24.6	Wilson	3,306	765	23.1
PENNSYLVANIA				Yadkin	2,830	660	23.3
Luzerne	70,171	14,029	20.0	Sampson	3,976	936	23.5
VIRGINIA				Polk	1,284	303	23.6
Pittsylvania	5,859	1,185	20.2	Clay	927	220	23.7
Smyth	3,755	770	20.6	Cherokee	2,429	579	23.8
Wythe	4,016	845	21.0	Johnston	5,407	1,296	24.0
Washington	5,981	1,275	21.2	Franklin	3,068	746	24.3
Gloucester	1,524	346	22.7	Haywood	3,283	802	24.4
Carroll	3,908	905	23.2	Gates	1,290	319	24.7
Franklin	4,119	975	23.6	Swain	1,553	394	25.4
Lee	4,003	961	24.0	Greene	1,507	386	25.6
Stafford	1,636	397	24.2	Jackson	2,360	609	25.8
Scott	4,787	1,193	24.9	Madison	4,074	1,077	26.4
Dickenson	1,521	380	25.0	Mitchell	2,980	816	27.4
Russell	3,817	1,003	26.2	Person	2,132	603	28.2
Patrick	2,923	914	31.2	Surry	5,019	1,414	28.2
Greene	1,058	331	31.3	Yancey	2,295	707	30.8
Buchanan	1,957	696	35.6	Wilkes	5,081	1,568	30.9
WEST VIRGINIA				Stokes	3,607	1,174	32.5
McDowell	3,700	747	20.2	**SOUTH CAROLINA**			
Wyoming	1,710	375	21.9	Horry	3,553	752	21.2
Boone	1,725	449	26.0	Pickens	3,190	689	21.6
Lincoln	3,336	868	26.0	Chesterfield	2,681	702	26.2
Mingo	2,617	698	26.7	**GEORGIA**			
Logan	1,475	405	27.5	Murray	1,733	354	20.4
NORTH CAROLINA				Twiggs	701	144	20.5
Hertford	1,441	290	20.1	Gilmer	2,104	442	21.0
Rockingham	4,903	988	20.2	Miller	798	171	21.4
Macon	2,328	479	20.6	Rabun	1,234	265	21.5
Onslow	2,045	426	20.8	Dawson	1,040	227	21.8
Lenoir	2,609	545	20.9	Paulding	2,493	557	22.3
Montgomery	2,412	507	21.0	Glascock	666	149	22.4
Dare	1,072	227	21.2	Pickens	1,750	395	22.6
Harnett	2,439	517	21.2	Fannin	2,268	535	23.6
Ashe	3,847	823	21.3	Union	1,665	393	23.6
Davie	2,184	467	21.4	Lumpkin	1,544	410	26.6
Martin	1,907	409	21.4	**FLORIDA**			
Davidson	4,515	975	21.5	Taylor	776	194	25.0
Pitt	3,792	816	21.5	Holmes	1,389	357	25.7
Watauga	2,689	579	21.5	**KENTUCKY**			
Caldwell	2,963	646	21.8	Lewis	4,477	896	20.0
Stanly	2,716	593	21.8	Grayson	4,471	914	20.4
Camden	808	178	22.0	Menifee	1,478	301	20.4
Cleveland	4,333	958	22.1	Marion	3,193	653	20.5
Tyrrell	850	188	22.1	Marshall	2,582	540	20.9
Burke	3,341	753	22.5	Allen	3,378	720	21.3
Graham	838	191	22.8	Johnson	2,879	614	21.3

TABLE VIII — CONTINUED

	Total	Illiterate	Per cent		Total	Illiterate	Per cent
KENTUCKY — con.				**ALABAMA**			
Adair	3,084	668	21.6	St. Clair	3,416	688	20.1
Rockcastle	2,787	609	21.9	Winston	1,905	393	20.6
Rowan	1,875	415	22.1	Franklin	3,038	639	21.0
Lawrence	4,180	961	23.0	Chilton	2,908	624	21.5
Butler	3,568	830	23.3	Covington	2,817	612	21.7
Metcalfe	2,178	514	23.6	Cherokee	3,913	867	22.2
Bell	3,220	764	23.7	Cleburne	2,644	595	22.5
Carter	4,389	1,046	23.8	Coffee	3,517	844	24.0
Casey	3,365	813	24.2	**MISSISSIPPI**			
Wayne	3,079	746	24.2				
Lee	1,627	395	24.3	Hancock	1,892	387	20.4
Knox	3,530	861	24.4	**LOUISIANA**			
Greenup	3,497	859	24.6				
Clinton	1,667	421	25.3	West Baton Rouge	635	136	21.4
Edmonson	2,101	555	26.4	Iberville	2,541	640	25.2
Estill	2,491	657	26.4	Livingston	1,486	377	25.3
Cumberland	1,778	481	27.1	Point Coupee	1,620	442	27.3
Letcher	1,777	493	27.7	Plaquemines	1,678	476	28.4
Owsley	1,435	397	27.7	Iberia	3,416	1,049	30.7
Jackson	2,119	593	28.0	St. John the Baptist	1,279	397	31.0
Martin	1,171	338	28.9	St. Bernard	771	246	31.9
Magoffin	2,387	709	29.7	St. James	2,202	712	32.3
Elliott	2,038	609	29.9	St. Mary	3,566	1,224	34.3
Harlan	1,888	567	30.0	Ascension	2,755	950	34.5
Floyd	3,074	939	30.5	Cameron	739	261	35.3
Perry	1,570	493	31.4	Avoyelles	3,621	1,443	39.9
Pike	4,462	1,432	32.1	St. Charles	830	332	40.0
Breathitt	2,748	890	32.4	Acadia	4,301	1,786	41.5
Clay	2,789	983	35.2	Lafayette	2,863	1,192	41.6
Leslie	1,272	448	35.2	St. Landry	5,268	2,305	43.7
Knott	1,561	559	35.8	St. Martin	1,109	986	47.1
TENNESSEE				Assumption	2,776	1,313	47.3
				Terrebonne	3,282	1,627	49.6
Benton	2,581	526	20.4	Jefferson	1,511	752	49.8
Meigs	1,465	307	20.9	Lafourche	4,510	2,277	50.5
Bledsoe	1,377	291	21.1	Vermilion	3,494	1,768	51.2
Polk	2,583	546	21.1	**TEXAS**			
Campbell	3,799	806	21.2				
Van Buren	688	147	21.4	Refugio	285	57	20.0
Marion	3,523	768	21.5	Zavalla	211	45	21.3
Scott	2,257	483	21.5	Wilson	2,889	620	21.5
Union	2,818	608	21.6	Uvalde	1,113	257	23.1
Clay	1,837	409	22.2	Dimmit	303	72	23.8
Anderson	3,858	866	22.4	Live Oak	526	128	24.3
Perry	1,816	407	22.4	McMullen	268	65	24.3
Morgan	2,126	476	22.4	Bee	1,682	411	24.4
Jackson	3,087	702	22.7	Frio	941	232	24.6
Sevier	4,321	980	22.7	Karnes	1,946	525	26.9
Monroe	3,815	871	22.8	Jeff Davis	323	91	28.2
Hancock	2,217	514	23.2	Atascosa	1,519	452	29.8
Grainger	2,623	804	23.4	El Paso	7,300	2,199	30.1
Unicoi	1,296	314	24.2	Valverde	1,449	470	32.4
Cocke	3,803	937	24.6	Brewster	699	229	32.8
Pickett	1,132	284	25.1	Kinney	580	193	33.3
Hawkins	4,757	1,212	25.4	Nueces	2,451	898	36.6
Claiborne	4,326	1,105	25.6	Maverick	1,005	378	37.6
Fentress	1,324	343	25.9	San Patricio	577	227	39.3
Macon	2,773	719	25.9	Pecos	914	367	40.1
Johnson	2,130	573	26.9	Ward	404	162	40.1
Carter	3,588	989	27.6	La Salle	587	236	40.2

TABLE VIII — CONCLUDED

	Total	Illiter-ate	Per cent		Total	Illiter-ate	Per cent
TEXAS — con.				**NEW MEXICO — con.**			
Reeves . .	513	211	41.1	Grant . . .	4,451	1,098	24.6
Zapata . . .	1,128	484	42.9	Sierra . . .	963	247	25.8
Presidio . .	903	391	43.3	Socorro . .	3,411	981	25.8
Duval . . .	1,883	862	45.7	San Miguel .	5,749	1,749	30.4
Webb . . .	5,841	2,874	49.2	**ARIZONA**			
Cameron . .	3,423	1,721	50.3	Guadalupe . .	1,344	427	31.8
Starr . . .	2,593	1,369	52.8	Valencia . .	2,712	871	32.1
Hidalgo . .	1,522	808	53.1	Mora . . .	2,453	819	33.4
ARKANSAS				Rio Arriba .	3,092	1,113	36.0
Randolph . .	3,898	780	20.0	Donna Ana .	2,818	1,163	41.3
Newton . .	2,608	527	20.2	Apache . .	538	138	20.4
MISSOURI				Graham . .	4,722	1,084	23.0
Washington . .	3,257	756	23.2	Pinal . . .	1,658	406	24.5
NEW MEXICO				Pima . . .	3,844	985	25.6
Union . . .	1,268	283	22.3	Santa Cruz .	1,347	412	30.6
Taos . . .	2,974	555	22.4	**COLORADO**			
				Huerfano . .	2,269	698	30.8

TABLE IX

SHOWING THE RANK OF EACH STATE IN PERCENTAGE OF ILLITERACY OF THE NATIVE WHITE POPULATION 10 YEARS OF AGE AND OVER: 1900

Rank	STATE OR TERRITORY	Per cent	Rank	STATE OR TERRITORY	Per cent
1	Washington . . .	0.5	26	Ohio . . .	2.4
2	South Dakota . .	0.6	27	Maine	2.4
3	Montana . . .	0.6	28	Oklahoma . .	2.5
4	Nevada . . .	0.6	29	Colorado . . .	2.7
5	Wyoming . . .	0.7	30	Vermont . . .	2.9
6	Massachusetts . .	0.8	31	Indiana . . .	3.6
7	Minnesota . . .	0.8	32	Maryland . . .	4.1
8	Nebraska . . .	0.8	33	Missouri . .	4.8
9	Connecticut . .	0.8	34	Delaware . . .	5.6
10	Oregon . . .	0.8	35	Texas . . .	6.1
11	Utah . . .	0.8	36	Arizona . . .	6.2
12	District of Columbia	0.8	37	Mississippi . .	8.0
13	North Dakota . .	0.9	38	Florida . . .	8.6
14	Idaho . . .	0.9	39	West Virginia .	10.0
15	California . . .	1.0	40	Virginia . . .	11.1
16	New York . . .	1.2	41	Arkansas . . .	11.6
17	Iowa . . .	1.2	42	Georgia . . .	11.9
18	Wisconsin . . .	1.3	43	Kentucky . .	12.8
19	Kansas . . .	1.3	44	South Carolina .	13.6
20	New Hampshire .	1.5	45	Indian Territory	14.0
21	Michigan . . .	1.7	46	Tennessee . .	14.2
22	New Jersey . .	1.7	47	Alabama . . .	14.8
23	Rhode Island . .	1.8	48	Louisiana . . .	17.3
24	Illinois . . .	2.1	49	North Carolina .	19.5
25	Pennsylvania . .	2.3	50	New Mexico . .	29.4

APPENDIX B

CHILD LABOR IN ALABAMA[1]

A CORRESPONDENCE

A DISCUSSION OF NEW ENGLAND'S PART IN THE COMMON RESPONSIBILITY FOR THE CHILD-LABOR CONDITIONS OF THE SOUTH

IN the summer of the year 1901 the Executive Committee on Child Labor in Alabama observed, in the New England press, certain criticisms of the child-labor conditions of the South. Knowing that the South was not alone at fault, and that Eastern men have been partly responsible for the failure of child-labor legislation in the Southern States, the Committee addressed a public statement of the facts to the people and the press of New England.

The object of this statement was to awaken the public opinion of New England in order that this opinion might operate to control — not the South — but the New England man who is doing at the South what he cannot and dare not do at home.

A REPLY TO THE COMMITTEE

On Wednesday, October 30, the following communication appeared in the *Evening Transcript* of Boston, Massachusetts.

To the Editor of the *Transcript*:

My attention has been called to an article in your paper of the 23d inst., signed by gentlemen from Alabama, in reference to child labor.

[1] A reprint of one of the series of pamphlets circulated by the Alabama Committee in behalf of factory legislation.

309

As treasurer of a mill in that State, erected by Northern capital, I am interested in the subject. From the starting of our mill, I have never been South without protesting to the agent, and overseer of spinning (the only department in which small help can be employed), against allowing children under twelve years of age to come into the mill, as I did not consider them intelligent enough to do good work. On a visit last June, annoyed that my instructions were not more carefully observed, before leaving I wrote the agent a letter of which the following is a copy : —

"Every time I visit this mill, I am impressed with the fact that it is a great mistake to employ small help in the spinning room. Not only is it wrong from a humanitarian standpoint but it entails an absolute loss to the mill. We prepare the stock and make it into roving, and, because of the small spinners, send back to the pickers an excessive amount of roving waste, and meantime lose the work of the spindles. I again express the wish that you prevent the overseer, as far as possible, from employing children under twelve years of age. I know it is sometimes difficult to get at the real age — and in some cases the parents may threaten to leave our employ unless we give work to their small children, but we must take this stand — and I trust an honest effort will be made to carry out my wishes."

In defence of our officials, it is doubtless true that the trouble comes largely from the parents, who make every effort to get their children into the mill, and often because of refusal, take their families containing needed workers, to other mills, where no objection is made to the employment of children. The statement that twice as many children under twelve years of age are employed in mills under Northern control as in Southern mills, if it means, as it should, in proportion to spindles on same number of yarns, is absolutely false so far as relates to our company, and I have reason to believe the same can be said of other mills under Northern ownership.

Now in regard to the attempted legislation of last winter: The labor organizations at the North imported from England a very bright and skilful female labor agitator and sent her to Alabama. She held meetings at central points, and when the Legislature convened appeared at Montgomery with her following, and a bill against employing children was promptly introduced. The manufacturers and other business men of Alabama resented this outside interference, well knowing the source from which it came, and they were also aware that manufacturers at the North were being solicited for funds with which to incite labor troubles in the South.

As they recognized that this bill was only the entering wedge, they determined that action must come from within the State, and not outside. They also felt that the adjoining State of Georgia, having double the number of spindles, should act first. With these considerations in mind, the manufacturers selected among others our agent, a native Alabamian, to appear before the legislative committee, with the result that the bill was defeated. I think it may be said with truth, that the interference of Northern labor agitators is retarding much needed legislation in all the manufacturing States of the South.

As to our mill and the little town of 2300 people which has grown up around it, there is nothing within the mill or without, of which any citizen of Massachusetts need be ashamed. On the contrary, I challenge either of the gentlemen from Alabama whose names are attached to the letter referred to, to mention among the forty mills in the State, of which only four are directly operated from the North, any one which will compare with ours, in the expenditure which has been made for the comfortable housing of the operatives, and the appliances introduced for their comfort and uplift. From the inception of this enterprise, the purpose has been to build up a model town that should be an object lesson to the South, and we are assured that its influences have been helpful. In addition to a school supported by public tax, the company has always carried on a school of its own, with an experienced and devoted teacher, who has been instructed to make special effort to get in the young children, and thus allure them from the mill. We have built and have in operation a beautiful library — the first erected for this special purpose in the State of Alabama, and we have a church building which would be an ornament in any village of New England, and is in itself an education to our people. We are now building a modern schoolhouse from plans by Boston architects which will accommodate all the children of our community. These are a few of the things we have done and are doing, in our effort to meet the responsibility we have assumed, in dealing with a class of people who have some most excellent traits, and who appeal to us strongly, because many of them have hitherto been deprived of needed comforts and largely of elementary advantages.

What we are attempting to do for our operatives may seem to the gentlemen who signed the appeal in your columns as " spectacular philanthropy " and a " heartless policy "; but this is not the opinion of our employees, nor of visitors who have acquainted themselves with the facts, nor of the communities adjacent to us.

J. HOWARD NICHOLS,
Treasurer Alabama City Mill, Alabama.

A REJOINDER FROM ALABAMA

On the afternoon of November 2d, Mr. Edgar Gardner Murphy, of Montgomery, Alabama, the chairman of the Alabama Child-labor Committee, received a copy of the above letter. Mr. Murphy at once wrote and forwarded the following rejoinder : —

To the Editor of the *Transcript*:

I note in your issue of October 30th a reply to a statement to the press and the people of New England, on the subject of child labor in Alabama. Our statement bore the signatures of six [1] representative citizens of Alabama, among them the Superintendent of Public Schools of Birmingham and ex-Governor Thomas G. Jones, of Montgomery. The reply to the address of the committee is signed, not by a disinterested citizen of the State, but by Mr. J. Howard Nichols, Treasurer of the Alabama City Mill, at Alabama City.

[1] The full membership of the Alabama Committee was, at a later date, as follows : Judge J. B. Gaston, Dr. B. J. Baldwin, Rev. Neal L. Anderson, Judge Thos. G. Jones, S. B. Marks, Jr., Judge W. H. Thomas, Father O'Brien, and Edgar Gardner Murphy, of Montgomery; John Craft, Erwin Craighead, Jos. E. Rich, of Mobile; (the Hon. Richard H. Clarke was a member of the local committee at Mobile) ; and A. J. Reilly, Rev. John G. Murray, Hon. A. T. London, and Dr. J. H. Phillips, Superintendent of Schools, of Birmingham.

I thank you for publishing Mr. Nichols's letter. The well-known citizens of Alabama with whom I have the honor to be associated, have welcomed the discussion of this subject, and they desire the frankest and fullest showing of the facts.

I note, however, with some amazement, that the Treasurer of the Alabama City Mill begins his argument by conceding the two fundamental principles for which we are contending — the social wrong and the economic error of child labor under twelve. He declares that from the starting of that mill he has repeatedly protested against the use of children under this age and that last June he wrote to his local agent that the employment of such help "is not only wrong from a humanitarian standpoint, but it entails an absolute loss to the mill." Now this is substantially, and in admirable form, the whole case of our committee.

Yet what must be our added amazement when, in the next paragraph but one, we read the further admission that, in order to continue this economic and social wrong and in order to defeat a simple and effective remedy for this wrong, the salaried representative of his own mill, during the preceding February, had appeared in this city before our Legislature, in aggressive and persistent antagonism to the protection of little children under twelve! This, in the teeth of protests which Mr. Nichols declares he has made since "the starting" of his mill. Who, then, is the responsible representative of the actual policy of the Alabama City Mill — its Treasurer or its representative before the Legislature? Or is the policy of the mill a policy which concedes the principle, only to deny the principle its fruit? If this be the true interpretation of the conditions, what are we to say to the explanations which are suggested; explanations offered "in defence of our [Mr. Nichols's] officials."

Mr. Nichols assures us that the officials have been put under grave pressure from the parents. Let us concede that this is true. Yet Mr. Nichols himself is not satisfied with this "defence," and he declares wisely and bravely that his officials must take their stand against the pressure of unscrupulous and idle parents. His agents must resist the threat of such parents to leave the Alabama City Mill for mills having a lower standard of employment. Does not Mr. Nichols see that our legislation was precisely directed toward ending this pressure, toward breaking up this ignoble competition, and toward the preservation of the standard of employment which he professes? There could be no pressure to withdraw the children and to enter them in other mills, if such labor were everywhere prohibited by statute. But we are grateful to Mr. Nichols for his declaration. And yet, is he ignorant of the need of legislation in the State at large? His very argument is a confession of knowledge. If the Alabama City Mill is fairly represented by the profession of Mr. Nichols, why should the paid and delegated agent of that mill labor here for weeks to thwart a simple legislative remedy for the abuses he deplores?

Is it sufficient for your correspondent to declare that this legislation met with local opposition simply because such reforms should come "from within the State and not from outside"? This is a strange objection upon the part of one who represents investments from outside. The evils may be supported from the East, but the remedies (sic) must be indigenous! Nor is there the slightest ground for the suggestion that the initiative for our movement of reform came from "a skilful female labor agitator imported from England." We yield sincere gratitude to the American Federation of Labor for their earnest, creditable, and effective coöperation. Their interest in the situation is entirely intelligible. When the younger children are thrust into the labor market in competition with the adult, they contend that the adult wage is everywhere affected. But the agent of the Federation of Labor — earnest and devoted woman that she is — did her work, not in the spirit of interference, but in the spirit of helpfulness. She was not responsible for the beginning of the agitation. The demand for this legislative protection of our children was made by the Ministers' Union of Montgomery and by the Woman's Christian Temperance Union of Alabama, before she was ever heard of in the South.

Nothing could be more baseless than the assumption that our local effort for reforms is due to outside forces. But if it were — what of it? There is at stake here to-day the welfare of our little children, the happiness and efficiency of our future operatives, the moral standard of our economic life; and this committee frankly proposes, in every honorable way, to secure all the aid, from every quarter of our common country, which we can possibly command. The criticism of such a policy is a little out of place from the representative of a mill here operated upon investments from Massachusetts.

Mr. Nichols then informs us that the reform legislation was defeated because " the adjoining State of Georgia, having double the number of spindles, should act first." This, we have contended, is to miss the very essence of the statesmanship of the situation. The very fact that Georgia has twice as many spindles as Alabama, makes it twice as hard for Georgia to precede us. The cost of such an economic readjustment must be obviously twice as great in Georgia as in Alabama. That Alabama is not so deeply involved in the system of child labor as some other Southern States is clearly the reason why Alabama should take the lead.

It has been conservatively estimated that in some of the Southern States more than twenty per cent of the mill operatives are under fourteen years of age. Does Mr. Nichols wish Alabama to delay until that becomes the condition of the industry in this State? According to the logical demand of his argument, the State having the most spindles, the State most deeply and inextricably involved, must be the first to face the delicate and difficult problem of readjustment!

Mr. Nichols also declares that our reform measure was defeated because it was believed to be " the entering wedge" of other troublesome labor legislation. We must not protect our little children under twelve, we must not do a compassionate and reasonable thing, because, forsooth, somebody might then demand an inconsiderate and unreasonable thing! Do the corporate interests in Alabama wish to predicate their liberties upon such an argument?

Yet, says Mr. Nichols, " with these considerations in mind, the manufacturers selected, among others, our agent, a native Alabamian, to appear before the Legislative Committee, with the result that the bill was defeated." Mr. Nichols neglects to state that on the second hearing of the bill, his agent appeared alone as the chosen spokesman of all the opponents of reform. He, too, made much of this hoary scare about " the entering wedge."

What iniquities of reaction, what bitter stultification of human progress has that argument not supported! In such a case as this, it is not an argument, it is a provocation. It is a challenge to the common sense and the common humanity of our people. If the corporate interests of this State, whether operated by Northerners or Southerners, are to rest the great cause of their unrestricted development upon the cruel refusal of protection to our younger children, then let them beware lest, having rejected " the entering wedge," they invite the cyclone. What greater folly, viewed from the strictly selfish standpoint of certain corporate interests, than to involve their fate in the issues of so odious an argument?

Such a course must gradually invite the hatred of the people, must inevitably goad the great masses of our population into the fixed belief that the corporation desires to live, not by production, but through destruction ; that it is a force to be feared and bound rather than a force to be trusted and liberated. The course of humanity is always the course of wisdom. If the corporate interests of this State desire a long and prosperous career, untrammelled by restrictive legislation, let them disabuse the people of the impression that their liberties represent the refusal of compassion to our children ; let them persuade the people of Alabama that they wish to grow, not out of the soil of ignorance and wretchedness, but out of the rich and human fertilities of social justice and the social welfare. Let them go to the popular heart, and base themselves there, not upon the negation, but upon the extension of privilege.

I concur in the claim that the Alabama City Mill is in some respects wholly exceptional. Says Mr. Nichols: " I challenge either of the gentlemen from Alabama to mention among the mills of the State . . . any one which compares with ours in the expenditure which has been made for the comfortable housing of the operatives and the appliances introduced for their comfort and uplift." In one breath the friends of this mill ask us to believe it exceptional, and yet in the next breath they ask that the need for reform legislation in relation to all the mills of the State, shall be determined from the conditions it presents! If the Alabama City Mill is so unique, then it is not representative or typical. If it is not representative of the average conditions of child labor in Alabama, it has nothing to do with this argument.

As to the proportionate number of little children in our Southern and Northern mills, the facts have been accurately stated by the committee. The statement of Mr. Nichols that there are only four mills in the State " directly operated from the North " is unintelligible to me. Upon my desk, as I write, there are the figures from eleven Alabama mills which, upon the word of their own managers, are controlled by Northern capital.

It seems to have grieved Mr. Nichols that we should have characterized certain unique philanthropies in connection with one or two of our Eastern mills as "spectacular." The gentlemen of this committee have no desire to express themselves in the language of impulsive epithet. We are sincerely grateful for every motive and for every work which touches and blesses the lot of the unprivileged. But when large photographs of the exceptional philanthropies of a single mill are seriously brought before the committee of our Legislature as an argument for the perpetuation of the general conditions of child labor in this State, when the advertisements of a unique establishment are used to cloak the wretched lot of the average factory; when, upon the basis of the representations of Alabama City, men are taught to ignore the essential cruelty of the whole miserable system, and are made blind to the misery of hundreds whom that factory can never touch, then I frankly declare that such philanthropies are indeed "spectacular," for they have actually cursed more than they have ever blessed. They have become a mockery of love. They may have benefited the employees of one mill; but they have served to rivet the chains of a heart-breaking and wretched slavery upon hundreds of our little children in the State at large. And no philanthropy, however exceptional, and no institutional compassion, however effective, can ever justify the refusal, at the door of the factory, of legislative protection to the little child under twelve years of age. That is the sole contention of this committee.

Is that asking too much? If Massachusetts protects at fourteen years, may not Alabama protect at twelve? Is this too drastic a demand upon the exceptional philanthropy of the mill at Alabama City? I hope not. I do not mean to write with the slightest personal unkindness, but I do write with an intense earnestness of concern in behalf of the sad and unnatural fate of the little people of our factories. We, for their sakes, do not

want enemies anywhere. We want friends everywhere. It is
with pleasure therefore that I recur to the instructions forwarded
by Mr. Nichols to his agent. Speaking of the employment of
little children, he said, "Not only is it wrong from a humanitarian standpoint, but it entails an absolute loss to the mill." There
speaks the man of wisdom and the man of heart. Does Mr.
Nichols mean it? Does the mill at Alabama City mean it? Will
Massachusetts join hands with Alabama?

That mill, with its great influences, has led the fight in this
State against the protection of our factory children. Will it continue to represent a policy of opposition and reaction? Or, will
it represent a policy of coöperation and of progress? Will it
send its representative, with this committee, before our next
Legislature and there declare that the cotton industry of the
South, as here undertaken by Massachusetts, is too important in
its dignity and its value to be longer involved in the odium and
the horror of an industrial system which all the world has cast
off? If so, that representative may indeed find himself in the
company of some of the nobler forces from "outside." The
whole world has a way of taking the little child to its heart. But
he will also find himself in the company — the increasingly reso-
lute company — of thousands of the people of Alabama.

EDGAR GARDNER MURPHY.

MONTGOMERY, ALA., November 2, 1901.

ANOTHER REPLY TO THE COMMITTEE

The following letter, in reply to the statement of Ala-
bama's Executive Committee, is from Mr. Horace Sears, of
Boston. The communication first appeared in the *Evening
Transcript*, of Boston, and was reprinted in the December
issue of the *Monthly Leader* — the organ of the Christian
Social Union. It appeared as follows in the *Leader:* —

Editor the *Leader:*

It would be difficult to think that such misleading statements
as those which appeared under the communication entitled,
"Child Labor in Alabama," were intended seriously, were it not
for the importance of the subject and the evident stress of feeling

under which its authors labored. Such appeals do far more to hinder than to help the welfare of the children, which many manufacturers have more truly at heart than have the professional labor agitator and the well-meaning but ill-advised humanitarian. But I have read with interest, and wish to indorse throughout, the thoughtful and dispassionate reply to this appeal in your issue of October 30 by Mr. J. Howard Nichols, treasurer of the Alabama City Mill. In the light of his statement, a statement with which I, in common with most manufacturers, agree, that the employment of child labor is not only " wrong from a humanitarian standpoint, but entails absolute loss to the mill," the fervid rhetoric of the executive committee " of the exploitation of childhood for the creation of dividends " seems just a little strained.

If, instead of giving utterance to sentimental heroics and berating those who are in no wise responsible for, but are trying to better, these conditions (which conditions are not nearly as deplorable as this over-wrought appeal would indicate), the executive committee would join the manufacturers in trying to obtain remedial legislation that would strike at the root of the trouble, and to awaken a deeper sense of parental responsibility, much would be gained towards improving the industrial system as far as it affects the employment of children in the cotton mills of the South.

At the hearing before the legislative committee at Montgomery last winter (which I am constrained to believe none of this executive committee attended or they would have a more intelligent conception of the situation to-day), the president of our mill joined with other manufacturers in urging that the Legislature pass a compulsory education law. If such a law were passed and then adequately enforced after enactment, it would be impossible for the children to work in the mills for a large part of the year, a condition which most manufacturers would welcome as gladly as the executive committee. As it is, no mill can afford, as Mr. Nichols states, to lose some of its most desirable and skilful operatives, through the parents' insisting that their children be given employment to swell the family revenues, and removing to a mill that will grant such employment, if the mill where they are located refuses to do so. At our mill the superintendent has sometimes taken this risk, and refused to allow children to work unless the parents would first agree to have them attend school for a part of the term at least. All possible pressure is brought to bear to get the children into school, but many will not go at all of their own volition, neither will their parents always require it. And without a compulsory education law we know they are better off in the mill than running wild in the streets and fields, exposed to the danger of growing up into an ignorant, idle, and vicious citizenship.

Any compulsory education law which is passed, however, should be made operative only upon the passage of similar laws by the States of Georgia, South Carolina, and North Carolina. Otherwise it would be prejudicial to the interests of Alabama as a cotton manufacturing State and make it very difficult for the mills to retain some of their best and most skilful hands. While I doubt not that the people of New England would be glad, as always, to do anything in their power for the elevation of the toiling masses, especially of the children, and for the amelioration of any adverse conditions that surround them, yet there is little in this instance that they can do, except to advise our friends in Alabama, who have interested themselves in the matter, to cultivate a calm and judicial mind, study the situation with intelligence and wise discrimination, and then act under the responsibility which they state that they feel rests upon them. Nor can they do better than to follow the lead of Massachusetts, which long ago successfully grappled with the problem, by

1st — Awakening a sense of parental responsibility, so that parents will deny themselves and make any reasonable sacrifice to win an education for their children.

2d — The enactment of a compulsory education law.

3d — Its energetic enforcement.

The statement that the actual number of children employed in mills representing Northern investments is twice as great as in the mills controlled by Southern capital is unworthy of attention. I challenge its accuracy, and deplore the partisan spirit which leads to such an unfounded accusation.

The executive committee appears to include representatives of the Church, the school, and the State. Let me call their attention to the fact that many of the families who are now happy in their work and growing into finer manhood and womanhood at the mills, came from isolated and distant homes where the Church and the school never reached them, and where the State was felt only through its unsympathetic and restraining, although necessary, laws. Through the opportunity which the mills have offered, and under their watchful and sympathetic care, many a community has been built up and surrounded with Christianizing, educational, and civilizing influences, that the Church, the school, and the State would never have been able to throw around them.

Although our mill village is provided with a church which was built at the expense of the mill in its very inception, with schools supported in part by the State, in part by the parents, and in part by the mill, whose superintendent is instructed to see that the tuition of every child desiring to attend school is paid by the mill if not otherwise provided for, with an assembly hall, a library, and a reading room, it did not occur to us that this was "spectacular philanthropy," for we neither knew nor cared whether it came to the notice of the outside world, save as it would influence other corporations to do likewise. Indeed, we do not consider it philanthropy at all, but simply rendering willing service in our turn to those who are faithfully serving us.

The neighboring factory village at Lanett, Ala., is similarly provided for at the expense and under the fostering care of the Lanett Cotton Mill, and my personal observation and knowledge lead me to believe that instead of one or two mills of a "spectacular philanthropy," the majority of the mills throughout the South, and especially those under Northern management, have, without any appeal to the galleries, quietly and gladly given their operatives and their families all desired privileges of church and school and social and literary life, that were not already offered by the town in which they were located.

Turning from the appeal of the executive committee, a picture arises before me of the peaceful, happy mill settlement at Langdale, with its pretty church filled to the doors on Sundays with an attentive, God-fearing congregation, with its large and enthusiastic Sunday-school, with its fine school and kindergarten department, with its well-selected library of over 1000 volumes, with its pleasant reading room open every week-day evening, with its assembly hall often filled with an audience attracted by a programme of the debating club, or the literary society, or the entertainment com-

mittee, with its streets lighted by electricity, and with the mill agent and his beloved wife going in and out among the homes of the people, participating in all their joys and sorrows ; and knowing that this is typical of many another manufacturing village in the South, especially of those under Northern management or controlled by Northern capital, I rub my eyes and wonder whether the animus of this appeal of the executive committee is that of ignorance, or of mischievous labor agitation, or of sectional hatred, which we had hoped was long since deservedly laid away in its grave-clothes. HORACE S. SEARS,
Treasurer of the West Point Manufacturing Company, Langdale, Ala.

On reading the above communication, Mr. Murphy, the Chairman of the Alabama Executive Committee, replied as follows : —

A REJOINDER TO MR. SEARS

To the Editor of the *Monthly Leader :*

A number of the considerations presented by Mr. Horace S. Sears I have dealt with in my reply to Mr. J. Howard Nichols. This reply was published in the *Evening Transcript* of Boston, and I will gladly forward a copy of it to any of your readers upon receipt of a postal card request.

There are, however, a few additional suggestions in the letter of Mr. Sears.

He contends that, while "the employment of little children is not only wrong from a humanitarian standpoint, but entails absolute loss to the mill," yet Alabama should not provide any legislative protection for her children under twelve, until the State can be won to the acceptance of a compulsory education law. In other words, we are not to attempt a possible reform until we have first secured another reform which every practical man in Alabama knows is just now impossible.

But granting that Mr. Sears is right, and admitting that Massachusetts may fairly labor to defeat one method of reform because Alabama will not adopt another, is Mr. Sears really ready for his remedy? Not by any means. If our Executive Committee should adopt his advice, should abandon its own conception of the statesmanship of the situation, and should "join the manufacturers" in first assisting upon a comprehensive scheme of compulsory education, would the forces represented by Mr. Sears stand by the compact? Not for a moment! He is quite frank in his disavowal of any such intention. Says Mr. Sears, "any compulsory education law which is passed, however, should be operative only upon the passage of similar laws by the States of Georgia, South Carolina, and North Carolina."

This enthusiasm for reform, only on condition that all the rest of the world will reform too, is very familiar to the students of economic progress. Over in Georgia and the Carolinas, some of the mill men are claiming that they "are only waiting upon Alabama." And there you are!

The suggestion from Mr. Sears that the members of our Committee were not present at the legislative hearings last winter is, I think, unworthy of this discussion. If Mr. Sears was there himself, he knows that one of the members of our Committee was Chairman of the Legislative Committee of the lower House which had the Child-labor Bill under consideration, that he presided at the public hearing on this bill given by the joint Committee of both Houses, and that he was personally in charge of the compulsory education bill (which Mr. Sears claims to have favored); that the writer of these lines appeared in behalf of the Child-labor Bill at both hearings; that those who fought our Child-labor law selected, as the most prominent man in Alabama whom they could get to oppose us, the State's most conspicuous opponent of compulsory education; and that the representative of Massachusetts investments who so vigorously fought the proposed legislative protection of our children, took no part whatever in the public discussion of the bill for compulsory education.

Moreover, Mr. Sears neglects to state that the compulsory education law, which he declares the president of his mill supported, owed its origin not to Massachusetts, nor to the mills, but to the same devoted woman whom Mr. Nichols condemns as "a skilful female labor agitator imported from England," which description Mr. Sears approves! In other words, the very remedy which Mr. Sears suggests with such commendable unction was offered to Alabama, not by the forces of Massachusetts, nor by the mills, but by the forces which Mr. Sears has so persistently opposed and which he ventures to charge with "sentimental heroics."

At the hearings upon the compulsory education bill I was not personally present, for, realizing the utter futility of then placing our dependence upon the practical coöperation of the mill men, I knew the bill was doomed. But other members of our Committee were untiring in its support, and had the mill forces expended one-fifth of the energy in favor of this bill that they expended in opposition to our Child-labor Bill, the compulsory education measure might at least have been put upon its passage.

In the face of such facts and in the face of all the convenient conditions suggested, under which "any compulsory education law should be made operative only upon the passage of similar laws by the States of Georgia, South Carolina, and North Carolina," it is not strange that suspicion should be abroad, and that some of our reform forces should have adopted the opinion that all this strenuous talk about compulsory education is but part of an attempt to block a reform which is possible, by the safe proposal of a reform which is impossible — that the effort is simply a neat and effective element in the diplomacy of estoppel.

Is the suspicion totally unfounded? I do not doubt that, in the hearts of some, the proposal is sincere. Those who are not face to face with our local conditions, may think compulsory education a practical alternative. But that the representative of the cotton mill, the representative of the system of child labor in this State, should sincerely advocate a policy of compulsory education, is something which many of our hard-headed, sensible people cannot understand. These people are confronted, not merely by a few exceptional mills, but by the average conditions of the child-labor system. They see little children under twelve, sometimes as young as six, working eight and twelve and thirteen hours a day — sometimes sent into the mills at night; they see the burden and the wretchedness of this system; and they cannot see how a man who is identified with such conditions can be sincerely an advocate of the system of compulsory education — and for the very obvious reason that he himself, in supporting the child-labor system of Alabama, is manifestly supporting a system of compulsory ignorance.

"But," Mr. Sears may say, "it is not true that I am identified with such conditions. Our mill is a good mill." The claim cannot stand. I am not prepared to charge the darkest conditions upon the mills controlled by Massachusetts, but I do contend that when the representatives of the Massachusetts mills, upon their own published confession, unite in public opposition to legislative reform for our abuses, when they themselves continue to oppose the legislative protection of children under twelve, and when they are actually employing hundreds of such children, then they are morally responsible for the general evils which they have labored to continue. We must have the aid of the law, not primarily for the good mill, but for the bad mill, just as every community needs a law against theft, not to protect it from the honest, but from the dishonest. In urging this suggestion upon our many friends in New England, I ask them to realize that any factory here, whatever its advantages, stands intimately related to the whole industrial system of the State. There are true men and true women associated with some of these factories. But the effort of the good mill to prevent the legislative protection of children under twelve, means, in its effect, the continuation of the present conditions in the worst mills of the State. Kindness may modify the evils of child labor in one mill without legislation, yet nothing but legislation will enable us to protect the child which has fallen into the hands of the unkind.

I am personally of the opinion that there is no mill on earth good enough to be permitted to work a little child under twelve years of age, but, if there be such a mill and if that mill be controlled by brave and good men, it will make its sacrifices and will put forth its labors, not only to continue the supposed good fortune of the few, but to avert the pitiable misfortunes of the many.

New England might find analogies in our situation. Was New England solicitous for the policy of "non-interference" from outside the State, in relation to the evils of slavery? Yet Mr. Nichols and Mr. Sears do not wish anybody outside of Alabama to take an interest in the local question of child labor! More than a generation ago it was argued, for the system of slavery, that there were good plantations upon which the slaves were well treated. The statement was true, but the argument was weak. The presence of the good plantation could not offset the perils and evils of the system in itself, any more than the "good factory" can justify the system of child labor. The need for any social or economic reform may never be determined from the conditions presented by the best phases of a system, but from the essential genius of the system, and from the average conditions which it presents. The very idea of enforced labor for the child under twelve is monstrous, both from a moral and an economic standpoint. The very essence of the system, as with the system of slavery, is an error. There can be no "good" child labor. And this system is monstrous, not only in principle, but in results.

Mr. Sears is sure that we have exaggerated the evil of these results. I would respectfully ask, who are the more likely to make accurate report of the results — Mr. Sears and Mr. Nichols, living in Boston and directly interested in the system they defend, or a representative committee of seven men who are passing their lives in Alabama and who have no financial connection whatever, direct or indirect, with the system they attack? Among these men are Dr. Phillips, the Superintendent of Public Schools at Birmingham, and ex-Governor Thos. G. Jones, lately selected by President Roosevelt for the Federal bench (although a Democrat) upon the ground of his breadth of learning, his sterling integrity, and his judicial capacity and temper. It is hardly necessary for Mr. Sears to accuse such men of "sentimental heroics" or to exhort such men "to cultivate a calm and judicial mind and to study the situation with intelligence and wise discrimination."

Let us take another of the issues of fact. Mr. Sears, in urging a compulsory education law and in opposition to a child-labor law, declares in support of his mill, that "all possible pressure is brought to bear to get the children into school, but many will not go at all of their own volition, neither will their parents always require it." The impression is created even upon the mind of the editor of the *Leader* (in whose large-heartedness I have every confidence) that present conditions are possibly better than they would be under the law proposed by the Committee. This rather ignores the fact that the law proposed by the Committee had an admirable educational provision — as good a provision as we thought it possible to pass. But, is it true that these children are stubbornly opposed to education? Conditions vary.

No man can speak for the children of every mill in Alabama. Yet, as Mr. Sears has told about the children in one factory, I will tell of those in another. The mill is less than twenty miles from my study. There are about seventy-five children in it. They are worked twelve hours out of twenty-four, from 6 A.M. to 6.30 P.M., allowing a half-hour for dinner. Last year they were refused a holiday, even on Thanksgiving. A night school, taught by volunteers, has been opened near them, through those whom Mr. Sears has called "well-meaning but ill-advised humanitarians." I have watched the experiment with some hesitation, because the teaching is real teaching and I am not sure that any child, after twelve hours of work, should be wearied with much of an effort at education. But fifty children out of the seventy-five are flocking into this school voluntarily, eager to learn, and disappointed when the crowded session is brought to its early end. Now, which law is the more needed by these children — a provision for compulsory education, or a provision which will strike at the system of compulsory ignorance surrounding them; which will close for them the door of the mill, and open to them the opportunities of knowledge by daylight?

Says Mr. Sears, "We know that they are better off in the mill than running wild in the streets and fields, exposed to the dangers of growing up into an ignorant, idle, and vicious citizenship." Mr. Sears seems to miss the point. He seems to forget that our legislation is directed simply toward the protection of the freedom of children under twelve. In view of this cardinal fact, I may suggest, in the words of Mr. Sears himself, that his language "seems just a little strained." What are the perils of vice "in the fields," or even in the streets of our rural South (or even in the streets of the model villages of Mr. Nichols and Mr. Sears), for the little child under twelve?

In attempting to arrive at the "animus" of the appeal of our Committee, Mr. Sears seems inclined to attribute our statement to "ignorance," or to "mischievous labor agitation," or to "sectional hatred." Sectional hatred! And which is the more likely to induce that malignant and excuseless passion — the spectacle of the attitude of the South toward the capital of Massachusetts, or the attitude of the capital of Massachusetts toward the little children of the South? The fact that these are white children, and that Massachusetts — always solicitous for the negro — should be largely indifferent to the fate of our white children, does not relieve the situation. Suppose the conditions were reversed, and that the mills of Southern men were full of negro children under twelve — how quickly and how justly New England would ring with denunciation!

The fundamental principle of our appeal is not that Alabama is guiltless, or that gentlemen like Mr. Nichols and Mr. Sears are intentionally brutal. That would be unjust to them and unjust to our own sense of right and truth. Our elementary contention is, simply, that the common conscience will hold, and should hold, the capital of Massachusetts to the moral and economic standards of Massachusetts. Both Mr. Nichols and Mr. Sears have admitted that the employment of little children is "wrong" from an economic and a humanitarian standpoint. Neither gentleman has told us, and no single representative of New England investments in Alabama has yet told us, that he is ready to join with us to right this wrong by direct and effective legislation.

But the appeal of our Committee has not been without response. We care to indulge in no recriminations for the past. We have prayed that, in our approaching struggle, New England will stand with us and not against us, for we have no intention whatever of seeing her investments here embarrassed by complex and oppressive labor legislation. Our motives cannot long be misunderstood. For such response as has come to us from the New England press, and from many of the people of New England, we are sincerely grateful. I close this letter with an expression which has just reached me. It is a telegram from Seth Low, the Mayor-elect of Greater New York, in reference to our bill now pending before the Legislature of the State of Georgia. It reflects what we believe will be the real, the ultimate, response of the North to the situation at the South. It is as follows: —

" I am heartily glad to throw whatever influence I can exert, in favor of protective legislation for the children of Georgia, strictly defining the permitted age and hours of labor in factories, on lines of similar legislation in Massachusetts and New York. Georgia ought to profit by the experience of other States. She ought not to pay for her own experience with the lives of her children. I say this as one having indirectly an interest in the Massachusetts mills in Georgia.

"SETH LOW."

That is statesmanship, that is religion, that is intersectional fraternity, and that is "Education."

EDGAR GARDNER MURPHY.
MONTGOMERY, ALA., December 15, A.D. 1901.

The above correspondence is included in this Appendix in order to illustrate the truth that the influence of that section of the country which has the broadest industrial experience and the highest industrial standards should be felt — within the newer regions of manufacturing enterprise — upon the side of humane and wholesome policies.

A Child-labor Law is now upon the statute books of Alabama. The bill, as originally proposed, prohibited *night* work for children under sixteen. This bill — at the demand of a committee of the manufacturers representing the factories of the State — had to be so amended as to permit night labor for all children of thirteen years and upward.

The South has no disposition to evade her own primary responsibility for her industrial conditions. She must face, and deal with, the problem of her own guilt. But, for the growing number of New England stockholders — drawing dividends from Southern industrial properties — the press and pulpit of New England might have, perhaps, a more frequent word of earnest and explicit suggestion. One Southern State — Georgia — is still without any direct factory legislation. In the States in which legislation has been secured there is still the task of adequate enforcement.

APPENDIX C

"WHERE contact already exists, a further question arises : Can the evils incident to it be mitigated through leading the Advanced and the Backward races to blend by intermarriage, a method slow but sure, and one by which many nations have been brought to unity and strength out of elements originally hostile? This is a question which Nature usually answers, settling the matter by the attractions or repulsions she implants. Yet legislation may so far affect it as to make it deserve to be pondered by those who are confronted by such a problem.

"We have already noted that races which are near one another in physical aspect and structure tend to mix, and that the race produced by their mixture is equal or superior to either of the progenitors.

"We have also noted that where races are dissimilar in aspect, and especially in colour, one at least is generally repelled by the other, so that there is little admixture by intermarriage. This is more plainly the case as regards whites (especially North European whites) and blacks than it is as regards other races.

"We have been further led to conclude, though more doubtfully, for the data are imperfect, that the mixture of races very dissimilar, and especially of European whites with blacks, tends rather to lower than to improve the

330

resultant stock. That it should be lower than the higher progenitor seems natural. But does it show a marked improvement upon the inferior progenitor ? May not the new mixed race stand, not halfway between the two parent stocks, but nearer the lower than the higher ?

" Should this view be correct, it dissuades any attempt to mix races so diverse as are the white Europeans and the negroes. The wisest men among the coloured people of the Southern States of America do not desire the intermarriage of their race with the whites. They prefer to develop it as a separate people, on its own lines, though of course with the help of the whites. The negro race in America is not wanting in intelligence. It is fond of learning. It has already made a considerable advance. It will cultivate self-respect better by standing on its own feet than by seeking blood alliances with whites, who would usually be of the meaner sort.

" In India, some sections of the native population are equal in intellectual aptitude to their European rulers, and may pride themselves upon even longer traditions of intellectual culture. One cannot call this part of the population a Backward race. Yet it does not seem desirable that they and the whites should become fused by intermarriage ; nor do they themselves appear to desire that result.

" The matter ought to be regarded from the side neither of the white nor of the black, but of the future of mankind at large. Now for the future of mankind nothing is more vital than that some races should be maintained at the highest level of efficiency, because the work they can do for thought and art and letters, for scientific discovery, and for raising the standard of conduct, will determine the general progress of humanity. If therefore we were to suppose the blood of the races which are now most advanced to be diluted, so to speak, by that of those most backward, not only would more be lost to the former than would be gained to the latter, but there would be a loss, possibly an irreparable loss, to the world at large.

" It may therefore be doubted whether any further mixture of Advanced and Backward races is to be desired. In some regions, however, that mixture seems probable. Brazil may see the Portuguese whites and the blacks blent into one after some centuries. The Spaniards of Central and South America (except perhaps Uruguay and Argentina, where there are very few natives, and Chile) may be absorbed into the Indian population, who will have then become a sort of Spaniards. In the Far East there may be a great mixing of Chinese and Malays, and in Central Africa a further mixture of the Sudanese Arabs with the negroes. But the Teutonic races, as well as the French, seem likely to keep their blood quite distinct from all the coloured races, whether in Asia, in Africa, or in America.

" It remains to consider what can be done to minimize the evils and reduce the friction which are incident to the contact of an Advanced and a Backward race, and which may sometimes become more troublesome with the forward movement of the latter.

" On the legal side of this question, one thing is clear. The Backward race ought to receive all such private civil rights as it can use for its own benefit. It ought to have as full a protection in person and property, as complete an access to all professions and occupations, as wide a power of entering into contracts, as ready an access to the courts, as the more advanced race enjoys. The only distinctions should be those which may be needed for its own defence against fraud, or to permit the continuance of the old customs (so far as harmless) to which it clings. This is the policy which the Romans followed in extending citizenship over their dominions. It has been followed with admirable consistency and success by the English in India, as well as by the French in Algeria, and by the Americans when they liberated the slaves during and after the Civil War. It has the two great merits of creating a respect for the lower race among the higher one, and of soothing the lower one by the feeling that in all that touches the rights of private life they are treated with strict justice.

" When we pass to the sphere of politics, more debatable questions emerge. Equality of rights might seem to be here also that which is fairest and most likely to make for unity and peace. But the Backward race may be really unfit to exercise political power, whether from ignorance, or from an indifference that would dispose it to sell its votes, or from a propensity to sudden and unreasoning impulses. The familiar illustration of the boy put to drive a locomotive engine might in some communities be no extreme way of describing the risks a democracy runs when the suffrage is granted to a large mass of half-civilized men.

" Those who rule subject races on despotic methods, as the Russians rule Transcaucasia and the English India, or as the Hispano-American minorities virtually rule the native Indians in most of the so-called republics of Central and South America, do not realize all the difficulties that arise in a democracy. The capital instance is afforded by the history of the Southern States since the Civil War. . . .

. . . " The moral to be drawn from the case of the Southern States seems to be that you must not, however excellent your intentions and however admirable your sentiments, legislate in the teeth of facts. The great bulk of the negroes were not fit for the suffrage ; nor under the American Federal system was it possible (without incurring other grave evils) to give them effective protection in the exercise of the suffrage. It would, therefore, have been better to postpone the bestowal of this dangerous boon. True it is that rocks and shoals were set thick round every course : true that it is easier to perceive the evils of a course actually taken than to realize other evils that might have followed some other course. Nevertheless, the general opinion of dispassionate men has come to deem the action taken in A.D. 1870 a mistake.

"The social relations of two races which cannot be fused raise problems even more difficult, because incapable of being regulated by law. Law may attempt to secure equal admission to public conveyances or public entertainments. But the look of scorn, the casual blow, the brutal oath thrown at one who dare not resent it — these are injuries which cannot be prevented where the sentiment of the dominant race allows them. Impunity corrupts the ordinary man ; and even the better sort suffer from the consciousness of their own superiority, not merely in rank, but also in strength and volition. One must have lived among a weaker race in order to realize the kind of irritation which its defects produce in those who deal with it, and how temper and self-control are strained in resisting temptations to harsh or arbitrary action. It needs something more than the virtue of a philosopher — it needs the tenderness of a saint to preserve the same courtesy and respect towards the members of a backward race as are naturally extended to equals.

. . . "The tremendous problem presented by the Southern States of America, and the likelihood that similar problems will have to be solved elsewhere, as, for instance, in South Africa and the Philippine Isles, bid us ask, What should be the duty and the policy of a dominant race where it cannot fuse with a backward race? Duty and policy are one, for it is equally to the interest of both races that their relations should be friendly.

"The answer seems to be that as regards political rights, race and blood should not be made the ground of discrimination. Where the bulk of the coloured race are obviously unfit for political power, a qualification based on property and education might be established which should permit the upper section of that race to enjoy the suffrage. Such a qualification would doubtless exclude some of the poorest and most ignorant whites, and might on that ground be resisted. But it is better to face this difficulty than to wound and alienate the whole of the coloured race by placing them without the pale of civic functions and duties."

See the Romanes Lecture, 1902: The Relations of the Advanced and the Backward Races of Mankind. By JAMES BRYCE, *D.C.L., Honorary Fellow of Oriel and Trinity Colleges. Delivered in the Sheldonian Theatre, Oxford, June 7, 1902. Oxford: The Clarendon Press, 1902.*